ISBN 0-8293-0831-8
C-831   CAREER EXAMINATION SERIES

This is your
PASSBOOK® for...

Electronic Technician

Test Preparation Study Guide
Questions & Answers

EAST NORTHPORT PUBLIC LIBRARY
EAST NORTHPORT, NEW YORK

NLC®
NATIONAL LEARNING CORPORATION®

Copyright © 2014 by

National Learning Corporation

212 Michael Drive, Syosset, New York 11791

All rights reserved, including the right of reproduction in whole or in part, in any form or by any means, electronic or mechanical, including photocopying, recording, or by any information storage and retrieval system, without permission in writing from the Publisher.

(516) 921-8888
(800) 645-6337
FAX: (516) 921-8743
www.passbooks.com
sales @ passbooks.com
info @ passbooks.com

PRINTED IN THE UNITED STATES OF AMERICA

PASSBOOK®
NOTICE

This book is SOLELY intended for, is sold ONLY to, and its use is RESTRICTED to *individual*, bona fide applicants or candidates who qualify by virtue of having seriously filed applications for appropriate license, certificate, professional and/or promotional advancement, higher school matriculation, scholarship, or other legitimate requirements of educational and/or governmental authorities.

This book is NOT intended for use, class instruction, tutoring, training, duplication, copying, reprinting, excerption, or adaptation, etc., by:

(1) Other publishers

(2) Proprietors and/or Instructors of "Coaching" and/or Preparatory Courses

(3) Personnel and/or Training Divisions of commercial, industrial, and governmental organizations

(4) Schools, colleges, or universities and/or their departments and staffs, including teachers and other personnel

(5) Testing Agencies or Bureaus

(6) Study groups which seek by the purchase of a single volume to copy and/or duplicate and/or adapt this material for use by the group as a whole without having purchased individual volumes for each of the members of the group

(7) Et al.

Such persons would be in violation of appropriate Federal and State statutes.

PROVISION OF LICENSING AGREEMENTS. — Recognized educational commercial, industrial, and governmental institutions and organizations, and others legitimately engaged in educational pursuits, including training, testing, and measurement activities, may address a request for a licensing agreement to the copyright owners, who will determine whether, and under what conditions, including fees and charges, the materials in this book may be used by them. In other words, a licensing facility exists for the legitimate use of the material in this book on other than an individual basis. However, it is asseverated and affirmed here that the material in this book *CANNOT* be used without the receipt of the express permission of such a licensing agreement from the Publishers.

NATIONAL LEARNING CORPORATION
212 Michael Drive
Syosset, New York 11791

Inquiries re licensing agreements should be addressed to:
The President
National Learning Corporation
212 Michael Drive
Syosset, New York 11791

PASSBOOK® SERIES

THE *PASSBOOK® SERIES* has been created to prepare applicants and candidates for the ultimate academic battlefield — the examination room.

At some time in our lives, each and every one of us may be required to take an examination — for validation, matriculation, admission, qualification, registration, certification, or licensure.

Based on the assumption that every applicant or candidate has met the basic formal educational standards, has taken the required number of courses, and read the necessary texts, the *PASSBOOK® SERIES* furnishes the one special preparation which may assure passing with confidence, instead of failing with insecurity. Examination questions — together with answers — are furnished as the basic vehicle for study so that the mysteries of the examination and its compounding difficulties may be eliminated or diminished by a sure method.

This book is meant to help you pass your examination provided that you qualify and are serious in your objective.

The entire field is reviewed through the huge store of content information which is succinctly presented through a provocative and challenging approach — the question-and-answer method.

A climate of success is established by furnishing the correct answers at the end of each test.

You soon learn to recognize types of questions, forms of questions, and patterns of questioning. You may even begin to anticipate expected outcomes.

You perceive that many questions are repeated or adapted so that you can gain acute insights, which may enable you to score many sure points.

You learn how to confront new questions, or types of questions, and to attack them confidently and work out the correct answers.

You note objectives and emphases, and recognize pitfalls and dangers, so that you may make positive educational adjustments.

Moreover, you are kept fully informed in relation to new concepts, methods, practices, and directions in the field.

You discover that you are actually taking the examination all the time: you are preparing for the examination by "taking" an examination, not by reading extraneous and/or supererogatory textbooks.

In short, this PASSBOOK®, used directedly, should be an important factor in helping you to pass your test.

ELECTRONIC TECHNICIAN

DUTIES:
    Performs advanced, skilled technical work in the installation, maintenance, repair and testing of precision electronic equipment and control systems. Performs related duties as required.

SUBJECT OF EXAMINATION:
Written test will cover knowledge, skills, and/or abilities in such areas as:
1. Basic electronics, including circuitry, schematics, and wiring diagrams;
2. Use of electronic test equipment;
3. Repair, maintenance, and operating characteristics of electronic equipment;
4. Mathematics; and
5. Mechanical comprehension and tool knowledge.

SAMPLE QUESTIONS
ELECTRONICS TECHNICIAN EXAMINATION

DIRECTIONS: The examination will consist of questions designed to test abilities which are important for satisfactory performance of the position.

The first section of the examination consists of a series of aptitude tests. Sample questions 1 through 3 illustrate this group.

The second section of the examination tests technical knowledge. Sample questions 4 through 9 illustrate this group.

Each question has a number of suggested answers lettered A, B, C, etc. Decide which one is the BEST answer to the question. PRINT THE LETTER OF THE CORRECT ANSWER IN THE SPACE AT THE RIGHT.

1. There is a design at the left and four drawings at the right. One or more of the four drawings contain the design in the correct position, that is, the design may not be *turned*. The designs in the drawings must be the same size as the original design, but they need not be in alignment with the original design. Print the letter or letters of the drawings that contain(s) the design.   1.____

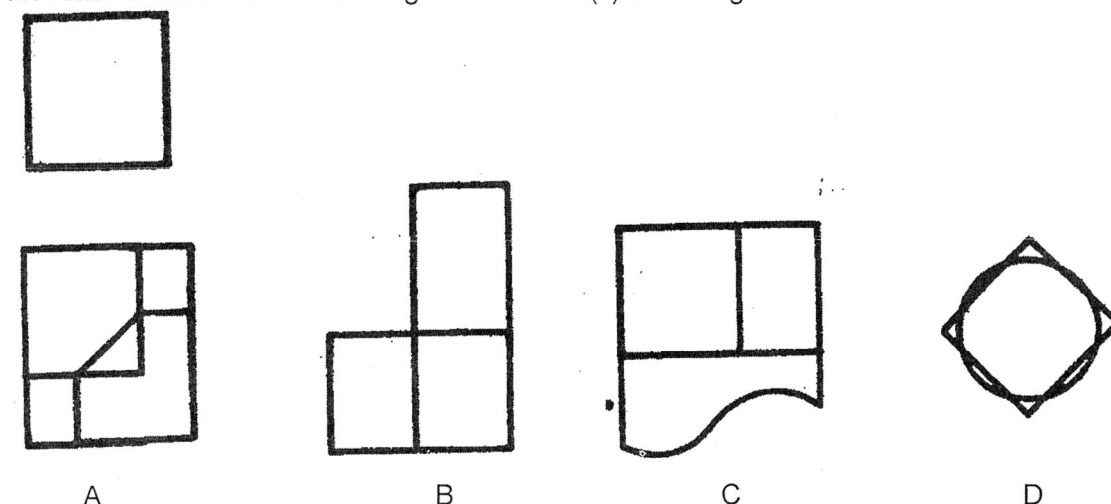

    A   B   C   D

2. This question consists of a series of numbers in which the numbers follow some definite order. Look at the numbers in the series and determine what the order is; then from the suggested answers, choose the answer that gives the next two numbers in the series. The rule for the order may involve adding, subtracting, multiplying, dividing, squaring, etc., or a combination of these operations.   2.____
   6 7 9 12 16
     A. 21 17   B. 26 33   C. 28 35   D. 30 37   E. 33 35

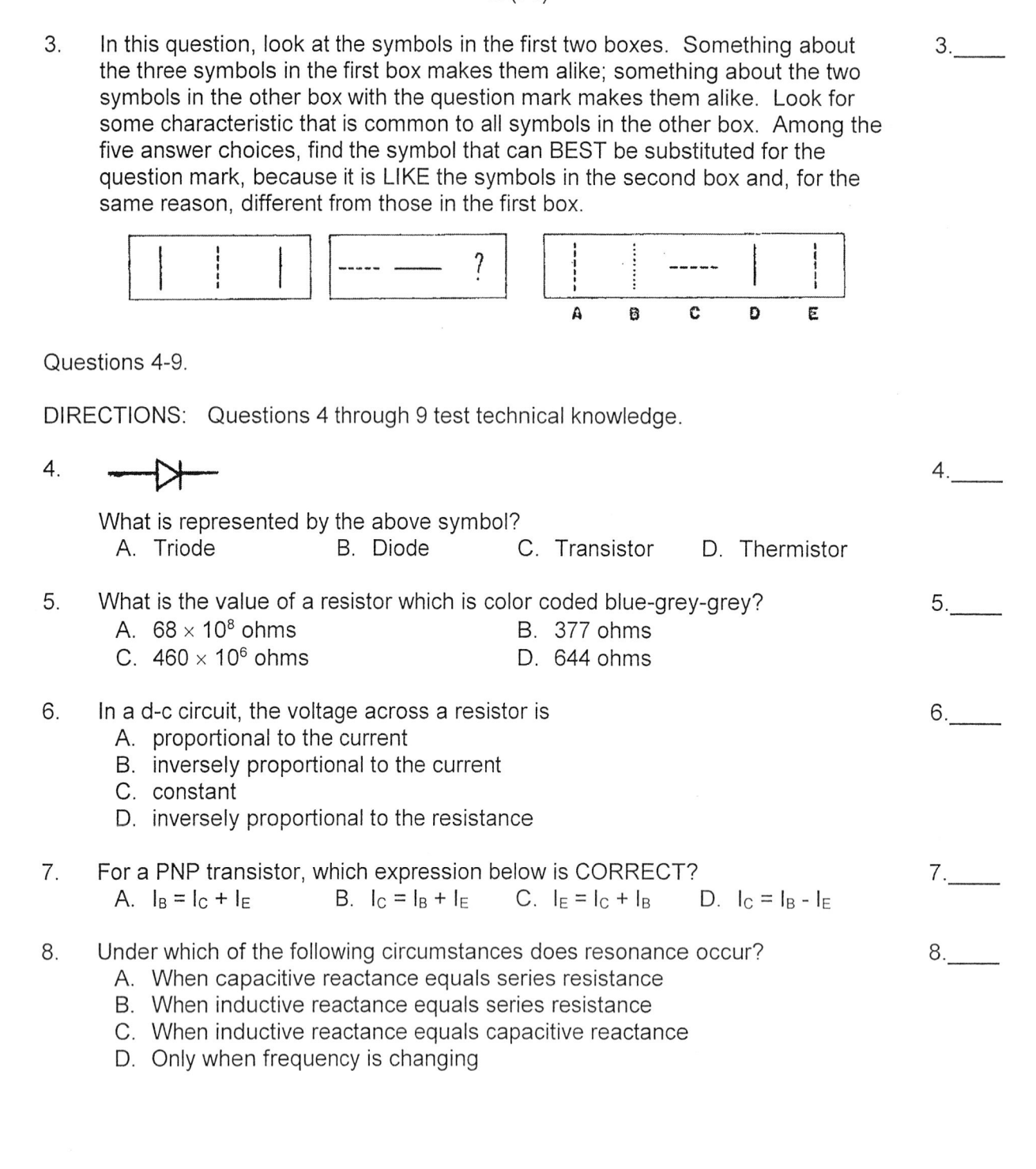

3. In this question, look at the symbols in the first two boxes. Something about the three symbols in the first box makes them alike; something about the two symbols in the other box with the question mark makes them alike. Look for some characteristic that is common to all symbols in the other box. Among the five answer choices, find the symbol that can BEST be substituted for the question mark, because it is LIKE the symbols in the second box and, for the same reason, different from those in the first box.

3.____

			?			-----			
				A B C D E

Questions 4-9.

DIRECTIONS: Questions 4 through 9 test technical knowledge.

4. ─▷|─

   What is represented by the above symbol?
   A. Triode B. Diode C. Transistor D. Thermistor

4.____

5. What is the value of a resistor which is color coded blue-grey-grey?
   A. 68×10^8 ohms
   B. 377 ohms
   C. 460×10^6 ohms
   D. 644 ohms

5.____

6. In a d-c circuit, the voltage across a resistor is
   A. proportional to the current
   B. inversely proportional to the current
   C. constant
   D. inversely proportional to the resistance

6.____

7. For a PNP transistor, which expression below is CORRECT?
   A. $I_B = I_C + I_E$ B. $I_C = I_B + I_E$ C. $I_E = I_C + I_B$ D. $I_C = I_B - I_E$

7.____

8. Under which of the following circumstances does resonance occur?
   A. When capacitive reactance equals series resistance
   B. When inductive reactance equals series resistance
   C. When inductive reactance equals capacitive reactance
   D. Only when frequency is changing

8.____

9.

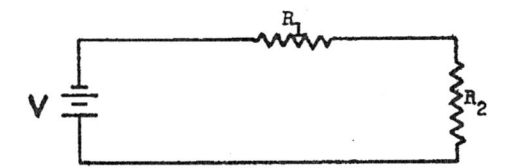

In the above figure, what is the resistance of R_2 when the voltage at V is 50v, the current in the circuit is 1 amp., and the voltage drop across R_1 is 10 volts?
    A. 10 ohms   B. 20 ohms   C. 40 ohms   D. 50 ohms

KEY (CORRECT ANSWERS)

1. A/C
2. A
3. C
4. B
5. A

6. A
7. C
8. C
9. C

Electronic Technician Test Battery

Practice Questions

From the official announcement for educational purposes

Workplace Learning
Instructions

This section contains sample items for the Workplace Learning Test. The items contained in this section are meant to provide individuals with an idea of what to expect when they take the actual Workplace Learning Test.

This is a test of your ability to remember and follow directions. During the test, you will listen to instructions given by an audio CD explaining how to complete certain jobs. Once each set of instructions ends, you will be asked to answer a series of questions. You should take notes as the instructions are given. Note-taking sheets will be provided in the test booklet.

The following page provides a passage like the one that would be read for you during the test. You should read through the sample passage and then answer the sample questions provided.

Remember, on the actual test, the instructions or conversation will be read aloud to you via an audio CD. You will need to listen to the instructions or conversation and then answer the questions.

Sample Questions

Use the passage below to answer sample questions 1-4.

In italics below is a sample passage that would be read aloud to you during the test. The equipment problem tag referred to in the instructions is shown below the passage.

> ***Lead Mechanic:*** *When problems occur with your machine contact your supervisor if it's a minor problem and the machine has been in service for more than a year. If a major problem comes up or the machine has been in service for less than one year report that problem to the maintenance department.*

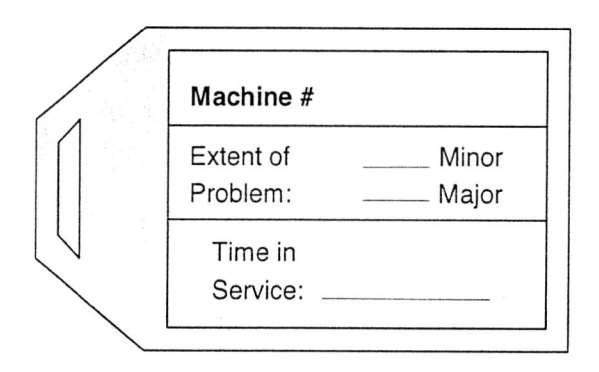

Machine #	
Extent of Problem:	____ Minor ____ Major
Time in Service:	____

Indicate what action should be taken in sample questions 1-4.

1

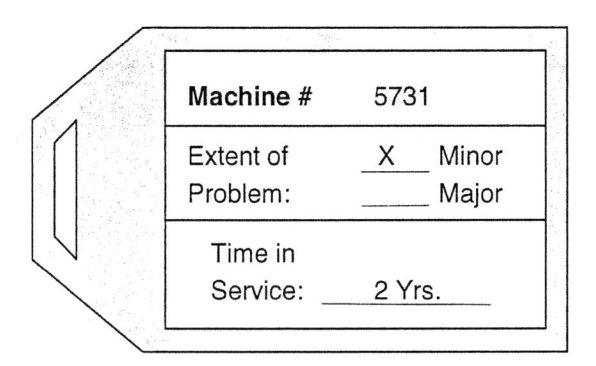

Machine # 5731

Extent of Problem: __X__ Minor ____ Major

Time in Service: __2 Yrs.__

A Report to supervisor
B Report to maintenance
C Need additional information

2

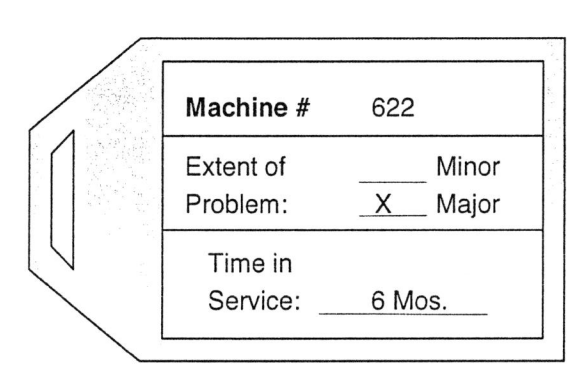

Machine # 622

Extent of Problem: ____ Minor __X__ Major

Time in Service: __6 Mos.__

A Report to supervisor
B Report to maintenance
C Need additional information

3

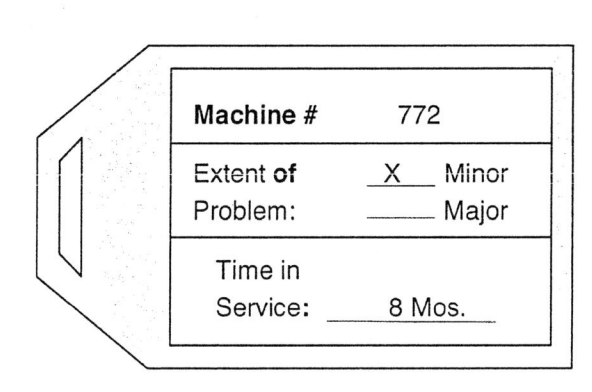

Machine # 772

Extent of Problem: __X__ Minor ____ Major

Time in Service: __8 Mos.__

A Report to supervisor
B Report to maintenance
C Need additional information

4

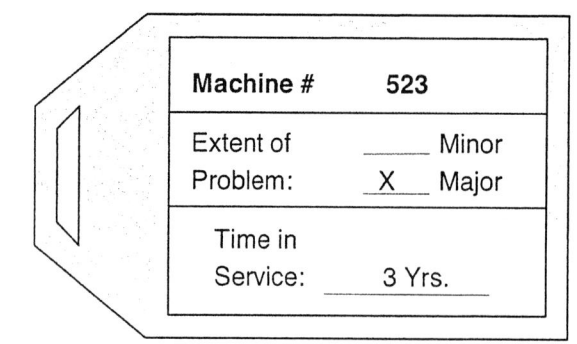

Machine #	523
Extent of Problem:	____ Minor _X_ Major
Time in Service:	3 Yrs.

A Report to supervisor
B Report to maintenance
C Need additional information

Answers

1. A 2. B 3. B 4. B

Workplace Practices 2.0
Instructions

This section contains sample items for the Workplace Practices 2.0 Test. The items contained in this section are meant to provide individuals with an idea of what to expect when they take the actual Workplace Practices 2.0 Test.

This test has two sub-sections. Both sections include questions that describe peoples' attitudes about themselves and their work. Please answer each question in a way that best describes your own experiences, judgments, and opinions. It is very important that you answer each item honestly and as accurately as possible. There are no right or wrong answers to this test.

In one section you are asked to read each statement, then decide whether you agree or disagree with what it says, and select your answer. If you **strongly agree** with the statement, select choice "A." If you **somewhat agree** with the statement, select choice "B." If you **somewhat disagree** with the statement, select choice "C." Finally, if you **strongly disagree** with the statement, select choice "D."

Section two contains two types of questions. Some questions ask you about work practices. Other questions describe a situation and ask you what to do. Read each question and choose the **one** answer that most accurately reflects your opinion. For some questions, more than one answer may seem appropriate. In these instances, choose the one answer that most accurately reflects your opinion.

Sample Questions

Section 1: Sample questions 1-4.

1	I dislike performing repetitive tasks.	A	Strongly Agree
		B	Somewhat Agree
		C	Somewhat Disagree
		D	Strongly Disagree

2	I prefer to be spontaneous and do things on the "spur of the moment."	A	Strongly Agree
		B	Somewhat Agree
		C	Somewhat Disagree
		D	Strongly Disagree

3	I am conscious of the effect my behavior and actions have on others.	A	Strongly Agree
		B	Somewhat Agree
		C	Somewhat Disagree
		D	Strongly Disagree

4	I agree with the saying, "the devil is in the details."	A	Strongly Agree
		B	Somewhat Agree
		C	Somewhat Disagree
		D	Strongly Disagree

Section 2: Sample questions 5-8

5	How many absences do you think the typical worker would have over a six-month period?	A	None
		B	One day
		C	Two to three days
		D	Four or five days
		E	Six or more days

6	Suppose we contacted your most recent supervisor. How would he/she rate your adherence to company policies and procedures?	A	Well above average
		B	Somewhat above average
		C	Average
		D	Below average
		E	I have never been employed

7	Toni, a line worker, has an idea to improve the assembly procedure that would allow workers to produce more widgets per hour. She has presented her idea to her supervisor on more than one occasion, but her supervisor is reluctant to listen to the ideas of his subordinates. Toni really believes that if her idea were implemented, it would improve company profits. If you were Toni, what would you do?	A	Go ahead and make the improvements anyway. After all, if the supervisor could see the improvements, he would have no choice but to agree to the change.
		B	Talk to coworkers about the idea and enlist their help in obtaining the supervisor's buy-in.
		C	Go to the supervisor's boss with the idea.
		D	File a complaint with the company's HR office. It is unfair that the supervisor will not listen to the ideas of his subordinates.
		E	Do nothing. After all, it is the company's loss.

8	**During your shift, a co-worker is working with a piece of heavy machinery and has an accident. As a result, he must be rushed to the hospital. Based on your experience, and without knowing more about the situation, what do you think the *most likely* cause of the accident was?**	A	Poor maintenance of equipment
		B	Bad luck
		C	Co-worker's failure to adhere to company policies
		D	Lack of attention to safety procedures
		E	Distractions caused by other coworkers

Arithmetic Computations
Instructions

This section contains sample items for the Arithmetic Computations Test. The items contained in this section are meant to provide individuals with an idea of what to expect when they take the actual Arithmetic Computations Test.

This is a test of your ability to solve arithmetic problems. This test will ask you to perform general arithmetic computations (addition, subtraction, multiplication, division) to test questions involving whole numbers, fractions, decimals and percentages. On the actual test, you will not be allowed to use a calculator, but you will be given a piece of scratch paper for your calculations.

When completing this test, you will need to work quickly and accurately to complete as many items as possible. Your score is based on the total number of items you answer correctly.

Sample Questions

1. 12.4 + 6.4 =
   - A 16.4
   - B 16.8
   - C 18.4
   - D 18.8
   - E other

2. 672 - 95 =
   - A 576
   - B 577
   - C 586
   - D 587
   - E other

3. 5.6 x 30 =
   - A 16.8
   - B 33.0
   - C 168
   - D 330
   - E other

4. 1/5 of 60 =
   - A .20
   - B 5
   - C 12
   - D 60.5
   - E other

5	618 ÷ 12 =	A	51.0
		B	51.5
		C	61.0
		D	61.5
		E	other

6	1/3 + 3/4 =	A	4/3
		B	1
		C	1 1/12
		D	1 1/3
		E	other

7	15% of 650 =	A	39
		B	43.3
		C	95.5
		D	97.5
		E	other

8	75.368 + 152.74 =	A	227.108
		B	227.442
		C	228.108
		D	228.442
		E	other

Answers

1. D 2. B 3. C 4. C 5. B 6. C 7. D 8. C

Advanced Industrial Skills
Instructions

This section contains sample items for the Advanced Industrial Skills Test. The items contained in this section are meant to provide individuals with an idea of what to expect when they take the actual Advanced Industrial Skills Test.

This is a test of your ability to identify and use standard work instructions and procedures like those you might find on the job. This test contains a number of work instructions presented in text, tables, or diagrams. Each set of work instructions is followed by several questions. Your task on this test is to apply the work instructions to determine the best answer for each question.

Sample Questions

Use the work instructions below to answer Sample Questions 1 - 4.

WORK INSTRUCTIONS

When monitoring the assembly machine, it is important to react to the warning indicator. When the status changes, you must take the following actions depending upon the numbered warning.

If the warning is a:	Then the required action is:
1	No action required, continue processing
2	First, check product quality and then call maintenance
3	Shut off machine and contact supervisor immediately

The warning indicator may, on occasion, turn off. If this happens, you should press the reset button and wait 30 seconds for the machine to run a self-test. If resetting the machine fails to fix the problem, then shut off the machine and contact your supervisor.

1 If the warning indicator shows a 1, what action is required?

A. No action is required
B. Check product quality
C. Shut off machine
D. Press the reset button
E. Need more information

2 What action should you take last if the warning indicator shows a 2?

A. No action is required
B. Check product quality
C. Contact supervisor
D. Call maintenance
E. Shut off machine

3 What action should you take first if the warning indicator shows a 3?

A. No action is required
B. Check product quality
C. Contact supervisor
D. Call maintenance
E. Shut off machine

4	If the warning indicator turns off and resetting the machine does not correct the problem, what is the last action you should take?	A	No action is required
		B	Check product quality
		C	Contact supervisor
		D	Call maintenance
		E	Shut off machine

Answers

1. A 2. D 3. E 4. C

Advanced Industrial Problem Solving
Instructions

This section contains sample items for the Advanced Industrial Problem Solving Test. The items contained in this section are meant to provide individuals with an idea of what to expect when they take the actual Advanced Industrial Problem Solving Test.

This is a test of your ability to locate and use information presented in tables and charts like those you might find on the job. The test contains a number of tables, charts or graphs, each followed by several questions. Your task on this test is to use information from the tables, charts or graphs to make calculations and determine the correct answer for each question.

Sample Questions

Use the table below to answer Sample Questions 1 - 4.

Per-minute telephone call charges by area code

	From →	200-245	315-355	401-485	509-599
	To ↓				
AREA CODES	200-245	$.15	$.28	$.47	$.43
	315-355	$.25	$.15	$.13	$.46
	401-485	$.40	$.25	$.15	$.32
	509-599	$.50	$.40	$.30	$.15

1	How much would a two-minute call from area code 205 to area code 403 cost?	A	$ .30
		B	$ .40
		C	$ .63
		D	$ .80
2	What is the difference in cost for a call from area code 320 to area code 470 versus one made from area code 470 to area code 320?	A	$ .12
		B	$ .13
		C	$ .25
		D	$ .38
3	How much would a five-minute call from area code 425 to area code 405 cost?	A	$ .15
		B	$ .60
		C	$ .65
		D	$ .75

4. What is the difference in cost for a two-minute call from area code 205 to area code 530 versus one made from area code 530 to area code 205?

A $ .07
B $ .10
C $ .14
D $ .20

Answers

1. D 2. A 3. D 4. C

Tool Knowledge Test
Instructions

This section contains sample items for the Tool Knowledge Test. The items contained in this section are meant to provide individuals with an idea of what to expect when they take the actual Tool Knowledge Test.

This is a test of your ability to identify tools and standard hardware and how they are commonly used. The test contains figures and pictures of tools and hardware. Your task is to read each question and select the best answer from the alternatives given. All the information you need to answer the questions will be provided.

Sample Questions

Use the pictures above each question to answer sample questions 1-4.

1	**The tool shown in the figure above is called a(n):**	A	Pliers
		B	Scissors
		C	Wrench
		D	Awl

2	**The item shown in the figure above is a:**	A	Beater
		B	Socket extension
		C	Tap handle
		D	Ratchet handle
		E	Torque wrench

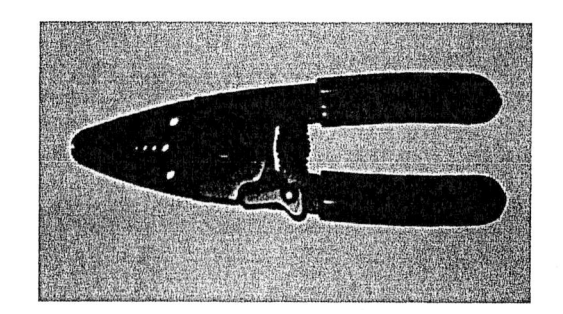

3	The tool shown in the figure above is a:	A	Slip-joint pliers
		B	Sire stripper
		C	Snips
		D	Lineman's pliers

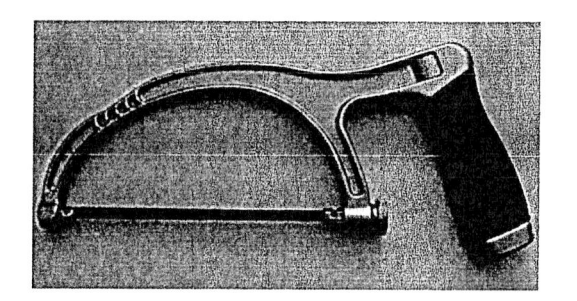

4	The tool shown in the figure above is called a:	A	Bow saw
		B	Coping saw
		C	Back saw
		D	Hack saw

Answers

1. B 2. D 3. B 4. D

Mechanical Comprehension
Instructions

This section contains sample items for the Mechanical Comprehension Test. The items contained in this section are meant to provide individuals with an idea of what to expect when they take the actual Mechanical Comprehension Test.

This is a test of your ability to solve problems that involve mechanical principles and problems. The test contains questions that show you an illustration of a practical problem, and ask you to determine the correct answer. Use your experience and judgment to choose the answer you think is best.

Sample Questions

For sample questions 1-4, examine the pictures to the right of each question.

---

1. Which of the following two objects would be easier to tip over, assuming that both are made of the same material and weigh the same? (If no difference, mark C.)

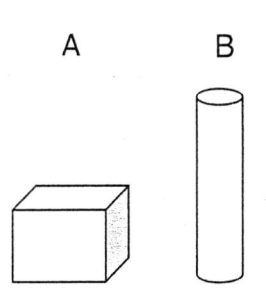

---

2. Which beam is more likely to break, assuming that both beams are of equal thickness and are made of the same material? (If no difference, mark C.)

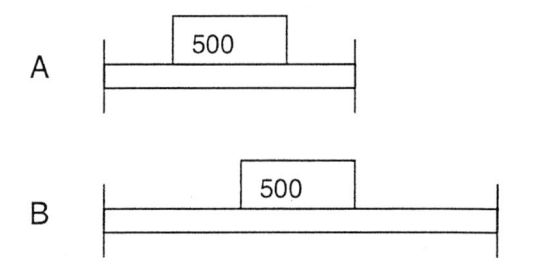

---

3. Which table is more likely to tip over, assuming that both tables are made of the same material, are the same size, and weigh the same? (If no difference, mark C.)

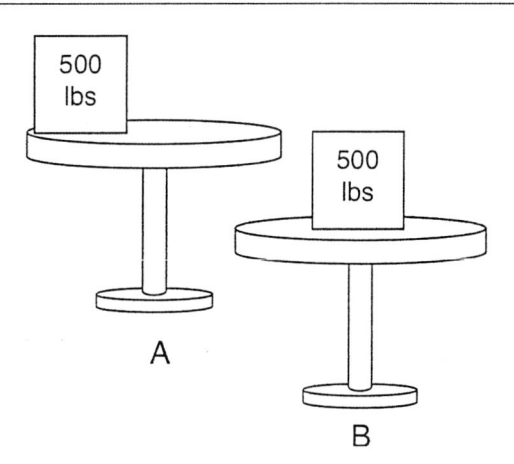

4. Which ball will be rolling faster when it reaches the bottom of the slide, assuming that both balls are made of the same material, are the same size, and weigh the same? (If no difference, mark C.)

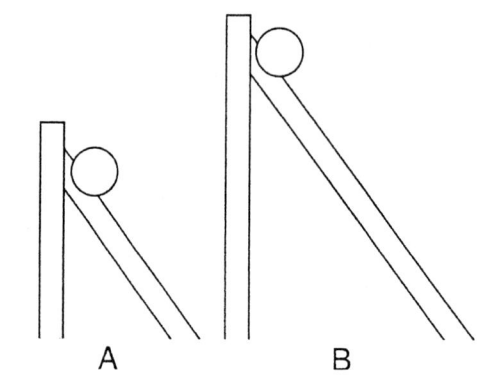

A   B

Answers

1. B 2. B 3. A 4. B

Systems Troubleshooting
Instructions

This section contains sample items for the Systems Troubleshooting Test. The items contained in this section are meant to provide individuals with an idea of what to expect when they take the actual Systems Troubleshooting Test.

This is a test of your ability to diagnose problems that can occur in systems. The test contains five systems, each followed by several questions. The "systems" are a collection of interconnected parts. Here is what a system looks like:

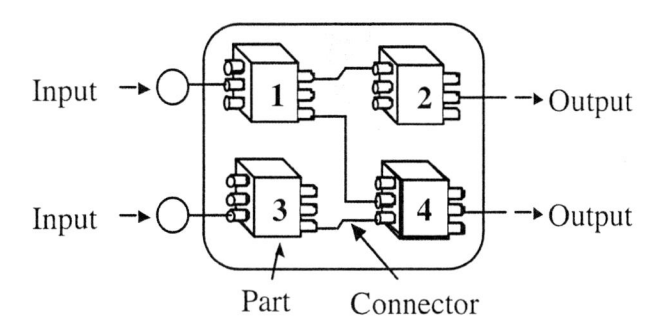

A "part" in a system can receive input signals or can output signals to another part through a connector. Input signals enter on the left side of a part and output signals leave on the right side of a part. In this test, your task will be to figure out why a system is not working or what will happen to the system if a part fails. You will need to use the two rules below to answer the test questions:

> Rule 1: A part will output a signal only if it receives an input signal from all other parts to which it is connected on its left side.

> Rule 2: If a part fails, then it will not output a signal to any other parts to which it is connected on its right side.

Sample Questions

Use the diagram below to answer sample questions 1-2.

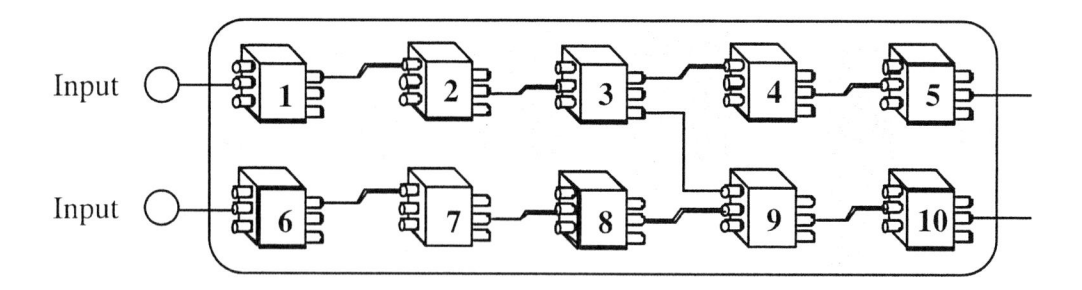

1	Part 5 has an output signal but Part 10 doesn't. Which of the following could be the failed part?	A	Part 1
		B	Part 3
		C	Part 4
		D	Part 7

2	Which of the following would not have an output signal if Part 3 suddenly failed?	A	Part 1
		B	Part 4
		C	Part 6
		D	Part 8

Use the diagram below to answer sample questions 3-4.

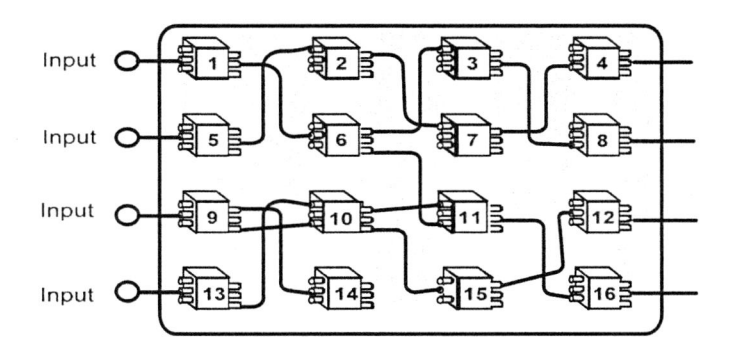

3	Parts 4 and 12 have output signals but Parts 8 and 16 don't. Which of the following could be the failed part?	A	Part 2
		B	Part 5
		C	Part 6
		D	Part 10

4	Which of the following could not have an output signal if Part 10 suddenly failed?	A	Part 7
		B	Part 12
		C	Part 13
		D	Part 14

Answers

1. D 2. B 3. C 4. B

HOW TO TAKE A TEST

I. YOU MUST PASS AN EXAMINATION

A. *WHAT EVERY CANDIDATE SHOULD KNOW*

Examination applicants often ask us for help in preparing for the written test. What can I study in advance? What kinds of questions will be asked? How will the test be given? How will the papers be graded?

As an applicant for a civil service examination, you may be wondering about some of these things. Our purpose here is to suggest effective methods of advance study and to describe civil service examinations.

Your chances for success on this examination can be increased if you know how to prepare. Those "pre-examination jitters" can be reduced if you know what to expect. You can even experience an adventure in good citizenship if you know why civil service exams are given.

B. *WHY ARE CIVIL SERVICE EXAMINATIONS GIVEN?*

Civil service examinations are important to you in two ways. As a citizen, you want public jobs filled by employees who know how to do their work. As a job seeker, you want a fair chance to compete for that job on an equal footing with other candidates. The best-known means of accomplishing this two-fold goal is the competitive examination.

Exams are widely publicized throughout the nation. They may be administered for jobs in federal, state, city, municipal, town or village governments or agencies.

Any citizen may apply, with some limitations, such as the age or residence of applicants. Your experience and education may be reviewed to see whether you meet the requirements for the particular examination. When these requirements exist, they are reasonable and applied consistently to all applicants. Thus, a competitive examination may cause you some uneasiness now, but it is your privilege and safeguard.

C. *HOW ARE CIVIL SERVICE EXAMS DEVELOPED?*

Examinations are carefully written by trained technicians who are specialists in the field known as "psychological measurement," in consultation with recognized authorities in the field of work that the test will cover. These experts recommend the subject matter areas or skills to be tested; only those knowledges or skills important to your success on the job are included. The most reliable books and source materials available are used as references. Together, the experts and technicians judge the difficulty level of the questions.

Test technicians know how to phrase questions so that the problem is clearly stated. Their ethics do not permit "trick" or "catch" questions. Questions may have been tried out on sample groups, or subjected to statistical analysis, to determine their usefulness.

Written tests are often used in combination with performance tests, ratings of training and experience, and oral interviews. All of these measures combine to form the best-known means of finding the right person for the right job.

II. HOW TO PASS THE WRITTEN TEST

A. NATURE OF THE EXAMINATION

To prepare intelligently for civil service examinations, you should know how they differ from school examinations you have taken. In school you were assigned certain definite pages to read or subjects to cover. The examination questions were quite detailed and usually emphasized memory. Civil service exams, on the other hand, try to discover your present ability to perform the duties of a position, plus your potentiality to learn these duties. In other words, a civil service exam attempts to predict how successful you will be. Questions cover such a broad area that they cannot be as minute and detailed as school exam questions.

In the public service similar kinds of work, or positions, are grouped together in one "class." This process is known as *position-classification*. All the positions in a class are paid according to the salary range for that class. One class title covers all of these positions, and they are all tested by the same examination.

B. FOUR BASIC STEPS

1) Study the announcement

How, then, can you know what subjects to study? Our best answer is: "Learn as much as possible about the class of positions for which you've applied." The exam will test the knowledge, skills and abilities needed to do the work.

Your most valuable source of information about the position you want is the official exam announcement. This announcement lists the training and experience qualifications. Check these standards and apply only if you come reasonably close to meeting them.

The brief description of the position in the examination announcement offers some clues to the subjects which will be tested. Think about the job itself. Review the duties in your mind. Can you perform them, or are there some in which you are rusty? Fill in the blank spots in your preparation.

Many jurisdictions preview the written test in the exam announcement by including a section called "Knowledge and Abilities Required," "Scope of the Examination," or some similar heading. Here you will find out specifically what fields will be tested.

2) Review your own background

Once you learn in general what the position is all about, and what you need to know to do the work, ask yourself which subjects you already know fairly well and which need improvement. You may wonder whether to concentrate on improving your strong areas or on building some background in your fields of weakness. When the announcement has specified "some knowledge" or "considerable knowledge," or has used adjectives like "beginning principles of…" or "advanced … methods," you can get a clue as to the number and difficulty of questions to be asked in any given field. More questions, and hence broader coverage, would be included for those subjects which are more important in the work. Now weigh your strengths and weaknesses against the job requirements and prepare accordingly.

3) Determine the level of the position

Another way to tell how intensively you should prepare is to understand the level of the job for which you are applying. Is it the entering level? In other words, is this the position in which beginners in a field of work are hired? Or is it an intermediate or advanced level? Sometimes this is indicated by such words as "Junior" or "Senior" in the class title. Other jurisdictions use Roman numerals to designate the level – Clerk I, Clerk II, for example. The word "Supervisor" sometimes appears in the title. If the level is not indicated by the title, check the description of duties. Will you be working under very close supervision, or will you have responsibility for independent decisions in this work?

4) Choose appropriate study materials

Now that you know the subjects to be examined and the relative amount of each subject to be covered, you can choose suitable study materials. For beginning level jobs, or even advanced ones, if you have a pronounced weakness in some aspect of your training, read a modern, standard textbook in that field. Be sure it is up to date and has general coverage. Such books are normally available at your library, and the librarian will be glad to help you locate one. For entry-level positions, questions of appropriate difficulty are chosen – neither highly advanced questions, nor those too simple. Such questions require careful thought but not advanced training.

If the position for which you are applying is technical or advanced, you will read more advanced, specialized material. If you are already familiar with the basic principles of your field, elementary textbooks would waste your time. Concentrate on advanced textbooks and technical periodicals. Think through the concepts and review difficult problems in your field.

These are all general sources. You can get more ideas on your own initiative, following these leads. For example, training manuals and publications of the government agency which employs workers in your field can be useful, particularly for technical and professional positions. A letter or visit to the government department involved may result in more specific study suggestions, and certainly will provide you with a more definite idea of the exact nature of the position you are seeking.

III. KINDS OF TESTS

Tests are used for purposes other than measuring knowledge and ability to perform specified duties. For some positions, it is equally important to test ability to make adjustments to new situations or to profit from training. In others, basic mental abilities not dependent on information are essential. Questions which test these things may not appear as pertinent to the duties of the position as those which test for knowledge and information. Yet they are often highly important parts of a fair examination. For very general questions, it is almost impossible to help you direct your study efforts. What we can do is to point out some of the more common of these general abilities needed in public service positions and describe some typical questions.

1) General information

Broad, general information has been found useful for predicting job success in some kinds of work. This is tested in a variety of ways, from vocabulary lists to questions about current events. Basic background in some field of work, such as sociology or economics, may be sampled in a group of questions. Often these are principles which have become familiar to most persons through exposure rather than through formal training. It is difficult to advise you how to study for these questions; being alert to the world around you is our best suggestion.

2) Verbal ability

An example of an ability needed in many positions is verbal or language ability. Verbal ability is, in brief, the ability to use and understand words. Vocabulary and grammar tests are typical measures of this ability. Reading comprehension or paragraph interpretation questions are common in many kinds of civil service tests. You are given a paragraph of written material and asked to find its central meaning.

3) Numerical ability

Number skills can be tested by the familiar arithmetic problem, by checking paired lists of numbers to see which are alike and which are different, or by interpreting charts and graphs. In the latter test, a graph may be printed in the test booklet which you are asked to use as the basis for answering questions.

4) Observation

A popular test for law-enforcement positions is the observation test. A picture is shown to you for several minutes, then taken away. Questions about the picture test your ability to observe both details and larger elements.

5) Following directions

In many positions in the public service, the employee must be able to carry out written instructions dependably and accurately. You may be given a chart with several columns, each column listing a variety of information. The questions require you to carry out directions involving the information given in the chart.

6) Skills and aptitudes

Performance tests effectively measure some manual skills and aptitudes. When the skill is one in which you are trained, such as typing or shorthand, you can practice. These tests are often very much like those given in business school or high school courses. For many of the other skills and aptitudes, however, no short-time preparation can be made. Skills and abilities natural to you or that you have developed throughout your lifetime are being tested.

Many of the general questions just described provide all the data needed to answer the questions and ask you to use your reasoning ability to find the answers. Your best preparation for these tests, as well as for tests of facts and ideas, is to be at your physical and mental best. You, no doubt, have your own methods of getting into an exam-taking mood and keeping "in shape." The next section lists some ideas on this subject.

IV. KINDS OF QUESTIONS

Only rarely is the "essay" question, which you answer in narrative form, used in civil service tests. Civil service tests are usually of the short-answer type. Full instructions for answering these questions will be given to you at the examination. But in case this is your first experience with short-answer questions and separate answer sheets, here is what you need to know:

1) Multiple-choice Questions

Most popular of the short-answer questions is the "multiple choice" or "best answer" question. It can be used, for example, to test for factual knowledge, ability to solve problems or judgment in meeting situations found at work.

A multiple-choice question is normally one of three types—
- It can begin with an incomplete statement followed by several possible endings. You are to find the one ending which *best* completes the statement, although some of the others may not be entirely wrong.
- It can also be a complete statement in the form of a question which is answered by choosing one of the statements listed.

- It can be in the form of a problem – again you select the best answer.

Here is an example of a multiple-choice question with a discussion which should give you some clues as to the method for choosing the right answer:

When an employee has a complaint about his assignment, the action which will *best* help him overcome his difficulty is to
   A. discuss his difficulty with his coworkers
   B. take the problem to the head of the organization
   C. take the problem to the person who gave him the assignment
   D. say nothing to anyone about his complaint

In answering this question, you should study each of the choices to find which is best. Consider choice "A" – Certainly an employee may discuss his complaint with fellow employees, but no change or improvement can result, and the complaint remains unresolved. Choice "B" is a poor choice since the head of the organization probably does not know what assignment you have been given, and taking your problem to him is known as "going over the head" of the supervisor. The supervisor, or person who made the assignment, is the person who can clarify it or correct any injustice. Choice "C" is, therefore, correct. To say nothing, as in choice "D," is unwise. Supervisors have and interest in knowing the problems employees are facing, and the employee is seeking a solution to his problem.

2) True/False Questions

The "true/false" or "right/wrong" form of question is sometimes used. Here a complete statement is given. Your job is to decide whether the statement is right or wrong.

SAMPLE: A roaming cell-phone call to a nearby city costs less than a non-roaming call to a distant city.

This statement is wrong, or false, since roaming calls are more expensive.
This is not a complete list of all possible question forms, although most of the others are variations of these common types. You will always get complete directions for answering questions. Be sure you understand *how* to mark your answers – ask questions until you do.

V. RECORDING YOUR ANSWERS

Computer terminals are used more and more today for many different kinds of exams.
For an examination with very few applicants, you may be told to record your answers in the test booklet itself. Separate answer sheets are much more common. If this separate answer sheet is to be scored by machine – and this is often the case – it is highly important that you mark your answers correctly in order to get credit.
An electronic scoring machine is often used in civil service offices because of the speed with which papers can be scored. Machine-scored answer sheets must be marked with a pencil, which will be given to you. This pencil has a high graphite content which responds to the electronic scoring machine. As a matter of fact, stray dots may register as answers, so do not let your pencil rest on the answer sheet while you are pondering the correct answer. Also, if your pencil lead breaks or is otherwise defective, ask for another.

Since the answer sheet will be dropped in a slot in the scoring machine, be careful not to bend the corners or get the paper crumpled.

The answer sheet normally has five vertical columns of numbers, with 30 numbers to a column. These numbers correspond to the question numbers in your test booklet. After each number, going across the page are four or five pairs of dotted lines. These short dotted lines have small letters or numbers above them. The first two pairs may also have a "T" or "F" above the letters. This indicates that the first two pairs only are to be used if the questions are of the true-false type. If the questions are multiple choice, disregard the "T" and "F" and pay attention only to the small letters or numbers.

Answer your questions in the manner of the sample that follows:

32. The largest city in the United States is
    A. Washington, D.C.
    B. New York City
    C. Chicago
    D. Detroit
    E. San Francisco

1) Choose the answer you think is best. (New York City is the largest, so "B" is correct.)
2) Find the row of dotted lines numbered the same as the question you are answering. (Find row number 32)
3) Find the pair of dotted lines corresponding to the answer. (Find the pair of lines under the mark "B.")
4) Make a solid black mark between the dotted lines.

VI. BEFORE THE TEST

Common sense will help you find procedures to follow to get ready for an examination. Too many of us, however, overlook these sensible measures. Indeed, nervousness and fatigue have been found to be the most serious reasons why applicants fail to do their best on civil service tests. Here is a list of reminders:

- Begin your preparation early – Don't wait until the last minute to go scurrying around for books and materials or to find out what the position is all about.
- Prepare continuously – An hour a night for a week is better than an all-night cram session. This has been definitely established. What is more, a night a week for a month will return better dividends than crowding your study into a shorter period of time.
- Locate the place of the exam – You have been sent a notice telling you when and where to report for the examination. If the location is in a different town or otherwise unfamiliar to you, it would be well to inquire the best route and learn something about the building.
- Relax the night before the test – Allow your mind to rest. Do not study at all that night. Plan some mild recreation or diversion; then go to bed early and get a good night's sleep.
- Get up early enough to make a leisurely trip to the place for the test – This way unforeseen events, traffic snarls, unfamiliar buildings, etc. will not upset you.
- Dress comfortably – A written test is not a fashion show. You will be known by number and not by name, so wear something comfortable.

- Leave excess paraphernalia at home – Shopping bags and odd bundles will get in your way. You need bring only the items mentioned in the official notice you received; usually everything you need is provided. Do not bring reference books to the exam. They will only confuse those last minutes and be taken away from you when in the test room.
- Arrive somewhat ahead of time – If because of transportation schedules you must get there very early, bring a newspaper or magazine to take your mind off yourself while waiting.
- Locate the examination room – When you have found the proper room, you will be directed to the seat or part of the room where you will sit. Sometimes you are given a sheet of instructions to read while you are waiting. Do not fill out any forms until you are told to do so; just read them and be prepared.
- Relax and prepare to listen to the instructions
- If you have any physical problem that may keep you from doing your best, be sure to tell the test administrator. If you are sick or in poor health, you really cannot do your best on the exam. You can come back and take the test some other time.

VII. AT THE TEST

The day of the test is here and you have the test booklet in your hand. The temptation to get going is very strong. Caution! There is more to success than knowing the right answers. You must know how to identify your papers and understand variations in the type of short-answer question used in this particular examination. Follow these suggestions for maximum results from your efforts:

1) Cooperate with the monitor

The test administrator has a duty to create a situation in which you can be as much at ease as possible. He will give instructions, tell you when to begin, check to see that you are marking your answer sheet correctly, and so on. He is not there to guard you, although he will see that your competitors do not take unfair advantage. He wants to help you do your best.

2) Listen to all instructions

Don't jump the gun! Wait until you understand all directions. In most civil service tests you get more time than you need to answer the questions. So don't be in a hurry. Read each word of instructions until you clearly understand the meaning. Study the examples, listen to all announcements and follow directions. Ask questions if you do not understand what to do.

3) Identify your papers

Civil service exams are usually identified by number only. You will be assigned a number; you must not put your name on your test papers. Be sure to copy your number correctly. Since more than one exam may be given, copy your exact examination title.

4) Plan your time

Unless you are told that a test is a "speed" or "rate of work" test, speed itself is usually not important. Time enough to answer all the questions will be provided, but this does not mean that you have all day. An overall time limit has been set. Divide the total time (in minutes) by the number of questions to determine the approximate time you have for each question.

5) Do not linger over difficult questions

If you come across a difficult question, mark it with a paper clip (useful to have along) and come back to it when you have been through the booklet. One caution if you do this – be sure to skip a number on your answer sheet as well. Check often to be sure that you have not lost your place and that you are marking in the row numbered the same as the question you are answering.

6) Read the questions

Be sure you know what the question asks! Many capable people are unsuccessful because they failed to *read* the questions correctly.

7) Answer all questions

Unless you have been instructed that a penalty will be deducted for incorrect answers, it is better to guess than to omit a question.

8) Speed tests

It is often better NOT to guess on speed tests. It has been found that on timed tests people are tempted to spend the last few seconds before time is called in marking answers at random – without even reading them – in the hope of picking up a few extra points. To discourage this practice, the instructions may warn you that your score will be "corrected" for guessing. That is, a penalty will be applied. The incorrect answers will be deducted from the correct ones, or some other penalty formula will be used.

9) Review your answers

If you finish before time is called, go back to the questions you guessed or omitted to give them further thought. Review other answers if you have time.

10) Return your test materials

If you are ready to leave before others have finished or time is called, take ALL your materials to the monitor and leave quietly. Never take any test material with you. The monitor can discover whose papers are not complete, and taking a test booklet may be grounds for disqualification.

VIII. EXAMINATION TECHNIQUES

1) Read the general instructions carefully. These are usually printed on the first page of the exam booklet. As a rule, these instructions refer to the timing of the examination; the fact that you should not start work until the signal and must stop work at a signal, etc. If there are any *special* instructions, such as a choice of questions to be answered, make sure that you note this instruction carefully.

2) When you are ready to start work on the examination, that is as soon as the signal has been given, read the instructions to each question booklet, underline any key words or phrases, such as *least, best, outline, describe* and the like. In this way you will tend to answer as requested rather than discover on reviewing your paper that you *listed without describing*, that you selected the *worst* choice rather than the *best* choice, etc.

3) If the examination is of the objective or multiple-choice type – that is, each question will also give a series of possible answers: A, B, C or D, and you are called upon to select the best answer and write the letter next to that answer on your answer paper – it is advisable to start answering each question in turn. There may be anywhere from 50 to 100 such questions in the three or four hours allotted and you can see how much time would be taken if you read through all the questions before beginning to answer any. Furthermore, if you come across a question or group of questions which you know would be difficult to answer, it would undoubtedly affect your handling of all the other questions.

4) If the examination is of the essay type and contains but a few questions, it is a moot point as to whether you should read all the questions before starting to answer any one. Of course, if you are given a choice – say five out of seven and the like – then it is essential to read all the questions so you can eliminate the two that are most difficult. If, however, you are asked to answer all the questions, there may be danger in trying to answer the easiest one first because you may find that you will spend too much time on it. The best technique is to answer the first question, then proceed to the second, etc.

5) Time your answers. Before the exam begins, write down the time it started, then add the time allowed for the examination and write down the time it must be completed, then divide the time available somewhat as follows:
   - If 3-1/2 hours are allowed, that would be 210 minutes. If you have 80 objective-type questions, that would be an average of 2-1/2 minutes per question. Allow yourself no more than 2 minutes per question, or a total of 160 minutes, which will permit about 50 minutes to review.
   - If for the time allotment of 210 minutes there are 7 essay questions to answer, that would average about 30 minutes a question. Give yourself only 25 minutes per question so that you have about 35 minutes to review.

6) The most important instruction is to *read each question* and make sure you know what is wanted. The second most important instruction is to *time yourself properly* so that you answer every question. The third most important instruction is to *answer every question*. Guess if you have to but include something for each question. Remember that you will receive no credit for a blank and will probably receive some credit if you write something in answer to an essay question. If you guess a letter – say "B" for a multiple-choice question – you may have guessed right. If you leave a blank as an answer to a multiple-choice question, the examiners may respect your feelings but it will not add a point to your score. Some exams may penalize you for wrong answers, so in such cases *only*, you may not want to guess unless you have some basis for your answer.

7) Suggestions
   a. Objective-type questions
      1. Examine the question booklet for proper sequence of pages and questions
      2. Read all instructions carefully
      3. Skip any question which seems too difficult; return to it after all other questions have been answered
      4. Apportion your time properly; do not spend too much time on any single question or group of questions

5. Note and underline key words – *all, most, fewest, least, best, worst, same, opposite,* etc.
6. Pay particular attention to negatives
7. Note unusual option, e.g., unduly long, short, complex, different or similar in content to the body of the question
8. Observe the use of "hedging" words – *probably, may, most likely,* etc.
9. Make sure that your answer is put next to the same number as the question
10. Do not second-guess unless you have good reason to believe the second answer is definitely more correct
11. Cross out original answer if you decide another answer is more accurate; do not erase until you are ready to hand your paper in
12. Answer all questions; guess unless instructed otherwise
13. Leave time for review

   b. Essay questions
   1. Read each question carefully
   2. Determine exactly what is wanted. Underline key words or phrases.
   3. Decide on outline or paragraph answer
   4. Include many different points and elements unless asked to develop any one or two points or elements
   5. Show impartiality by giving pros and cons unless directed to select one side only
   6. Make and write down any assumptions you find necessary to answer the questions
   7. Watch your English, grammar, punctuation and choice of words
   8. Time your answers; don't crowd material

8) Answering the essay question

Most essay questions can be answered by framing the specific response around several key words or ideas. Here are a few such key words or ideas:

M's: manpower, materials, methods, money, management
P's: purpose, program, policy, plan, procedure, practice, problems, pitfalls, personnel, public relations

   a. Six basic steps in handling problems:
   1. Preliminary plan and background development
   2. Collect information, data and facts
   3. Analyze and interpret information, data and facts
   4. Analyze and develop solutions as well as make recommendations
   5. Prepare report and sell recommendations
   6. Install recommendations and follow up effectiveness

   b. Pitfalls to avoid
   1. *Taking things for granted* – A statement of the situation does not necessarily imply that each of the elements is necessarily true; for example, a complaint may be invalid and biased so that all that can be taken for granted is that a complaint has been registered

2. *Considering only one side of a situation* – Wherever possible, indicate several alternatives and then point out the reasons you selected the best one
3. *Failing to indicate follow up* – Whenever your answer indicates action on your part, make certain that you will take proper follow-up action to see how successful your recommendations, procedures or actions turn out to be
4. *Taking too long in answering any single question* – Remember to time your answers properly

IX. AFTER THE TEST

Scoring procedures differ in detail among civil service jurisdictions although the general principles are the same. Whether the papers are hand-scored or graded by machine we have described, they are nearly always graded by number. That is, the person who marks the paper knows only the number – never the name – of the applicant. Not until all the papers have been graded will they be matched with names. If other tests, such as training and experience or oral interview ratings have been given, scores will be combined. Different parts of the examination usually have different weights. For example, the written test might count 60 percent of the final grade, and a rating of training and experience 40 percent. In many jurisdictions, veterans will have a certain number of points added to their grades.

After the final grade has been determined, the names are placed in grade order and an eligible list is established. There are various methods for resolving ties between those who get the same final grade – probably the most common is to place first the name of the person whose application was received first. Job offers are made from the eligible list in the order the names appear on it. You will be notified of your grade and your rank as soon as all these computations have been made. This will be done as rapidly as possible.

People who are found to meet the requirements in the announcement are called "eligibles." Their names are put on a list of eligible candidates. An eligible's chances of getting a job depend on how high he stands on this list and how fast agencies are filling jobs from the list.

When a job is to be filled from a list of eligibles, the agency asks for the names of people on the list of eligibles for that job. When the civil service commission receives this request, it sends to the agency the names of the three people highest on this list. Or, if the job to be filled has specialized requirements, the office sends the agency the names of the top three persons who meet these requirements from the general list.

The appointing officer makes a choice from among the three people whose names were sent to him. If the selected person accepts the appointment, the names of the others are put back on the list to be considered for future openings.

That is the rule in hiring from all kinds of eligible lists, whether they are for typist, carpenter, chemist, or something else. For every vacancy, the appointing officer has his choice of any one of the top three eligibles on the list. This explains why the person whose name is on top of the list sometimes does not get an appointment when some of the persons lower on the list do. If the appointing officer chooses the second or third eligible, the No. 1 eligible does not get a job at once, but stays on the list until he is appointed or the list is terminated.

X. HOW TO PASS THE INTERVIEW TEST

The examination for which you applied requires an oral interview test. You have already taken the written test and you are now being called for the interview test – the final part of the formal examination.

You may think that it is not possible to prepare for an interview test and that there are no procedures to follow during an interview. Our purpose is to point out some things you can do in advance that will help you and some good rules to follow and pitfalls to avoid while you are being interviewed.

What is an interview supposed to test?

The written examination is designed to test the technical knowledge and competence of the candidate; the oral is designed to evaluate intangible qualities, not readily measured otherwise, and to establish a list showing the relative fitness of each candidate – as measured against his competitors – for the position sought. Scoring is not on the basis of "right" and "wrong," but on a sliding scale of values ranging from "not passable" to "outstanding." As a matter of fact, it is possible to achieve a relatively low score without a single "incorrect" answer because of evident weakness in the qualities being measured.

Occasionally, an examination may consist entirely of an oral test – either an individual or a group oral. In such cases, information is sought concerning the technical knowledges and abilities of the candidate, since there has been no written examination for this purpose. More commonly, however, an oral test is used to supplement a written examination.

Who conducts interviews?

The composition of oral boards varies among different jurisdictions. In nearly all, a representative of the personnel department serves as chairman. One of the members of the board may be a representative of the department in which the candidate would work. In some cases, "outside experts" are used, and, frequently, a businessman or some other representative of the general public is asked to serve. Labor and management or other special groups may be represented. The aim is to secure the services of experts in the appropriate field.

However the board is composed, it is a good idea (and not at all improper or unethical) to ascertain in advance of the interview who the members are and what groups they represent. When you are introduced to them, you will have some idea of their backgrounds and interests, and at least you will not stutter and stammer over their names.

What should be done before the interview?

While knowledge about the board members is useful and takes some of the surprise element out of the interview, there is other preparation which is more substantive. It *is* possible to prepare for an oral interview – in several ways:

1) Keep a copy of your application and review it carefully before the interview

This may be the only document before the oral board, and the starting point of the interview. Know what education and experience you have listed there, and the sequence and dates of all of it. Sometimes the board will ask you to review the highlights of your experience for them; you should not have to hem and haw doing it.

2) Study the class specification and the examination announcement

Usually, the oral board has one or both of these to guide them. The qualities, characteristics or knowledges required by the position sought are stated in these documents. They offer valuable clues as to the nature of the oral interview. For example, if the job involves supervisory responsibilities, the announcement will usually indicate that knowledge of modern supervisory methods and the qualifications of the candidate as a supervisor will be tested. If so, you can expect such questions, frequently in the form of a hypothetical situation which you are expected to solve. NEVER go into an oral without knowledge of the duties and responsibilities of the job you seek.

3) Think through each qualification required

Try to visualize the kind of questions you would ask if you were a board member. How well could you answer them? Try especially to appraise your own knowledge and background in each area, *measured against the job sought*, and identify any areas in which you are weak. Be critical and realistic – do not flatter yourself.

4) Do some general reading in areas in which you feel you may be weak

For example, if the job involves supervision and your past experience has NOT, some general reading in supervisory methods and practices, particularly in the field of human relations, might be useful. Do NOT study agency procedures or detailed manuals. The oral board will be testing your understanding and capacity, not your memory.

5) Get a good night's sleep and watch your general health and mental attitude

You will want a clear head at the interview. Take care of a cold or any other minor ailment, and of course, no hangovers.

What should be done on the day of the interview?

Now comes the day of the interview itself. Give yourself plenty of time to get there. Plan to arrive somewhat ahead of the scheduled time, particularly if your appointment is in the fore part of the day. If a previous candidate fails to appear, the board might be ready for you a bit early. By early afternoon an oral board is almost invariably behind schedule if there are many candidates, and you may have to wait. Take along a book or magazine to read, or your application to review, but leave any extraneous material in the waiting room when you go in for your interview. In any event, relax and compose yourself.

The matter of dress is important. The board is forming impressions about you – from your experience, your manners, your attitude, and your appearance. Give your personal appearance careful attention. Dress your best, but not your flashiest. Choose conservative, appropriate clothing, and be sure it is immaculate. This is a business interview, and your appearance should indicate that you regard it as such. Besides, being well groomed and properly dressed will help boost your confidence.

Sooner or later, someone will call your name and escort you into the interview room. *This is it.* From here on you are on your own. It is too late for any more preparation. But remember, you asked for this opportunity to prove your fitness, and you are here because your request was granted.

What happens when you go in?

The usual sequence of events will be as follows: The clerk (who is often the board stenographer) will introduce you to the chairman of the oral board, who will introduce you to the other members of the board. Acknowledge the introductions before you sit down. Do not be surprised if you find a microphone facing you or a stenotypist sitting by. Oral interviews are usually recorded in the event of an appeal or other review.

Usually the chairman of the board will open the interview by reviewing the highlights of your education and work experience from your application – primarily for the benefit of the other members of the board, as well as to get the material into the record. Do not interrupt or comment unless there is an error or significant misinterpretation; if that is the case, do not hesitate. But do not quibble about insignificant matters. Also, he will usually ask you some question about your education, experience or your present job – partly to get you to start talking and to establish the interviewing "rapport." He may start the actual questioning, or turn it over to one of the other members. Frequently, each member undertakes the questioning on a particular area, one in which he is perhaps most competent, so you can expect each member to participate in the examination. Because time is limited, you may also expect some rather abrupt switches in the direction the questioning takes, so do not be upset by it. Normally, a board member will not pursue a single line of questioning unless he discovers a particular strength or weakness.

After each member has participated, the chairman will usually ask whether any member has any further questions, then will ask you if you have anything you wish to add. Unless you are expecting this question, it may floor you. Worse, it may start you off on an extended, extemporaneous speech. The board is not usually seeking more information. The question is principally to offer you a last opportunity to present further qualifications or to indicate that you have nothing to add. So, if you feel that a significant qualification or characteristic has been overlooked, it is proper to point it out in a sentence or so. Do not compliment the board on the thoroughness of their examination – they have been sketchy, and you know it. If you wish, merely say, "No thank you, I have nothing further to add." This is a point where you can "talk yourself out" of a good impression or fail to present an important bit of information. Remember, *you close the interview yourself.*

The chairman will then say, "That is all, Mr. _____, thank you." Do not be startled; the interview is over, and quicker than you think. Thank him, gather your belongings and take your leave. Save your sigh of relief for the other side of the door.

How to put your best foot forward
Throughout this entire process, you may feel that the board individually and collectively is trying to pierce your defenses, seek out your hidden weaknesses and embarrass and confuse you. Actually, this is not true. They are obliged to make an appraisal of your qualifications for the job you are seeking, and they want to see you in your best light. Remember, they must interview all candidates and a non-cooperative candidate may become a failure in spite of their best efforts to bring out his qualifications. Here are 15 suggestions that will help you:

1) Be natural – Keep your attitude confident, not cocky
If you are not confident that you can do the job, do not expect the board to be. Do not apologize for your weaknesses, try to bring out your strong points. The board is interested in a positive, not negative, presentation. Cockiness will antagonize any board member and make him wonder if you are covering up a weakness by a false show of strength.

2) Get comfortable, but don't lounge or sprawl
Sit erectly but not stiffly. A careless posture may lead the board to conclude that you are careless in other things, or at least that you are not impressed by the importance of the occasion. Either conclusion is natural, even if incorrect. Do not fuss with your clothing, a pencil or an ashtray. Your hands may occasionally be useful to emphasize a point; do not let them become a point of distraction.

3) Do not wisecrack or make small talk
This is a serious situation, and your attitude should show that you consider it as such. Further, the time of the board is limited – they do not want to waste it, and neither should you.

4) Do not exaggerate your experience or abilities

In the first place, from information in the application or other interviews and sources, the board may know more about you than you think. Secondly, you probably will not get away with it. An experienced board is rather adept at spotting such a situation, so do not take the chance.

5) If you know a board member, do not make a point of it, yet do not hide it

Certainly you are not fooling him, and probably not the other members of the board. Do not try to take advantage of your acquaintanceship – it will probably do you little good.

6) Do not dominate the interview

Let the board do that. They will give you the clues – do not assume that you have to do all the talking. Realize that the board has a number of questions to ask you, and do not try to take up all the interview time by showing off your extensive knowledge of the answer to the first one.

7) Be attentive

You only have 20 minutes or so, and you should keep your attention at its sharpest throughout. When a member is addressing a problem or question to you, give him your undivided attention. Address your reply principally to him, but do not exclude the other board members.

8) Do not interrupt

A board member may be stating a problem for you to analyze. He will ask you a question when the time comes. Let him state the problem, and wait for the question.

9) Make sure you understand the question

Do not try to answer until you are sure what the question is. If it is not clear, restate it in your own words or ask the board member to clarify it for you. However, do not haggle about minor elements.

10) Reply promptly but not hastily

A common entry on oral board rating sheets is "candidate responded readily," or "candidate hesitated in replies." Respond as promptly and quickly as you can, but do not jump to a hasty, ill-considered answer.

11) Do not be peremptory in your answers

A brief answer is proper – but do not fire your answer back. That is a losing game from your point of view. The board member can probably ask questions much faster than you can answer them.

12) Do not try to create the answer you think the board member wants

He is interested in what kind of mind you have and how it works – not in playing games. Furthermore, he can usually spot this practice and will actually grade you down on it.

13) Do not switch sides in your reply merely to agree with a board member

Frequently, a member will take a contrary position merely to draw you out and to see if you are willing and able to defend your point of view. Do not start a debate, yet do not surrender a good position. If a position is worth taking, it is worth defending.

14) Do not be afraid to admit an error in judgment if you are shown to be wrong

The board knows that you are forced to reply without any opportunity for careful consideration. Your answer may be demonstrably wrong. If so, admit it and get on with the interview.

15) Do not dwell at length on your present job

The opening question may relate to your present assignment. Answer the question but do not go into an extended discussion. You are being examined for a *new* job, not your present one. As a matter of fact, try to phrase ALL your answers in terms of the job for which you are being examined.

Basis of Rating

Probably you will forget most of these "do's" and "don'ts" when you walk into the oral interview room. Even remembering them all will not ensure you a passing grade. Perhaps you did not have the qualifications in the first place. But remembering them will help you to put your best foot forward, without treading on the toes of the board members.

Rumor and popular opinion to the contrary notwithstanding, an oral board wants you to make the best appearance possible. They know you are under pressure – but they also want to see how you respond to it as a guide to what your reaction would be under the pressures of the job you seek. They will be influenced by the degree of poise you display, the personal traits you show and the manner in which you respond.

ABOUT THIS BOOK

This book contains tests, divided into Examination Sections. Go through each test, answering every question in the margin. We have also attached a sample answer sheet at the back of the book that can be removed and used. At the end of each test look at the answer key and check your answers. On the ones you got wrong, look at the right answer choice and learn. Do not fill in the answers first. Do not memorize the questions and answers, but understand the answer and principles involved. On your test, the questions will likely be different from the samples. Questions are changed and new ones added. If you understand these past questions you should have success with any changes that arise. Tests may consist of several types of questions. We have additional books on each subject should more study be advisable or necessary for you. Finally, the more you study, the better prepared you will be. This book is intended to be the last thing you study before you walk into the examination room. Prior study of relevant texts is also recommended. NLC publishes some of these in our Fundamental Series. Knowledge and good sense are important factors in passing your exam. Good luck also helps. So now study this Passbook, absorb the material contained within and take that knowledge into the examination. Then do your best to pass that exam.

EXAMINATION SECTION

EXAMINATION SECTION
TEST 1

DIRECTIONS: Each question or incomplete statement is followed by several suggested answers or completions. Select the one that BEST answers the question or completes the statement. *PRINT THE LETTER OF THE CORRECT ANSWER IN THE SPACE AT THE RIGHT.*

1. The gray code minimizes the possibility of ambiguity when changing state by: 1._____
   A. Changing state on leading or trailing pulse edges.
   B. Using a common clock to synchronize inputs.
   C. Changing only one bit at a time.
   D. Requiring coincidence between two or more samples.

2. Convert the decimal number 164 to hex. 2._____
   A. 104. B. A4. C. 10110100. D. 5B.

3. A computer memory location is designated FO9Fh. The decimal equivalent is: 3._____

   A. 4367. B. 1010101. C. 10110100. D. 61599.

4. Which of the following items is not an ASCII item? 4._____
   A. 8. B. BS. C. END. D. A.

5. If the input lead to an operating TTL inverter became grounded, what would the output lead measure? 5._____
   A. +0 to +0.7 VDC.
   B. Ground.
   C. More than +5 VDC.
   D. Between +2.5 VDC and + 5VDC depending on load.

6. What is the range of supply voltage (VDD) to a CMOS logic IC? 6._____
   A. +4.5 to +5.5 VDC. C. +5 to +25 VDC.
   B. -3 VDC to +10 VDC. D. + 3 VDC to +15 VDC.

7. Using positive logic, a TTL IC will recognize the following voltages levels as valid "1" and "0" levels in an operational logic circuit: 7._____
   A. Binary 0 = +0.4 VDC, Binary 1 = +3.6 VDC.
   B. Binary 0 = 0.0 VDC, Binary 1 = +5.0 VDC.
   C. Binary 0 = +0.3 VDC, Binary 1 = +4.7 VDC.
   D. All of these.

8. If the output of a TTL gate measures 2.0VDC: 8._____
   A. There is a problem either in the gate or the loading.
   B. This is a normal high.
   C. This is a normal low.
   D. None of these.

9. A digital logic chip has a supply voltage of -5.2V. This chip belongs to which family? 9._____
   A. ECL B. TTL C. CMOS D. RTL

10. Which of the following integrated circuit or semiconductors devices normally require special handling to avoid damage by static electricity? 10._____
    A. TTL B. ECL C. MOV D. CMOS

Figure 9C-1

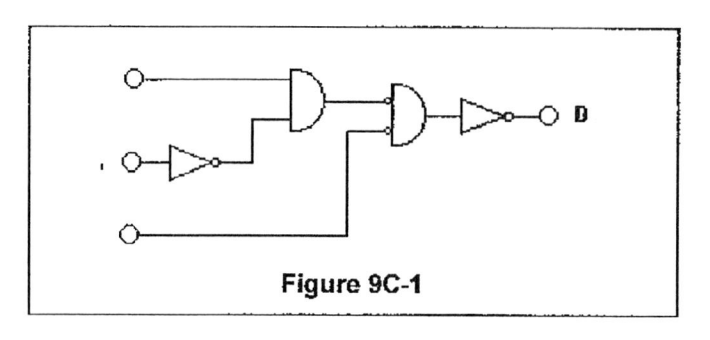

11. On Figure 9C-1, the function D is described as:
    A. AB (-C).   B. C + (-A) B.   C. C + AB.   D. A + BC.

11.____

12. ECL achieves high speed due to:
    A. The use of gallium arsenide conductors.
    B. Construction in small geometries.
    C. The operating transistors being unsaturated.
    D. Operation in low noise negative supply region.

12.____

13. By DeMorgan's Theorem, (X + Y) =
    A. -X + -Y   B. (X + Y)   C. -(X + Y)   D. X Y

13.____

14. The logic family which typically has the largest fanout is:
    A. CMOS.   B. ECL.   C. TTL.   D. RTL.

14.____

15. In order of highest to lowest speed, the logic families are ranked:
    A. ECL, CMOS, Schottky TTL, Standard TTL.
    B. Schottky, Standard TTL, ECL, CMOS.
    C. CMOS, Standard TTL, Schottky TTL, ECL.
    D. ECL, Schottky TTL, Standard TTL, CMOS.

15.____

16. In a three bit binary ripple counter, the state following 111 will be:
    A. 110.   B. 000.   C. 001.   D. 111.

16.____

17. In a 4 bit BCD ripple counter the state following 1001 will be:
    A. 1111.   B. 1011.   C. 0000.   D. 1000.

17.____

18. Synchronous counters are distinguished from ripple in that:
    A. Logic inputs are applied in parallel.
    B. Counter feedback is synchronous.
    C. The clock is applied to all flip flops simultaneously.
    D. There is no ripple on synchronous counters.

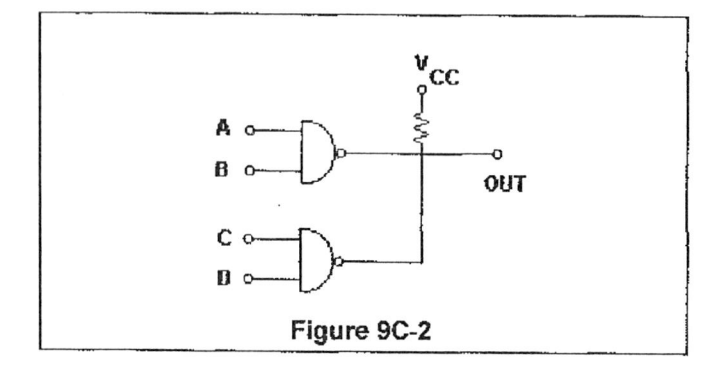

18.____

Figure 9C-2

19. The circuit shown on Figure 9C-2:   19._____
    A. Is a wired exclusive or.
    B. Is a wired or.
    C. Is used for high speed operation.
    D. Uses open collector gates.

20. What is the result of adding binary 110111 and 1001:   20._____
    A. 1000000.   B. 11111.   C. 100000.   D. 111111.

21. What is the binary result of multiplying hexadecimal 1C by 7?   21._____
    A. 11101100.   B. 11000100.   C. 11001100.   D. 11100100.

22. The value 123456 is based upon a number system which has a minimum radix of: 22._____
    A. 10.   B. 6.   C. 7.   D. 2.

23. A twos complement number is formed by the following method: 23._____
    A. Complement individual bits; then add 1.
    B. Add the number to all ones; then add 1.
    C. Subtract the number from all ones; then add 1.
    D. Add individual bits; then add 1.

24. Choose the correct solution to the following: 0101 + 0010 =19.   24._____
    A. 10111.   B. 1000.   C. 0111.   D. 01000.

Figure 9C-3

25. Refer to the waveforms shown on Figure 9C-3:20.   25._____
    With x and y as inputs to an "AND" gate, what is the output waveform?
    A. Waveform A   C. Waveform C
    B. Waveform B   D. Waveform D

26. Refer to the waveforms shown on Figure 9C-3:   26._____
    With x and y as inputs to an "OR" gate, what is the output waveform?
    A. Waveform D   C. Waveform B
    B. Waveform C   D. Waveform A

27. Refer to the waveforms shown on Diagram EL9C3C: With x and y as inputs to a   27._____
    "Exclusive OR" gate, what is the output waveform?
    A. Waveform A   C. Waveform C
    B. Waveform B   D. Waveform D

28. The standard serial output of a PC conforms to the following specification.   28.____
    A. 20 mA loop.   C. NMEA0180.
    B. RS232.@ @   D. Centronics

29. Which of the following logic levels are in a normal ran for TxD and Rxd signals on an   29.____
    RS232 interface line?
    A. 2.5 V and +2.5 V.   C. -10 V and +10 V.
    B. +0.20 V and + 4.5 V.   D. 10 V and 0 V.

30. What happens in a microprocessor system if electrical power input is interrupted?   30.____
    A.   Data stored in ROM is lost forever.
    B.   Data stored in ROM is lost, but can be restored by rebooting.
    C.   Data stored in RAM is lost.
    D.   Data stored in RAM is retained.

KEY (CORRECT ANSWERS)

1. C	11. B	21. B
2. B	12. C	22. C
3. D	13. D	23. A
4. C	14. A	24. B
5. B	15. D	25. B
6. D	16. A	26. D
7. D	17. C	27. C
8. A	18. C	28. B
9. A	19. D	29. C
10. D	20. A	30. C

TEST 2

DIRECTIONS: Each question or incomplete statement is followed by several suggested answers or completions. Select the one that BEST answers the question or completes the statement. *PRINT THE LETTER OF THE CORRECT ANSWER IN THE SPACE AT THE RIGHT.*

1. Complete the following sentence. A bit string manipulated by a computer in one operation is usually called: 1.____
   A. A bit. B. A word. C. A byte. D. A nibble.

2. In a microcomputer, the program counter contains: 2.____
   A. The address of the next instruction to be executed.
   B. Data.
   C. A sequential instruction set.
   D. An instruction set.

3. Choose the most correct statement.   3.____
   A. A RISC processor requires two or more clock cycles to execute a command.
   B. A RISC processor has fewer instructions available than an equivalent non-RISC processor.
   C. A RISC processor is inherently limited to a 32 bit architecture.
   D. RISC processors cannot implement a stack.

4. A one dimensional data structure in which values are entered and removed one item at a time at one end is called what?   4.____
   A. A ring counter.
   B. A FIFO.
   C. A stack pointer.
   D. A pushdown stack.

5. The output of an assembler is: 5____
   A. Used only for solving floating point problems.
   B. A higher level language.
   C. Equivalent machine language instructions called object code.
   D. Not in executable machine language form.

6. What is the DOS command used to copy files from one drive to another?   6.____
   A. RD. B. COPY. C. DEL. D. FC.

7. What is the command used to determine the version of DOS that the computer is currently using?   7.____
   A. MEM. B. VER. C. VERIFY. D. CHKDSK.

8. All DOS file names may contain a maximum of how many characters?   8.____
   A. 6.
   B. 11.@@
   C. 10.
   D. 7.

9. Compilers are used with which type of code?.
    A. High level languages.
    B. Assembly languages.
    C. Machine languages.
    D. High level languages and assembly languages.

10. Choose the correct answer:11._____
    A. A bit is one binary digit.
    B. A nibble is 4 bits.
    C. A byte is 8 bits.
    D. All answers are correct.

11. An interpreter is used with which type of code?
    A. Object codes.
    B. Assembly languages.
    C. High level languages.
    D. Machine codes.

12. An internal short between the base and collector of a bipolar transistor might be indicated by which of the following?
    A. A weak signal at the collector, in phase with the input.
    B. No signal at the output.
    C. DC supply voltage on the collector.
    E. Little or no signal at the collector and a reversal of phase.

13. When attempting to test a bipolar silicon or germanium transistor, which of the following is likely to be correct if the test is conducted after the device has been removed from its circuit?
    A. If an ohmmeter is used without an external limiting resistor, excessive base current will destroy the device.
    B. If A PNP transistor is being tested, forward junction resistance will be greater than reverse resistance.
    C. Forward junction resistance should be less than reverse junction resistance.
    D. Circuit effects which cannot be accounted for, preclude the use of resistance measurements.

14. When replacing a diac which is used with a silicon controlled rectifier, which way must the diac be installed?
    A. The anode must be connected to the gate.
    B. Either way will work.
    C. The cathode must be connected to the gate.
    D. Either way, depending on the polarity of the SCR.

15. Which of the following statements about diac bidirectional trigger diodes is incorrect?
    A. A diac is a three layer device with two terminals.
    B. A diac switch functions in either direction.
    C. The breakover voltage is usually between 28 and 36 volts.
    D. Lamps and battery chargers are typical loads for a diac.

16. Which of the following statements correctly describes photo diode operation?
    A. Photodiodes generate light in response to incident photons.
    B. Reverse biased photodiodes are photoresistive.
    C. Efficiency is a measure of photons per electron.
    D. Dark current flows in response to black light.

17. Which of the following statements distinguish phototransistors from photodiodes.
    A. Phototransistors are faster than photodiodes.
    B. Photodiodes are more sensitive than phototransistors.
    C. Photodarlingtons are the fastest photoconductors
    D. None of these.

18. Photodiode reverse current is called:
    A. Dark current in the absence of light.
    B. Zener current if the diode is reverse biased.
    C. Photocurrent if the diode is forward biased.
    D. Dark current in very low illumination.

19. What is the life expectancy of a light emitting diode operated continuously under normal operating conditions?
    A. Up to 100 years.
    B. Light emitting diodes may last up to 20 years.
    C. Unlimited life expectancy.
    D. Approximately 87660 hours.

20. How may the polarity of the leads of an LED be identified prior to installation in a circuit?
    A. The cathode lead is usually longer than the anode lead.
    B. There may be a flat edge on the body near the anode.
    C. If the cathode can be seen, it is usually smaller.
    D. The ground lead is usually lighter in color.

21. In testing a GaAs light emitting diode within the manufacturer's operating parameters of voltage and current, it appears that no light is emitted. What explanation could be given:
    A. The LED is connected backwards.
    B. The LED may have run out of GaAs.
    C. The LED may be emitting invisible light.
    D. The LED is connected backwards and may be emitting invisible light.

22. What is the typical minimum bias voltage required for normal operation of a GaAsP light emitting diode?
    A. The LED will operate at 1.2 volts reverse bias.
    B. The LED will operate at 0.6 volts forward bias.
    C. The LED will operate at 2 volts reverse bias.
    D. The LED will operate at 1.2 volts forward bias.

23. Which of the following statements is not true of light emitting diodes?
    A. They can be manufactured to emit various wavelengths.
    B. They can operate at very high speed.
    C. They can be made to emit nearly pure white light.
    D. They are vulnerable to failure due to overcurrent.

24. What is the usual method of protecting a light emitting diode from damage that would result if the operating voltage became too high?
    A. A series current limiting resistor is used.
    B. A zener voltage regulator is used.
    C. A fast-blow fuse is used in series with the LED.
    D. The LED is attached to a heat sink.

25. Assuming that a light emitting diode has an internal resistance of 5 ohms, what value of series current limiting resistor should be used if the power supply voltage is 6 volts and the diode current is to be 0.05 Amperes at 1.6 Volts DC?
    A. 83 Ohms.
    B. b} 120 Ohms.
    C. 88 Ohms.
    D. 32 Ohms.

26. With regard to a 7-segment LED display, which statement is correct?
    A. Only one segment at a time can be illuminated.
    B. An external decoder/driver is usually used.
    C. They are often used as simple on-off indicators.
    D. Segments must be illuminated in sets of two.

27. Identify the statement below which is incorrect with respect to infrared light emitting diodes:
    A. Light from an IR LED is invisible.
    B. Photodiodes can be used with IR LEDs.
    C. Phototransistors can be used with IR LEDs.
    D. IR LEDs are often used in optical couplers but not in opto-isolators.

28. When a power MOSFET has OV from gate to source the following is true:
    A. It is in pinch off.
    B. It is saturated.
    C. It is in a conducting region.
    D. It is drawing gate current.

Figure 9C-4

29. The purpose of the diode in the circuit shown on Figure 9C-4 is to:
    A. Speed switching time.
    B. Protect the transistor.
    C. Increase current capacity.
    D. Compensate for thermal variations.

30. In the silicon transistor circuit below, you test the input and find that it is a 0.5V p-p sine wave centered about 4V. The output is a 1.5Vp-p sine wave centered about 7V. The most likely fact is that:
    A. The circuit is operating normally and is driving a high impedance.
    B. The circuit is operating normally and is heavily loaded.
    C. The transistor is bad.
    D. One of the circuit components is bad.

KEY (CORRECT ANSWERS)

1. B	11. C	21. C
2. A	12. C	22. D
3. B	13. C	23. C
4. D	14. B	24. A
5. C	15. D	25. A
6. B	16. B	26. B
7. B	17. D	27. D
8. B	18. A	28. A
9. D	19. C	29. B
10. D	20. A	30. A

EXAMINATION SECTION
TEST 1

DIRECTIONS: Each question or incomplete statement is followed by several suggested answers or completions. Select the one that BEST answers the question or completes the statement. *PRINT THE LETTER OF THE CORRECT ANSWER IN THE SPACE AT THE RIGHT.*

1. What is the voltage range considered to be valid logic low input in a TTL device operating at 5 volts?
   A. 2.0 to 5.5 volts.
   B. -2.0 to -5.5 volts.
   C. Zero to 0.8 volts.
   D. 5.2 to 34.8 volts.

   1.____

2. What is the voltage range considered to be a valid logic high input in a TTL device operating at 5.0 volts?
   A. 2.0 to 5.5 volts.
   B. 1.5 to 3.0 volts.
   C. to 1.5 volts.
   D. 5.2 to 34.8 volts.

   2.____

3. What is the common power supply voltage for TTL series integrated circuits?
   A. 12 volts.
   B. 13.6 volts.
   C. 1 volt.
   D. 5 volts.

   3.____

4. TTL inputs left open develop what logic state?
   A. A high-logic state.
   B. A low-logic state.
   C. Open inputs on a TTL device are ignored.
   D. Random high- and low-logic states.

   4.____

5. Which of the following instruments would be best for checking a TTL logic circuit?
   A. VOM.
   B. DMM.
   C. Continuity tester.
   D. Logic probe.

   5.____

6. What do the initials TTL stand for?
   A. Resistor-transistor logic.
   B. Transistor-transistor logic.
   C. Diode-transistor logic.
   D. Emitter-coupled logic.

   6.____

7. What is a characteristic of an AND gate?
   A. Produces a logic "0" at its output only if all inputs are logic "1".
   B. Produces a logic "1" at its output only if all inputs are logic "1".
   C. Produces a logic "1" at its output if only one input is a logic "1".
   D. Produces a logic "1" at its output if all inputs are logic "0".

   7.____

8. What is a characteristic of a NAND gate?
    A. Produces a logic "0" at its output only when all inputs are logic "0".
    B. Produces a logic "1" at its output only when all inputs are logic "1".
    C. Produces a logic "0" at its output if some but not all of its inputs are logic "1".
    D. Produces a logic "0" at its output only when all inputs are logic "1".

8.____

9. What is a characteristic of an OR gate?
    A. Produces a logic "1" at its output if any input is logic "1".
    B. Produces a logic "0" at its output if any input is logic "1".
    C. Produces a logic "0" at its output if all inputs are logic "1".
    D. Produces a logic "1" at its output if all inputs are logic "0".

9.____

10. What is a characteristic of a NOR gate?
    A. Produces a logic "0" at its output only if all inputs are logic "0".
    B. Produces a logic "1" at its output only if all inputs are logic "1".
    C. Produces a logic "0" at its output if any or all inputs are logic "1".
    D. Produces a logic "1" at its output if some but not all of its inputs are logic "V.

10.____

11. What is a characteristic of a NOT gate?
    A. Does not allow data transmission when its input is high.
    B. Produces logic "0" at its output when the input is logic "1" and vice versa.
    C. Allows data transmission only when its input is high.
    D. Produces a logic "1" at its output when the input is logic "1" and vice versa.

11.____

12. Which of the following logic gates will provide an active high out when both inputs are active high?
    A. NAND.
    B. NOR.
    C. AND.
    D. XOR.

12.____

13. In a negative-logic circuit, what level is used to represent a logic 0?
    A. Low level.
    B. Positive-transition level.
    C. Negative-transition level
    D. High level

13.____

14. For the logic input levels shown in the following figure, what are the logic levels of test points A, B and C in this circuit? (Assume positive logic.)
    A. A is high, B is low and C is low.
    B. A is low, B is high and C is high.
    C. A is high, B is high and C is low.
    D. A is low, B is high and C is low.

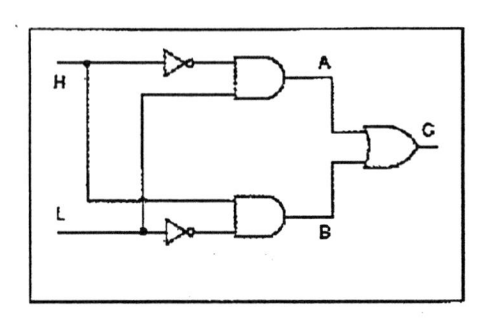

14.____

15. For the logic input levels given in the following figure, what are the logic levels of test points A, B and C in this circuit? (Assume positive logic.)
    A. A is low, B is low and C is high.
    B. A is low, B is high and C is low.
    C. A is high, B is high and C is high.
    D. A is high, B is low and C is low.

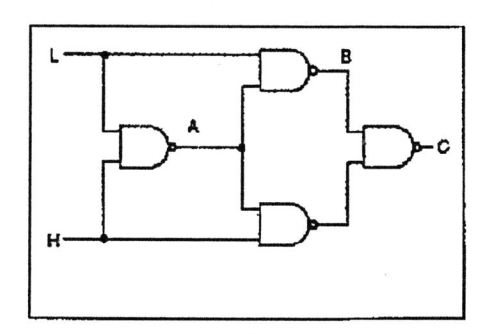

16. In a positive-logic circuit, what level is used to represent a logic 1?
    A. High level
    B. Low level
    C. Positive-transition level
    D. Negative-transition level

17. Given the input levels shown in the following figure, and assuming positive logic devices, what would the output be?
    A. A is low, B is high and C is high.
    B. A is high, B is high and C is low.
    C. A is low, B is low and C is high.
    D. None of the above are correct.

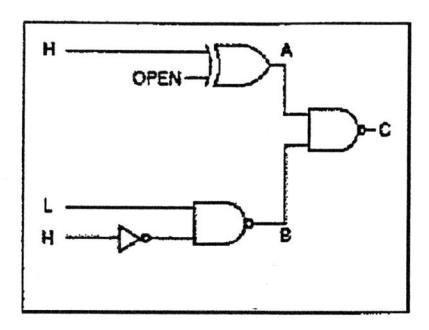

18. What is a truth table?
    A. A list of input combinations and their corresponding outputs that characterizes a digital device's function.
    B. A table of logic symbols that indicate the high logic states of an op-amp.
    C. A diagram showing logic states when the digital device's output is true.
    D. A table of logic symbols that indicates the low logic states of an op-amp.

19. It has been reported that a VHF transceiver is unusable, because the LCD display characters are "all black." Which of the following might get it working again?
    A. Warm the display up to 20 degrees C.
    B. Drain and replace the LCD liquid.
    C. Replace the display's current limiting resistor.
    D. Replace the crystal.

19.___

20. A flip-flop circuit is a binary logic element with how many stable states?
    A. 1
    B. 2
    C. 4
    D. 8

20.___

21. What is a flip-flop circuit? A binary sequential logic element with_____stable states.
    A. 1
    B. 4
    C. 2
    D. 8

21.___

22. How many flip-flops are required to divide a signal frequency by 4?
    A. 1
    B. 2
    C. 3
    D. 4

22.___

23. How many bits lof information can be stored in a single flip-flop circuit?.
    A. 1
    B. 2
    C. 3
    D. 4

23.___

24. How many R-S flip-flops would be required to construct an 8 bit storage register?
    A. 2
    B. 4
    C. 8
    D. 16

24.___

25. An R-S flip-flop is capable of doing all of the following except:
    A. Accept data input into R-S inputs with CLK initiated.
    B. Accept data input into PRE and CLR inputs without CLK being initiated.
    C. Refuse to accept synchronous data if asynchronous data is being input at same time.
    D. Operate in toggle mode with R-S inputs he ld constant and CLK initiated.

25.___

KEY (CORRECT ANSWERS)

1. C
2. A
3. D
4. A
5. D
6. B
7. B
8. D
9. A
10. C

11. B
12. C
13. D
14. B
15. C
16. A
17. B
18. A
19. A
20. B

21. C
22. D
23. A
24. C
25. D

TEST 2

DIRECTIONS: Each question or incomplete statement is followed by several suggested answers or completions. Select the one that BEST answers the question or completes the statement. *PRINT THE LETTER OF THE CORRECT ANSWER IN THE SPACE AT THE RIGHT.*

1. Which of the following procedures would be appropriate with metal oxide semiconductor integrated circuits while making equipment repairs:
    A. Use a non-conductive mat on the work surface.
    B. Wear a conductive wrist strap with a 1 million ohm resistor to ground.
    C. Touch each lead to equalize electrostatic potentials.
    D. Keep spare IC's neatly organized in styrofoam.

2. The frequency of an AC signal can be divided electronically by what type of digital circuit?
    A. Free-running multivibrator.
    B. Bistable multivibrator.
    C. OR gate.
    D. Astable multivibrator.

3. What is an astable multivibrator?
    A. A circuit that alternates between two stable states.
    B. A circuit that alternates between a stable state and an unstable state.
    C. A circuit set to block either a 0 pulse or a 1 pulse and pass the other.
    D. A circuit that alternates between two unstable states.

4. What is a monostable multivibrator?
    A. A circuit that can be switched momentarily to the opposite binary state and then returns after a set time to its original state.
    B. A "clock" circuit that produces a continuous square wave oscillating between 1 and 0.
    C. A circuit designed to store one bit of data in either the 0 or the 1 configuration.
    D. A circuit that maintains a constant output voltage, regardless of variations in the input voltage.

5. What is a bistable multivibrator circuit commonly named?
    A. AND gate.
    B. OR gate.
    C. Clock.
    D. Flip-flop.

6. What is a bistable multivibrator circuit?
    A. Flip-flop.
    B. AND gate.
    C. OR gate.
    D. Clock.

7. What wave form would appear on the voltage outputs at the collectors of an astable, multivibrator, common-emitter stage?
    A. Sine wave.
    B. Sawtooth wave.
    C. Square wave.
    D. Half-wave pulses.

8. What is the name of the semiconductor memory IC whose digital data can be written or read, and whose memory word address can be accessed randomly?
   A. ROM — Read-Only Memory.
   B. PROM — Programmable Read-Only Memory.
   C. RAM — Random-Access Memory.
   D. EPROM — Electrically Programmable Read-Only Memory.

9. What is the name of the semiconductor IC that has a fixed pattern of digital data stored in its memory matrix?
   A. RAM — Random-Access Memory.
   B. ROM — Read-Only Memory.
   C. Register.
   D. Latch.

10. What does the term "IO" mean within a microprocessor system?
    A. Integrated oscillator.
    B. Integer operation.
    C. Input-output.
    D. D Internal operation.

11. What is the name for a microprocessor's sequence of commands and instructions?
    A. Program.
    B. Sequence.
    C. Data string.
    D. Data execution.

12. How many individual memory cells would be contained in a memory IC that has 4 data bus input/output pins and 4 address pins for connection to the address bus?
    A. 8
    B. 16
    C. 32
    D. 64

13. What is the name of the random-accessed semiconductor memory IC that must be refreshed periodically to maintain reliable data storage in its memory matrix?
    A. ROM — Read-Only Memory.
    B. DRAM — Dynamic Random-Access Memory.
    C. PROM — Programmable Read-Only Memory.
    D. PRAM — Programmable Random-Access Memory.

14. In a microprocessor-controlled two-way radio, a "watchdog" timer:
    A. Verifies that the microprocessor is executing the program.
    B. Assures that the transmission is exactly on frequency.
    C. Prevents the transmitter from exceeding allowed power out.
    D. Connects to the system RADAR presentation.

15. What does the term "DAC" refer to in a microprocessor circuit?
    A. Dynamic access controller.
    B. Digital to analog converter.
    C. Digital access counter.
    D. Dial analog control.

16. Which of the following is not part of a MCU processor?
    A. RAM
    B. ROM
    C. I/O
    D. Voltage Regulator

17. What portion of a microprocessor circuit is the pulse generator?
    A. Clock
    B. RAM
    C. ROM
    D. PLL

18. In a microprocessor, what is the meaning of the term "ALU"?
    A. Automatic lock/unlock.
    B. Arithmetical logic unit.
    C. Auto latch undo.
    D. Answer local unit.

19. What circuit interconnects the microprocessor with the memory and input/output system?
    A. Control logic bus.
    B. PLL line.
    C. Data bus line.
    D. Directional coupler.

20. What is the purpose of a prescaler circuit?
    A. Converts the output of a JK flip-flop to that of an RS flip-flop.
    B. Multiplies an HF signal so a low-frequency counter can display the operating frequency.
    C. Prevents oscillation in a low frequency counter circuit.
    D. Divides an HF signal so that a low-frequency counter can display the operating frequency.

21. What does the term "BCD" mean?
    A. Binaural coded digit.
    B. Bit count decimal.
    C. Binary coded decimal.
    D. Broad course digit.

22. What is the function of a decade counter digital IC?
    A. Decode a decimal number for display on a seven-segment LED display.
    B. Produce one output pulse for every ten input pulses.
    C. Produce ten output pulses for every input pulse.
    D. Add two decimal numbers.

23. What integrated circuit device converts an analog signal to a digital signal?
    A. DAC
    B. DCC
    C. ADC
    D. CDC

24. What integrated circuit device converts digital signals to analog signals?
    A. ADC
    B. DCC
    C. CDC
    D. DAC

25. In binary numbers, how would you note the quantity TWO?
    A. 0010
    B. 0002
    C. 2000
    D. 0020

KEY (CORRECT ANSWERS)

1. B	11. A
2. B	12. D
3. D	13. B
4. A	14. A
5. D	15. B
6. A	16. D
7. C	17. A
8. C	18. B
9. B	19. C
10. C	20. D

21. C
22. B
23. C
24. D
25. A

EXAMINATION SECTION
TEST 1

DIRECTIONS: Each question or incomplete statement is followed by several suggested answers or completions. Select the one that BEST answers the question or completes the statement. *PRINT THE LETTER OF THE CORRECT ANSWER IN THE SPACE AT THE RIGHT.*

1. The *primary* function of a take-up pulley in a belt conveyor is to

    A. carry the belt on the return trip
    B. track the belt
    C. maintain proper belt tension
    D. change the direction of the belt
    E. regulate the speed of the belt

    1.____

2. Which device is used to transfer power and rotary mechanical motion from one shaft to another?

    A. Bearing B. Lever C. Idler roller
    D. Gear E. Bushing

    2.____

3. A circuit has two resistors of equal value in series. The voltage and current in the circuit are 20 volts and 2 amps respectively.
What is the value of each resistor?

    A. 5 ohs B. 10 ohms C. 20 ohms
    D. Not enough information given

    3.____

4. Which of the following circuits is shown in the figure below?

    A. Series B. Parallel
    C. Series, parallel D. Solid state
    E. None of the above

    4.____

5. The total net capacitance of two 60-farad capacitors connected in series is _____ farads.

    A. 30 B. 60 C. 90 D. 120 E. 360

    5.____

6. If two 30-mH inductors are connected in series, the total net inductance of the combination is _____ mH.

    A. 15 B. 20 C. 30 D. 45 E. 60

    6.____

7. Select the Boolean equation that matches the circuit diagram at the right.

   A. Z = AB+CD+EF
   B. Z = (A+B)(C+D)(E+F)
   C. Z = A+B+C+D+EF
   D. Z = ABCD(E+F)

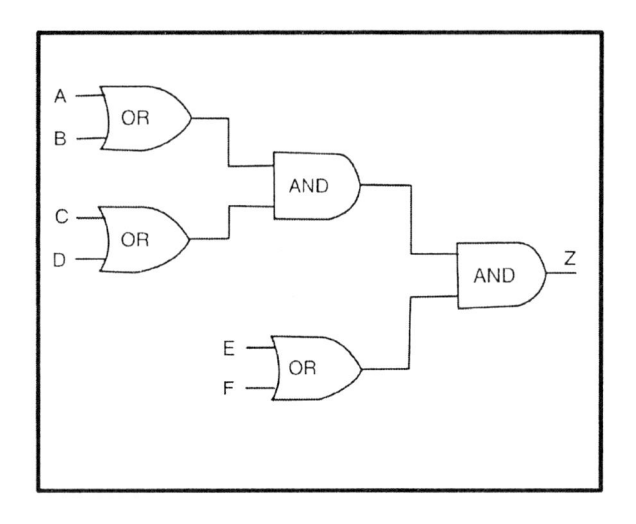

   7.____

8. In pure binary, the decimal number 6 would be expressed as

   A. 001   B. 011   C. 110   D. 111

   8.____

9. In the figure to the right, the scores that will be printed are an scores

   A. > 90 and < 60
   B. < 90
   C. ≤ 90 and ≥ 60
   D. < 60

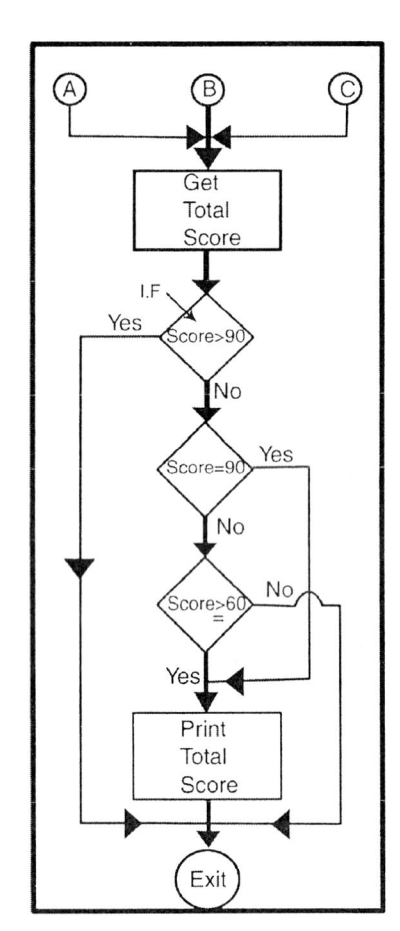

   9.____

10. Crowbars, light bulbs and vacuum bags are to be stored in the cabinet shown in the figure below. Considering the balance of weight, what would be the safest arrangement?

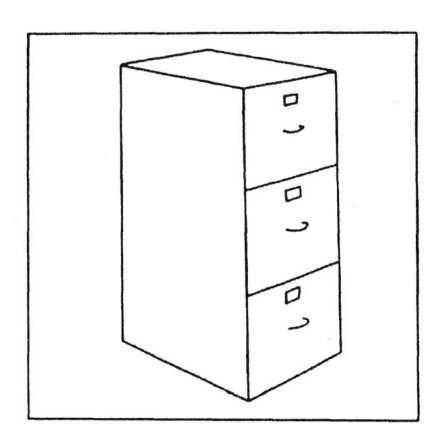

    A. Top drawer   - Crowbars
        Middle drawer - Light bulbs
        Bottom drawer - Vacuum bag
    B. Top drawer   - Crawbars
        Middle drawer - Vacuum bag
        Bottom drawer - Light bulbs
    C. Top drawer   - Vacuum bag
        Middle drawer - Crowbars
        Bottom drawer - Light bulbs
    D. Top drawer   - Vacuum bag
        Middle drawer - Light bulbs
        Bottom drawer - Crowbars
    E. Top drawer   - Light bulbs
        Middle drawer - Vacuum bag
        Bottom drawer - Crowbars

11. Which is the MOST appropriate for pulling a heavy load?

    A. Electric lift   B. Fork lift
    C. Tow conveyor   D. Dolly
    E. Pallet truck

12. The electrical circuit term "open circuit" refers to a closed loop being opened. When an ohmmeter is connected into this type of circuit, one can expect the meter to read

    A. infinity
    B. infinity and slowly return to zero
    C. zero
    D. zero and slowly return to infinity
    E. none of the above

13. Contaminants have caused bearings to fail prematurely. Which pair of the items listed below should be kept away from bearings?

    A. Dirt and oil   B. Grease and water
    C. Oil and grease   D. Dirt and moisture
    E. Water and oil

14. In order to operate a breast drill, which direction should you turn it?

    A. Clockwise   B. Counterclockwise   C. Up and down
    D. Back and forth   E. Right, then left

15. Which is the *correct* tool for tightening or loosening a water pipe?

    A. Slip joint pliers   B. Household pliers
    C. Monkey wrench   D. Water pump pliers
    E. Pipe wrench

16. What is the purpose of a chuck key?

    A. Opening doors   B. Removing drill bits
    C. Removing screws   D. Removing chucks
    E. Removing set screws

17. When smoke is generated as a result of cutting holes into a piece of angle iron using a portable electric drill, one should

    A. use a fire watch
    B. cease the drilling operation
    C. use an exhaust fan to remove smoke
    D. use a prescribed coolant solution to reduce friction
    E. call the fire department

18. The *primary* purpose of soldering is to

    A. melt solder to a molten state
    B. heat metal parts to the right temperature to be joined
    C. join metal parts by melting the parts
    D. harden the metal
    E. join metal parts

19. A soldering gun

    A. tip is not replaceable
    B. cannot be used in cramped places
    C. heats only when trigger is pressed
    D. not rated by the number of watts they use
    E. has no light

20. What unit of measurement is read on a dial torque wrench?

    A. Pounds   B. Inches   C. Centimeters
    D. Foot-pounds   E. Degrees

KEY (CORRECT ANSWERS)

1. C
2. D
3. A
4. A
5. A

6. E
7. B
8. C
9. C
10. E

11. E
12. A
13. D
14. A
15. E

16. B
17. D
18. E
19. C
20. D

EXAMINATION SECTION

DIRECTIONS: Each question in this part is followed by several suggested answers or completions. Select the one that BEST answers the question or completes the statement. *PRINT THE LETTER OF THE CORRECT ANSWER IN THE SPACE AT THE RIGHT.*

TEST 1

1. The length of a Marconi-type antenna is
   A. 1/4 wavelength B. 1/2 wavelength
   C. 3/4 wavelength D. one wavelength

2. A whip antenna of less than 1/4 wavelength will present an electrical impedance that is
   A. resistive B. capacitive
   C. inductive D. 180° out-of-phase

3. Frequency multiplication is achieved in transmitter stages by operating them as
   A. Class A amplifiers B. Class AB amplifiers
   C. Class B amplifiers D. Class C amplifiers

4. The power factor of a resonant circuit is
   A. lagging B. leading C. unity D. zero

5. The power factor of a <u>parallel</u> circuit consisting of a 51-ohm resistor and a 51-ohm capacitive reactance is
   A. .500 B. .667 C. .707 D. .887

6. A tunable <u>series</u> RLC circuit will have MINIMUM impedance when the
   A. capacitive reactance equals the inductive reactance
   B. inductive reactance or capacitive reactance equals zero
   C. capacitive reactance equals the resistance
   D. inductive reactance equals the resistance

7. At resonance, a tunable <u>parallel</u> RLC circuit will be characterized by
   A. broadest bandwidth B. lowest "Q"
   C. maximum impedance
   D. equal currents through the resistance, inductance, and capacitance

8. If the number of turns of an inductor is halved, the value of the inductance is
   A. doubled B. unchanged
   C. reduced to one-half D. reduced to one-quarter

9. The resistivity of copper is GREATER than that of the element
   A. silicon B. germanium C. silver D. gold

10. The MINIMUM number of 10-microfarad, 25-volt capacitors that can be connected up to yield an equivalent capacitance of 5 microfarads, usable on 150 volts, is
    A. 2 B. 6 C. 18 D. 24

11. The number of DB's(decibels) corresponding to a power ratio of 200 is, MOST NEARLY,
    A. 20 DB's B. 23 DB's C. 26 DB's D. 40 DB's

1. ...
2. ...
3. ...
4. ...
5. ...
6. ...
7. ...
8. ...
9. ...
10. ...
11. ...

12. The MAXIMUM current carrying capacity, in amperes, of a   12. ...
    resistor marked "5,000 ohms, 200 watts" is
    A. 1/25   B. 1/5   C. 5   D. 25
13. The combined equivalent resistance of a 12-ohm resistor,   13. ...
    a 6-ohm resistor, and a 4-ohm resistor connected in para-
    llel is
    A. ½ ohm   B. 1 ohm   C. 2 ohms   D. 3 ohms
14. The percentage regulation of a power supply with a no-load 14. ...
    voltage output of +25.3 volts and a full-load voltage out-
    put of +23.0 volts is
    A. 1.9%   B. 2.1%   C. 9%   D. 10%
15. A capacitance of .0015 microfarads is equal to   15. ...
    A. 150 picofarads   B. 1500 picofarads
    C. 150 nanofarads   D. 1500 nanofarads
16. A diode is color coded with a purple, a green and a red   16. ...
    ring in that order (the purple ring is at the end of the
    diode). It should be concluded from the coding that the
    diode is a
    A. 1N752   B. 1N7500   C. 1N75B   D. 1N7511
17. The time constant of a resistance and an inductance in   17. ...
    series can be increased by
    A. *increasing* either the resistance or the inductance
    B. *increasing* the resistance or decreasing the inductance
    C. *decreasing* the resistance or increasing the inductance
    D. *decreasing* either the resistance or the inductance
18. The combined equivalent impedance of a 50-ohm inductive   18. ...
    reactance connected in parallel with a 25-ohm capacitive
    reactance is
    A. 75 ohms inductive reactance
    B. 75 ohms capacitive reactance
    C. 50 ohms inductive reactance
    D. 50 ohms capacitive reactance
19. The three connections of an SCR are the   19. ...
    A. collector, emitter and gate
    B. base 1, base 2 and emitter
    C. anode, cathode and gate
    D. emitter 1, emitter 2 and base
20. FET is the abbreviation for a   20. ...
    A. fast epitaxial transistor B. field effect transistor
    C. frequency extended transistor
    D. forward emitting transistor
21. The resonant frequency of a .1 henry inductance and a   21. ...
    .001 microfarad capacitance "tank" circuit is, MOST NEARLY,
    A. 160 Hz   B. 1600 Hz   C. 16 KHz   D. 16 MHz
22. At 300 MHz, electromagnetic energy in air has a wavelength 22. ...
    of
    A. 1 centimeter   B. 10 centimeters
    C. 100 centimeters   D. 1000 centimeters
23. The frequency range from 300 MHz to 3000 MHz is designated 23. ...
    by RETMA and ASA as the
    A. HF range   B. VHF range   C. UHF range D. SHF range

24. A modulated carrier wave has a maximum magnitude of 150   24. ...
    volts and 50% modulation. If the modulation is removed,
    the carrier will have a magnitude of
       A. 50 volts   B. 75 volts   C. 100 volts   D. 150 volts
25. If 50 microamperes produces a full-scale deflection on a   25. ...
    DC voltmeter, the sensitivity of the instrument is
       A. 5,000 ohms/volt   B. 10,000 ohms/volt
       C. 20,000 ohms/volt   D. 50,000 ohms/volt
26. A "beat-frequency meter" is also called a   26. ...
       A. frequency synthesizer   B. distortion meter
       C. wave analyzer   D. heterodyne-frequency meter
27. Assume that a voltmeter uses the same scale for three   27. ...
    ranges, 0-300 volts, 0-75 volts and 0-15 volts. If the
    scale is marked only for the 0-300 volt range, then a
    scale reading of 120 when the 0-75 volt range is being
    used will correspond to an ACTUAL voltage of
       A. 10 volts   B. 12 volts   C. 24 volts   D. 30 volts
28. Variations in the signals introduced in the "Z" axis in-   28. ...
    put of an oscilloscope produce corresponding changes in the
       A. positioning of the time-delayed sweep
       B. intensity of the trace
       C. "Y" axis frequency response
       D. "X" axis sawtooth repetition rate
29. When using an ohmmeter to measure resistance, the GREATEST 29. ...
    accuracy is obtained when the range selected results in a
    deflection that is, APPROXIMATELY,
       A. $\frac{1}{4}$ full-scale   B. $\frac{1}{2}$ full-scale
       C. 3/4 full-scale   D. full-scale
30. A grid-dip meter is GENERALLY used to measure   30. ...
       A. Q   B. modulation   C. RF current   D. frequency
31. A 0-150 v. voltmeter has an accuracy of 2% F.S. When the   31. ...
    pointer shows 75 volts, the MAXIMUM error is plus or minus
       A. .5 volt   B. 1.5 volts   C. 2.0 volts   D. 3.0 volts
32. Certain attenuation probes used with oscilloscopes provide 32. ...
    for an adjustment to be made in each probe, prior to its
    use. The adjustment is required in order to
       A. match the probe to the circuitry on which it is used
       B. match the probe to the input of the scope on which it
          is used
       C. adjust the DC volts/division sensitivity of the input
          to the scope on which it is used
       D. adjust the DC balance of the input to the scope on
          which it it used
33. When an oscilloscope is set up to display a lissajous pat- 33. ...
    tern, the feature that is inhibited and NOT available is
    the
       A. "Y" axis manual positioning control
       B. "X" axis manual positioning control
       C. automatic retrace blanking
       D. trace intensity manual control

34. In order to minimize multiple reflections in a coaxial 34. ...
line, the MOST effective steps that should be taken are to
    A. drive the sending end with a low impedance source and terminate the receiving end with a resistance equal to the coaxial characteristic impedance
    B. drive the sending end with a source with output impedance equal to the coaxial characteristic impedance and terminate the receiving end with a resistance equal to the coaxial characteristic impedance
    C. drive the sending end with a low impedance source and terminate the receiving end with a high impedance
    D. drive the sending end with a source with output impedance to the coaxial characteristic impedance and terminate the receiving end with a high impedance
35. Of the following statements concerning a dual-trace oscil- 35. ...
loscope, the one which is CORRECT is that it
    A. requires a two-gun cathode-ray tube
    B. has two "Y" axis imputs that are chopped and displayed as a single trace
    C. uses a single time base when used in the "chopped" mode
    D. uses dual-time bases when used in the "chopped" mode
36. The type of display usually produced on oscilloscopes, 36. ...
where signal amplitude is converted to a "Y" axis displacement and a time base is introduced on the "X" axis, is CLOSEST in appearance to the radar indicator that is called a(n)
    A. A scan   B. B scan   C. J scan   D. PPI scan
37. Of the following, the BEST instrument for measuring very 37. ...
low resistances is the
    A. Wien bridge   B. Kelvin bridge
    C. Hay bridge   D. Maxwell bridge
38. Of the following, the instrument that should be used in 38. ...
measuring radiation patterns produced by antennas is the
    A. spectrum analyzer   B. field-strength meter
    C. curve tracer   D. distortion meter
39. Taut-band suspension is a feature which is incorporated in 39. ...
    A. the internal supporting of hermetic-sealed units
    B. low-friction meter movements
    C. dial cord assemblies
    D. vibration mounts for electronic packages
40. A "bolometer" is a device that can be used for measuring 40. ...
    A. microwave power   B. static charge
    C. magnetic-field strength D. vibration frequencies

TEST 2

1. One of the reasons why radiotelephones are operated in the 1. ...
30 MHz to 3000 MHz range is that
    A. skip transmission is very effective
    B. antenna orientation is not important
    C. the number of voice channels is great
    D. AM operation is less noisy than FM

TEST 2

2. The transmission of a distress message by a radiotelephone   2. ...
   station not itself in distress should include calling out
   three times the expression
      A. SOS   B. SOS relay   C. Mayday   D. Mayday relay
3. In specifying the characteristics of an oscillator crystal,   3. ...
   the information that should be given, together with the frequency tolerance, is the crystal
      A. age   B. operating temperature range
      C. manufacturer   D. power supply voltages
4. Records indicate that a component in a certain unit has   4. ...
   been replaced repeatedly, and no such history exists in
   other similar units with the same type of service and total
   operation time. Based on this information it should be con-
   cluded that
      A. the replacement components were defective
      B. the component was replaced at times when it had not
         failed
      C. the replacement components were connected into the
         circuit improperly
      D. there is something else wrong in the unit causing the
         component to fail
5. When trouble-shooting a large electronic unit, such as a   5. ...
   console, first, power should be removed and the NEXT step
   should be that
      A. internal capacitors be discharged by using a shorting
         connection to chassis
      B. ohmmeter checks be made according to the instruction
         manual
      C. the operating personnel be notified that the unit is
         out of operation
      D. the door and panel interlocks be by-passed
6. Metal enclosures and panels of electronic or electrical   6. ...
   equipment should be well grounded in order to
      A. protect operating personnel from getting electric shocks
      B. insure that the contained equipment has a good reference
         ground
      C. prevent static charges from building up on the frame
      D. provide a solid mounting for the equipment and keep it
         firmly in place
7. The main reason for NOT using carbon tetrachloride as a   7. ...
   cleaning agent on electrical equipment is that is
      A. is an electrical conductor   B. is too expensive
      C. generates toxic fumes
      D. coats equipment with an acid deposit
8. The MOST likely cause of damage occurring in transistorized   8. ...
   circuitry during the process of soldering is due to the application of too much
      A. pressure   B. heat   C. solder   D. rosin flux
9. A 2-inch diameter hole can be made quickly and cleanly in a   9. ...
   16-gauge aluminum plate by the use of a
      A. rat-tail file   B. nibbler
      C. chassis punch   D. jig saw

10. A reason for using teflon insulation rather than vinyl   10. ...
    on electrical wiring is that teflon is
       A. better for bonding   B. more flexible
       C. less expensive   D. more resistant to heat
11. Of the following statements concerning epoxy glue, the one   11. ...
    which is CORRECT is that it
       A. dissolves quickly upon contact with water
       B. is prepared from two components that are mixed together shortly before use
       C. is a long-time favorite for making temporary bonds
       D. generally does not require clamps, nails or presses on surfaces to be joined
12. Of the following chemicals, the one which will burn on con- 12. ...
    tact with a lighted match is
       A. carbon tetrachloride   B. acetone
       C. methylene chloride   D. sodium bicarbonate
13. Of the following, the BEST method of disposing of spray   13. ...
    cans that contain aerosol paints or solvents is
       A. puncturing the cans and then throwing them into an incinerator
       B. puncturing the cans and then having them picked up by the sanitation men
       C. throwing them into an incinerator
       D. having them picked up by the sanitation men
14. An ohmmeter of known polarity is connected from the base   14. ...
    to the emitter on a transistor in such manner that the positive lead is on the base. The ohmmeter registers continuity with such conditions and then registers an "open" circuit when the leads are reversed. Based on this information, it should be concluded that the transistor is
       A. good   B. defective   C. an NPN   D. a PNP
15. An ohmmeter registers "open" when connected from the emit- 15. ...
    ter to the collector of a transistor (base left disconnected) and also registers "open" when the leads are reversed. This information suggests that the transistor is
       A. possibly good   B. definitely defective
       C. an NPN   D. a PNP
16. In order to get good indications when checking a transis-   16. ...
    tor by using an ohmmeter, yet not cause damage, the voltage across the test leads should
       A. *exceed* 1.5 volts DC and the ohmmeter scale should be less than R x 100
       B. *exceed* 1.5 volts DC and the ohmmeter scale should not be less than R x 100
       C. *not exceed* 1.5 volts DC and the ohmmeter scale should be less than R x 100
       D. *not exceed* 1.5 volts DC and the ohmmeter scale should not be less than R x 100
17. If an audio amplifier requiring a 3200-ohm load is con-   17. ...
    nected to the primary winding of a 20:1 step-down output transformer, the matching speaker to be connected to the secondary winding should have an impedance of
       A. 4 ohms   B. 8 ohms   C. 16 ohms   D. 32 ohms

18. The Converter stage in a typical heterodyne receiver combines the functions of a(n) 18. ...
    A. RF stage and the Local Oscillator
    B. Mixer stage and the Local Oscillator
    C. RF stage and an IF stage
    D. Mixer stage and an IF stage
19. One of the reasons why RF stages improve the performance 19. ...
    of a typical heterodyne receiver is that they
    A. increase the sensitivity and broaden the bandwidth
    B. provide regenerative action and improve selectivity
    C. increase sensitivity and improve AVC action
    D. improve AVC action and broaden bandwidth
20. Of the following statements concerning the record heads in 20. ...
    typical magnetic-tape recorders, the one which is CORRECT
    is that they are
    A. self-cleaning and require occasional realignment
    B. automatically demagnetized by the signals in the tape-erase heads
    C. easily magnetized and should not be checked for continuity with an ohmmeter
    D. not self-cleaning and are demagnetized by over-driving the record amplifiers
21. Typical recording speeds on commercial magnetic-tape recorders are 21. ...
    A. 3½ ips., 7 ips., 15 ips., and 30 ips
    B. 3 3/4 ips., 7½ ips., 15 ips., and 30 ips
    C. 3 3/4 ips., 7 ips., 15 ips., and 25 ips
    D. 3½ ips., 7½ ips., 15 ips., and 30 ips
22. According to FCC regulations, the frequency and deviation 22. ...
    of a crystal-controlled FM transmitter must be checked BEFORE it is put into operation, and rechecked thereafter
    every
    A. month   B. 3 months   C. 6 months   D. year
23. According to FCC regulations, radio transmitters may be 23. ...
    tuned or adjusted only by persons possessing a
    A. first or second class commercial radiotelephone operator's license
    B. first class commercial radiotelephone operator's license
    C. first or second class commercial radiotelephone operator's license or by personnel working under their immediate supervision
    D. first class commercial radiotelephone operator's license or by personnel working under their immediate supervision
24. According to FCC regulations, transmitters whose oscillators are not crystal controlled should have their carrier 24. ...
    frequencies checked BEFORE they are put into operation,
    and rechecked thereafter every
    A. week   B. month   C. 3 months   D. 6 months

25. The FCC dictates that the power in the output stage(s) of   25. ...
    a 5-watt transmitter, whose modulation and power setting
    remain unaltered, should be checked at the time it is put
    into operation, and rechecked thereafter every
       A. month   B. 3 months   C. 6 months   D. year

Questions 26-40.
DIRECTIONS: Answer questions 26 through 40 based on the schematic
            diagram appearing on pages 11 and 12.

26. The circuits shown on the schematic represent the stages   26. ...
    of a(n)
       A. transmitter   B. receiver
       C. audio-intercom   D. pulse-generator
27. The types of transistors shown on the schematic are   27. ...
       A. all NPN's   B. all PNP's
       C. some NPN's and some PNP's
       D. interchangeable and usable as either NON's or PNP's
28. The power supply shown on the schematic supplies the   28. ...
    stages with
       A. one B + voltage, common to all stages
       B. two B + voltages
       C. one B + voltage and one B - voltage
       D. two B - voltages
29. The circuit element designated as Y101, in Oscillator F1 is 29. ...
    a A. remote-bias adjustment   B. compensated-crystal assembly
       C. solid-state switching device D. protective interlock
30. If the unmodulated frequency at the collector of Q107, of   30. ...
    the Final Amplifier, is 135 MHz, then the input frequency
    to the base of transistor Q103, in the Modulator is
       A. 3.75 MHz   B. 7.50 MHz
       C. 15.0 MHz   D. 22.5 MHz
31. The component in the Automatic Drive Limiter that has the   31. ...
    designation RT101,10K is a
       A. high-resistance incandescent lamp
       B. thermistor
       C. precision wire-wound resistor
       D. ballast lamp
32. The component in the power supply that has the designation   32. ...
    of CR103 is a
       A. double-anode clipper   B. tunnel diode
       C. zener diode   D. rectifier bridge
33. The transistor-stage configuration in which transistor   33. ...
    Q109 of the Integrator is connected is called a(n)
       A. emitter-follower connection B. phase-splitter connection
       C. Darlington connection   D. common-base connection
34. The component between the Amplifier-Clipper and the Inte-   34. ...
    grator that has the designation L116,0.8H is a(n)
       A. air-core choke   B. iron-core inductor
       C. ferrite inductor   D. saturable-core inductor

8

35. Trouble has developed in a unit whose schematic is the one 35. ...
    accompanying this test. DC measurements are taken and indi-
    cate that the voltage on the base of Q109 in the Integrator
    stage has gone to -5.6 volts and the emitter voltage has gone
    to 0.0 volts. Of the following, the condition that causes
    such voltage levels is
    A. the R128 potentiometer slider-arm is making poor contact
    B. Q109 has developed an "open" between base and emitter
    C. C153 has become shorted
    D. Q108, in the previous stage, has gone to cut-off
36. If, in the Pre-Amplifier stage shown in the schematic, ca- 36. ...
    pacitor C164 were to short, the result would be that
    A. Q110 would go harder into conduction
    B. Q110 would approach cut-off
    C. Q110 would become damaged
    D. C165 would break down in the reverse direction
37. In the power supply section, capacitor C156 is required 37. ...
    in shunt with C155 because
    A. the circuit requires a capacity of slightly more than
       15 microfarads; hence C156 would supply the addition-
       al amount
    B. C155 regulates the DC voltage while C156 shunts out
       rupple frequencies
    C. C155 is effective in filtering low frequencies, and
       C156 is effective in filtering high frequencies
    D. C155 and C156, in parallel, form a "pi" section of
       the filter network
38. R113 and C124 in the collector circuit of Q104 in the 38. ...
    2nd Tripler stage form what is COMMONLY called a
    A. self-bias network
    B. low-frequency peaking network
    C. parasitic-suppressor network
    D. decoupling network
39. The Z101 sub-miniature harmonic filter, at the output of 39. ...
    the Final Amplifier, is a
    A. lo-pass filter   B. hi-pass filter
    C. notch filter   D. bandpass filter
40. The purpose of C101, in Oscillator F1, is to 40. ...
    A. adjust the bias level of the stage
    B. slightly "pull" the frequency of oscillation
    C. tune out the inductance seen looking into the tran-
       sistor base
    D. suppress parasitic oscillations

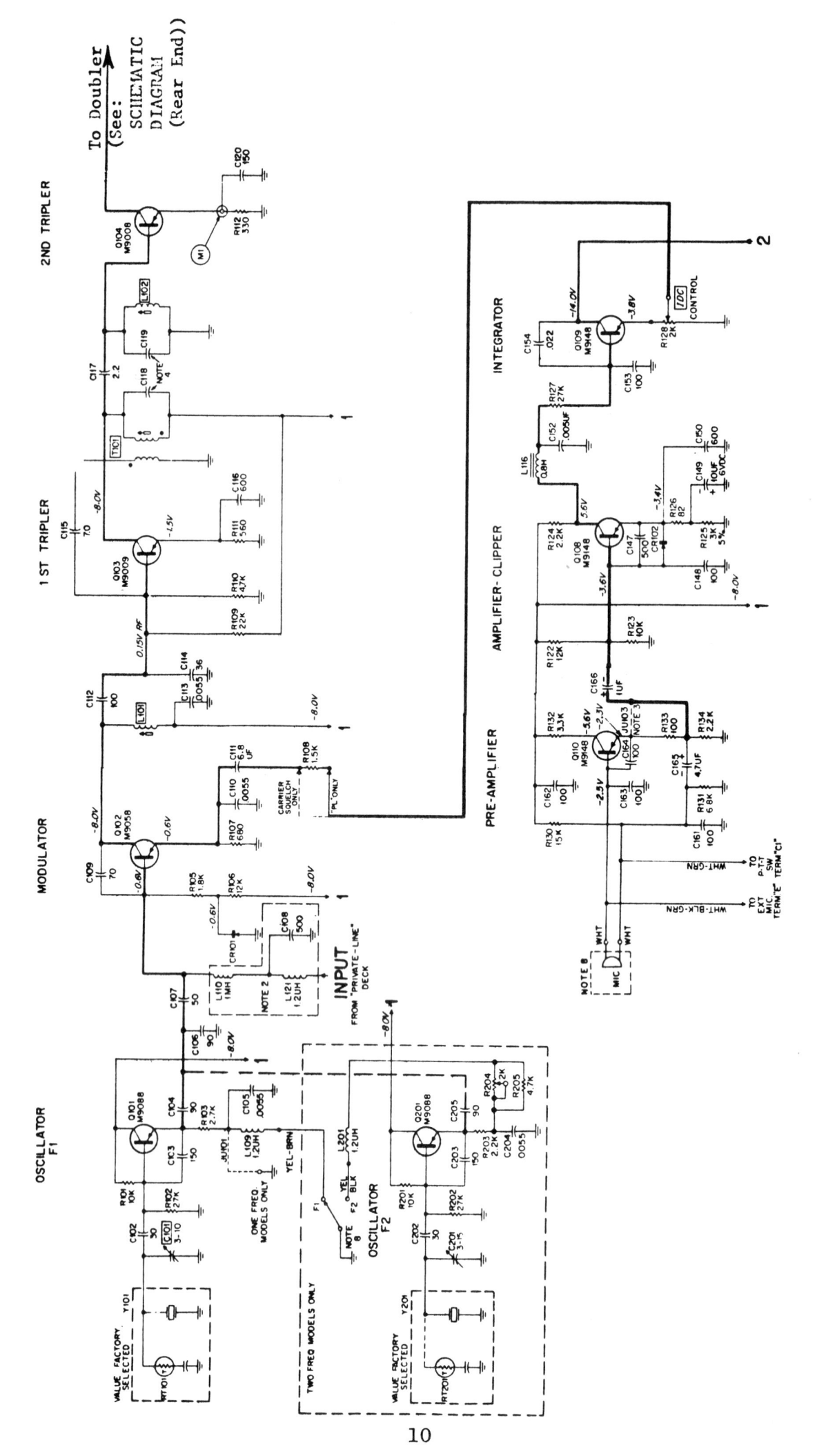

SCHEMATIC DIAGRAM (Front End)

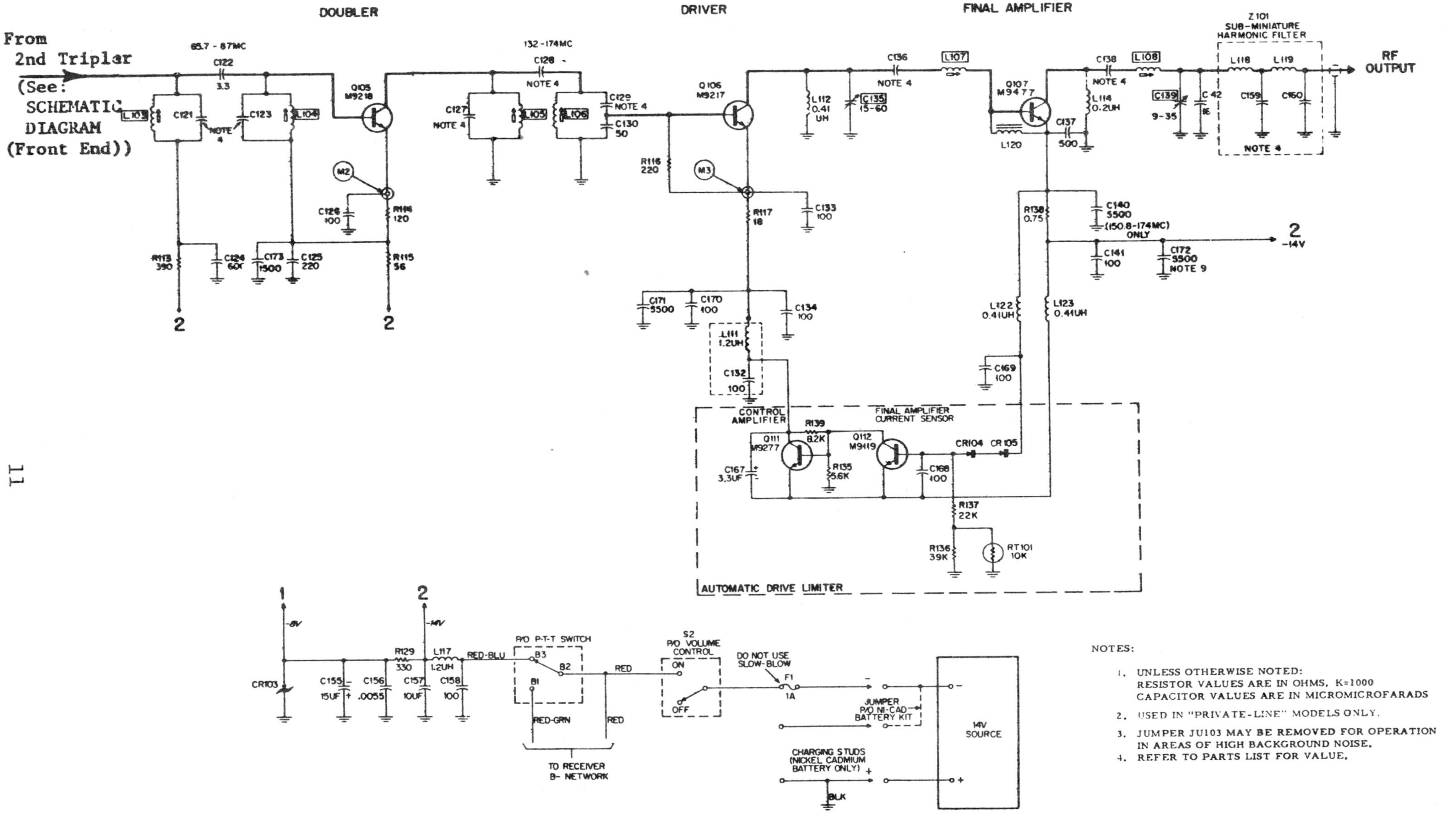

SCHEMATIC DIAGRAM (Rear End)

NOTES:
1. UNLESS OTHERWISE NOTED: RESISTOR VALUES ARE IN OHMS, K=1000 CAPACITOR VALUES ARE IN MICROMICROFARADS
2. USED IN "PRIVATE-LINE" MODELS ONLY.
3. JUMPER JU103 MAY BE REMOVED FOR OPERATION IN AREAS OF HIGH BACKGROUND NOISE.
4. REFER TO PARTS LIST FOR VALUE.

TEST 3

1. If an amplifier has three stages each having a gain of ten, the overall gain of the amplifier is
   A. 30 B. 300 C. 1,000 D. 1,000,000

2. An amplitude-modulated carrier is said to be overmodulated when the
   A. carrier amplitude sometimes is zero for an appreciable time
   B. audio frequencies exceed the assigned band width
   C. audio frequencies are close to the carrier frequency
   D. carrier amplitude sometimes exceeds the rated tank voltage

3. For a radio receiver in which the tuning is done with variable air condensers, the practical ratio of highest to lowest frequency that can be tuned with a single coil for each condenser is NEAREST to
   A. 1.5:1 B. 3:1 C. 6:1 D. 12:1

4. A 2k-ohm, a 4k-ohm, a 6k-ohm and an 8k-ohm resistor are connected in parallel to a 100-volt power source. The resistor which must have the HIGHEST rating, in watts, is the
   A. 2k-ohm B. 4k-ohm C. 6k-ohm D. 8k-ohm

5. A large number of 10-microfarad, 25-volt condensers are available in a particular laboratory. The MINIMUM number of these required to yield a capacitance of 5 microfarads for operation on 150 volts is
   A. 2 B. 6 C. 18 D. 24

6. The heaters of three vacuum tubes are to be operated in series with a resistor on a 120-volt circuit. If the ratings of the heaters are respectively 50, 35, and 12 volts, all at 0.15 amp., the MINIMUM rating of the resistor should be
   A. 250 ohms, 5 watts   B. 250 ohms, 10 watts
   C. 150 ohms, 10 watts D. 150 ohms, 5 watts

7. An audio amplifier is stated to have a frequency response of ± 3 db from 50 to 10,000 cps. If the response is down 3 db at 50 cycles, the voltage output at this frequency (50 cycles) compared to the average voltage output throughout the frequency range is ABOUT
   A. 50% B. 63% C. 67% D. 70%

8. The MAXIMUM limits of resistance of a resistor having yellow, green, and orange color bands (reading from left to right) are
   A. 44,100 - 45,900   B. 42,750 - 47,250
   C. 41,500 - 49,500   D. 36,000 - 54,000

9. A COMMONLY used IF for FM receivers in the 88-108 mc. range is
   A. 455 kc. B. 456 kc. C. 10.7 mc. D. 22.3 mc.

10. Crystal controlled oscillator frequency stability is maintained MOST closely by
    A. feeding the output into a tuned tank circuit
    B. enclosing the crystal in a temperature controlled oven
    C. mounting the crystal in a shock-proof container
    D. obtaining the input from a tuned tank circuit

11. One COMMONLY used dual triode vacuum tube has the designa-   11. ...
    tion
       A. 12AU7   B. 12BE6   C. 12SA7   D. 12SQ7
12. The base radiotelephone station used for contacting surface 12. ...
    line patrol cars in operation 24 hours per day would be meet-
    ing legal requirements if self-identification were made
       A. 24 times a day   B. every 2 hours
       C. at the end of each transmission
       D. at the beginning of each day
13. The alphabet used in radiotelephone communication is   13. ...
       A. Morse   B. international   C. telephonic
       D. phonetic
14. A d.c. meter which gives full-scale deflection at 50 micro- 14. ...
    amperes has a sensitivity of
       A. 1,000 ohms/volt   B. 5,000 ohms/volt
       C. 20,000 ohms/volt   D. 50,000 ohms/volt
15. A certain d.c.meter which gives full-scale deflection at   15. ...
    50 microamperes has a resistance of 250 ohms. When used to
    measure current, it reads .50 of fullscale with a 2.5-ohm
    re istor connected across the meter terminals. The measured
    current, in milliamperes, is NEAREST to
       A. 1.3   B. 2.5   C. 12.5   D. 25.3
16. A certain train to wayside communication system operates   16. ...
    at a frequency of 180 mc. This corresponds to a wavelength
    of
       A. 1667 meters   B. 166.7 meters
       C. 1667 centimeters   D. 166.7 centimeters
17. In an FM receiver using vacuum tubes, the tube having the   17. ...
    lowest voltage applied to the plate is USUALLY the
       A. mixer   B. IF amplifier   C. limiter   D. AF amplifier
18. A grid-dip meter is GENERALLY used to measure   18. ...
       A. frequency   B. RF current   C. AF current   D. modulation
19. To obtain a trapezoidal modulation pattern on the oscillo- 19. ...
    scope, the signal applied to the horizontal deflection
    plates should be a
       A. square wave
       B. saw-tooth wave
       C. sample of the final tank-circuit voltage
       D. sample of the audio modulating voltage
20. To obtain a wave-envelope modulation pattern on the oscil- 20. ...
    loscope, the signal applied to the horizontal deflection
    plates should be a
       A. square wave
       B. saw-tooth wave
       C. sample of the audio modulating voltage
       D. sample of the final tank-circuit voltage
21. When soldering transistorized circuitry, the transistors   21. ...
    are MOST likely to be damaged from the use of too much
       A. solder   B. rosin flux   C. heat   D. pressure

Questions 22-28.
DIRECTIONS: Questions 22 to 28 inclusive refer to the circuit below. Consult the circuit in answering these questions.

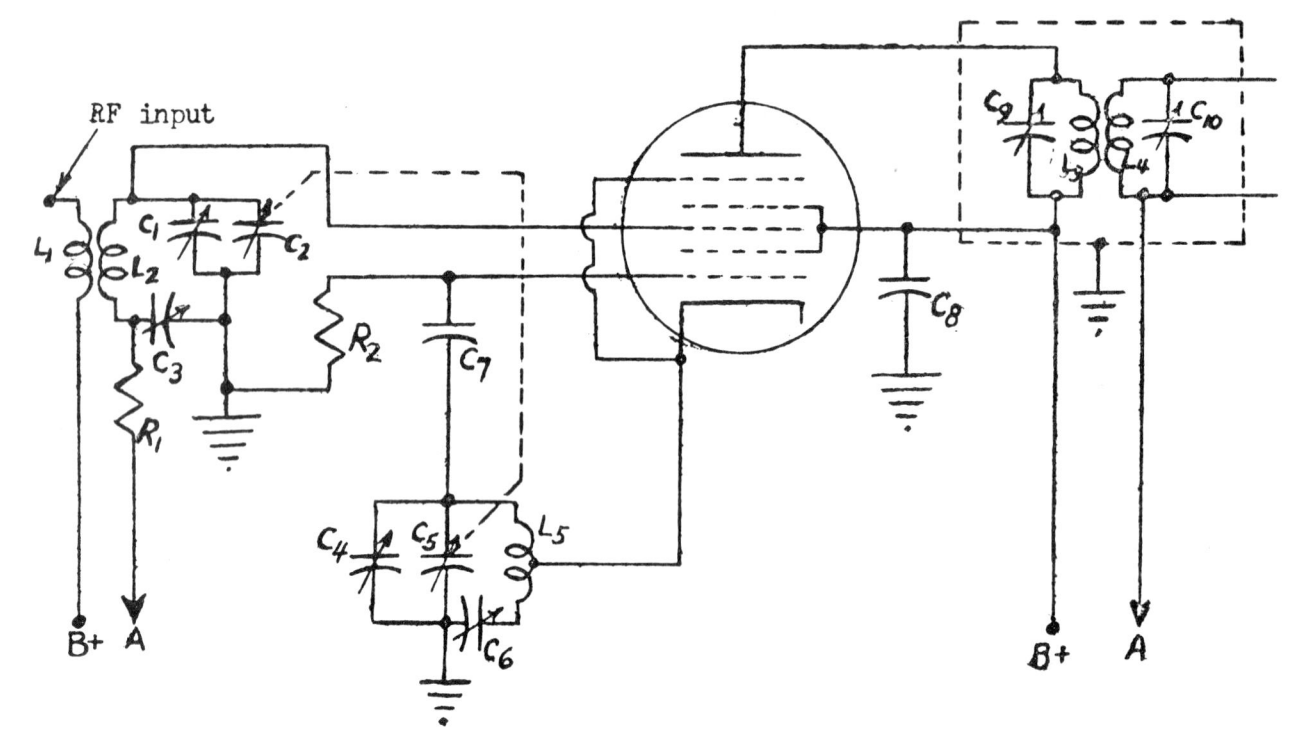

22. The name MOST commonly given to this circuit is 22. ...
    A. radio-frequency amplifier B. first detector
    C. intermediate frequency amplifier   D. ratio detector
23. The vacuum tube shown is a 23. ...
    A. power amplifier pentode   B. beam power pentode
    C. hexode mixer   D. pentagrid converter
24. The wires terminating in arrowheads and labeled A, MOST 24. ...
    likely connect to the
    A. chassis   B. AVC bus
    C. cathode bias resistors
    D. power supply screen grid bias
25. Tracking at the high-frequency end of the tuning range is 25. ...
    synchronized by adjusting
    A. C_1 and C_4 B. C_3 and C_6
    C. C_2 and C_5 D. C_3 and C_4
26. Tracking at the low-frequency end of the tuning range is 26. ...
    synchronized by adjusting
    A. C_1 and C_4 B. C_3 and C_6
    C. C_2 and C_5 D. C_3 and C_4
27. The circuit shows that there is shielding around the 27. ...
    A. RF tuning stage   B. oscillator
    C. vacuum tube   D. IF transformer
28. The type of oscillator shown is a 28. ...
    A. tickler   B. Colpitts   C. Hartley   D. TPTG

29. A 35-ohm, 2-watt, 10% tolerance resistor should have color   29. ...
    bands, reading from left to right, of
    A. orange,green,brown,silver   B. orange,green,brown,gold
    C. orange,green,black,silver   D. orange,green,black,gold
30. The resistor of Question 29 above has a current-carrying   30. ...
    capacity of
    A. .239 ma   B. 2.39 ma   C. 23.9 ma   D. 239 ma
31. The 20,000 ohms/volt meter   31. ...
    having a full-scale deflec-
    tion of 50 volts reads 45
    volts with switch S closed
    in position 1, and 21 volts
    when the switch is in posi-
    tion 2 as shown. The value
    of R is readily calculated
    to be
    A. .875 megohm   B. 1.14 megohms   C. 87,500 ohms
    D. 114,000 ohms
32. In the high rejection-ratio   32. ...
    trap circuit shown, the de-
    vice that must be connected
    between terminals 1 and 2
    for proper rejection is a(n)
    A. resistor   B. RF choke
    C. AF choke   D. capacitor
33. A band elimination filter is MOST accurately illustrated by 33. ...

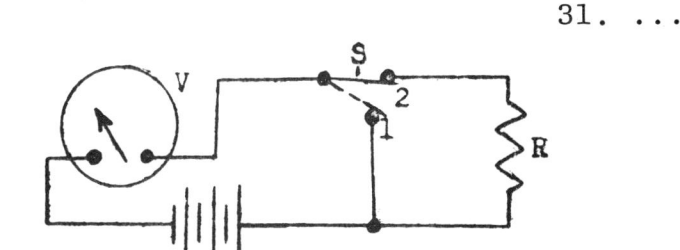

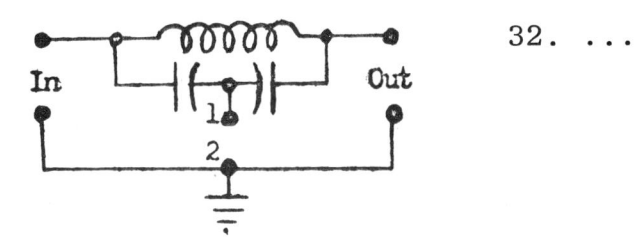

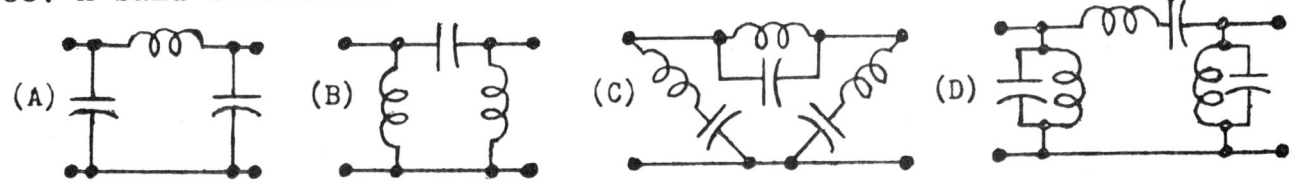

34. The circuit which can yield a relatively sharp pulse out-   34. ...
    put ( ) to the grid and cathode of a vacuum tube when
    a square wave is applied to the input is

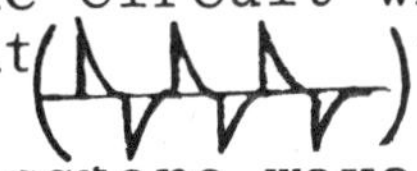

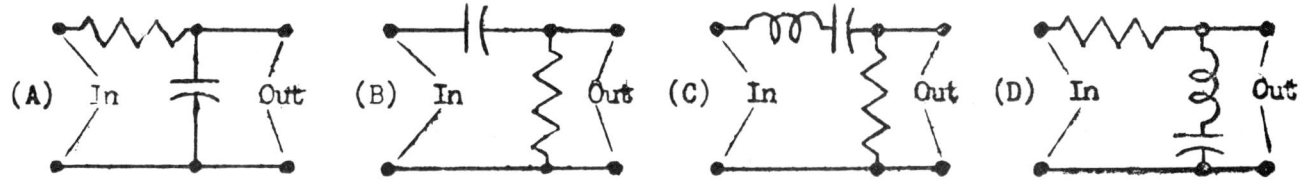

35. The figure which shows that two equal voltages of the same   35. ...
    frequency but 90° out of phase are applied to the horizon-
    tal and vertical deflecting plates of the CRO is

15

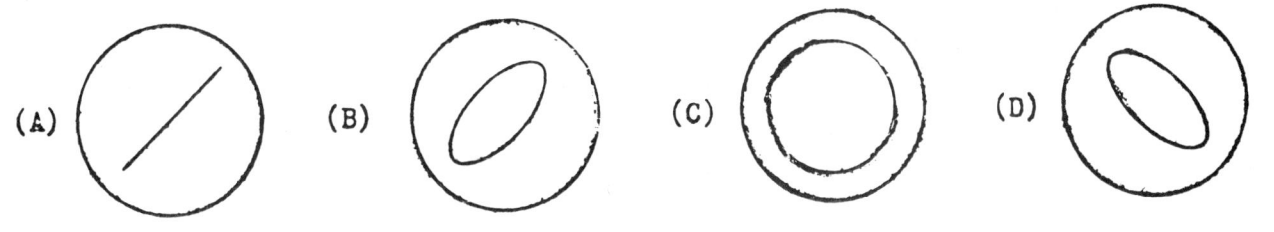

36. The electron tube which does NOT include an electron gun   36. ...
    in its construction is the
      A. Klystron   B. Kinescope   C. Iconoscope   D. Thyraton
37. The capacitance of a condenser does NOT depend on the   37. ...
      A. surface area of the conductors or plates in contact
         with the dielectric
      B. thickness of the dielectric
      C. insulation of the dielectric
      D. thickness of the plates
38. Frequency doublers and triplers are used in   38. ...
      A. CW transmitters   B. pulsed transmitters
      C. FM transmitters   D. keyed transmitters
39. Zener diodes are GENERALLY used for   39. ...
      A. AVC rectification   B. diode detection
      C. voltage regulation   D. current limitation
40. An AF amplifier transistor could have the designation   40. ...
      A. 2N242   B. 242N2   C. 1N105   D. 105N1
41. Carrier frequency voice transmission is used in wire tele- 41. ...
    phony PRIMARILY to increase the
      A. number of voice channels   B. clarity of tone
      C. transmission distance   D. transmitted power
42. The circuit shown at the   42. ...
    right is PROPERLY called
    a
      A. potentiometer
      B. voltage divider
      C. vol age decade
      D. current limiter
43. If R_1, R_2, and R_3 in the sketch of Question 42 above are 43. ...
    250k, 500k, and 50k ohms, respectively, the MAXIMUM grid
    bias (negative) voltage available for a tube with a grounded
    cathode is
      A. 12.5   B. 25   C. 125   D. 250
44. Automobiles now use alternators and rectifiers instead of   44. ...
    d.c. generators for supplying the cars' electrical demands.
    The rectifier that is MOST widely used is the
      A. copper oxide   B. galena   C. germanium   D. silicon
45. A circuit configuration which does NOT apply to transis-   45. ...
    tors is common
      A. emitter   B. base   C. cathode   D. collector
46. The microphone that is MOST likely to require a preampli-   46. ...
    fier to operate an audio amplifier is the
      A. crystal   B. carbon   C. ceramic   D. magnetic
47. If the oscillator of a tape recorder is faulty, the MOST   47. ...
    likely result will be
      A. incomplete erasure   B. weak recording
      C. excessive volume   D. variation in tape speed
48. Measurement of radiation from a radio antenna is made with 48. ...
    a A. Q meter   B. field strength meter   C. flux meter
      D. radiometer
49. If a 0-150 volt meter is guaranteed to have an accuracy of 49. ...
    2% of full scale deflection, then the MAXIMUM error of the
    indication when the pointer shows 25 volts is plus or minus
      A. 0.5 volt   B. 1.0 volt   C. 1.5 volts   D. 3.0 volts

50. The contacts of relays and switches used in communication work are frequently silver plated. The purpose of the silver plating is to
   A. improve conductivity of the contacts
   B. reduce arcing at the contacts
   C. improve the flexibility of the contacts
   D. reduce the amount of copper that would otherwise be necessary

50. ...

TEST 4

1. If a one microfarad condenser is connected in series with a two microfarad condenser, the capacity of the resulting combination in microfarads is
   A. three   B. one and one half   C. two-thirds   D. one-third

1. ...

2. A storage battery is charged from a 112-volt d-c line through a series resistance. If the charging rate is 10 amperes, the electromotive force of the battery is 12 volts and its internal resistance is 0.2 ohms, the value of the series resistance is
   A. 11.2 ohm   B. 10 ohm   C. 9.8 ohm   D. 1.2 ohm

2. ...

3. The resistance, in ohms, of a 10 ampere 50M.V shunt is, MOST NEARLY,
   A. 2   B. .05   C. .005   D. .002

3. ...

4. It is required to couple a 4 ohm voice coil of a loudspeaker to an output tube having a plate load of 10,000 ohms. This can best be done by using a transformer having a ratio of primary to secondary turns of, APPROXIMATELY,
   A. 5   B. 25   C. 50   D. 75

4. ...

5. A dynamoelectric amplifier for power control having high amplification ratio is commonly called a(n)
   A. Dynatron   B. Amplidyne   C. Amplitherm   D. Dynatherm

5. ...

6. An amplifier has an output voltage wave form that does not exactly follow that of the input voltage. This type of distortion is called
   A. amplitude distortion   B. modular distortion
   C. resonance distortion   D. variation distortion

6. ...

7. The frequency in cycles multipled by 2π is COMMONLY called
   A. annular frequency   B. heaviside frequency
   C. angular frequency   D. circular frequency

7. ...

8. An anion is a negative ion that moves toward the
   A. anode in an electrolytic cell
   B. cathode in a discharge tube
   C. positive terminal of a battery while being discharged
   D. negative terminal of a battery while being charged

8. ...

9. Silicon rectifiers as compared with selenium rectifiers of the same physical size have
   A. greater current ratings   B. smaller current ratings
   C. the same current ratings
   D. much greater resistance at 60 cycles

9. ...

10. The germanium rectifier as compared with other types of   10. ...
    rectifier, has
       A. a high forward drop
       B. a low reverse resistance
       C. no aging, and therefore has an indefinitely long life
       D. a narrow temperature range, from -5° to +40°C.
11. Transistors are ideally suited for Hi-Fi amplifiers since   11. ...
    they are inherently
       A. high impedance devices   B. low impedance devices
       C. non-linear devices   D. quadrature devices
12. An Air Condenser composed of two parallel flat plates of   12. ...
    area Z, separated by a distance Y, has a capacitance which
    is
       A. directly proportional to the distance Y
       B. directly proportional to the area Z
       C. inversely proportional to the area Z
       D. inversely proportional to the square of the area Z
13. For Audio Frequency amplifiers used for Hi-Fi work, it is   13. ...
    desirable to have a hum and noise level, at full output, of,
    APPROXIMATELY,
       A. -80 db   B. -20 db   C. +20 db   D. +80 db
14. The maximum Q of cavity resonators is, APPROXIMATELY,   14. ...
       A. 500   B. 5,000   C. 50,000   D. 5,000,000
15. To find out if a source of supply is D.C. or A.C., it is   15. ...
    BEST to use a(n)
       A. iron vane voltmeter
       B. neon tester
       C. test set made up of two ordinary lamps in series
       D. dynamometer-type voltmeter
16. A vacuum tube circuit having high input impedance, low out-16. ...
    put impedance, and a gain of less than unity is MOST likely
    a(n)
       A. anode-follower circuit   B. differentiating circuit
       C. ignitron circuit   D. cathode-follower circuit
17. A heart-shaped pattern obtained as the response or radia- 17. ...
    tion characteristic of certain directional antennae or as
    the response characteristic of certain microphones is called
    a A. cardioid pattern   B. sinusoidal pattern
      C. semicircular pattern   D. parabolic
18. A standard FM broadcast transmitter sends out a signal   18. ...
    with a swing of ± 60 kc. The percentage modulation of this
    signal is
       A. 60   B. 70   C. 80   D. 90
19. A standard method of securing a good signal-to-noise ratio 19. ...
    in an FM transmitter is to
       A. keep the filament power low to reduce thermal noise
       B. use pre-emphasis
       C. use squelch circuits
       D. use thermal agitation
20. The process of determining the correct values for different 20. ...
    positions of a meter, pointer or settings of a control is
    COMMONLY called
       A. adjusting   B. measuring   C. aligning   D. calibrating

Questions 21-23.
DIRECTIONS: Questions 21-23 inclusive refer to the diagram below.

[Diagram: rectangle with arrow on top, containing three dots labeled A, B, C]

21. In the standard RMA color code for the value of fixed capacitors, when only three color dotes are used, the working voltage is assumed to be
    A. 100   B. 300   C. 500   D. 600

22. In standard RMA color code for the value of fixed capacitors when only three color dots are given, the tolerance is assumed to be
    A. 5 percent   B. 10 percent   C. 15 percent   D. 20 percent

23. With reference to the above figure, the dot marked A represents the
    A. first significant figure   B. decimal multiplier
    C. working temperature   D. second significant figure

24. If 1000 watts of power are delivered to an antenna having a resistance of 10 ohms, the antenna current, in amperes, is, MOST NEARLY,
    A. 3.1   B. 5   C. 7.07   D. 10

25. A quarter-wave (90°) antenna comprised of thin wire without supporting structure and operating at a frequency of 5000 kilocycles, has a physical height of
    A. 24.6 feet   B. 49.2 feet   C. 93.8 feet   D. 98.4 feet

26. As compared with the series-fed antenna, the shunt-fed antenna
    A. permits the elimination of the base ground
    B. need not have an impedance match with the source for optimum operation
    C. permits the elimination of the base insulator
    D. permits the elimination of all insulators

27. The diagram below represents a(n)

[Diagram: ladder network with two series resistors and two shunt capacitors, e_{in} on left, e_{out} on right]

    A. differentiating circuit   B. high pass filter
    C. integrating circuit   D. band pass filter

28. Of the following, the type of bridge used for measuring inductance is the
    A. Kelvin Bridge   B. Wheatstone Bridge
    C. Maxwell Bridge   D. Newton Bridge

29. A certain circuit having an input of one volt and an output of 10 volts, has a power gain, in decibels, of
    A. 5   B. 10   C. 15   D. 20

30. In an A.M. transmitter, if the peak value of the modulated carrier current is 2 amps and that of the unmodulated carrier current is one amp, the percentage of modulation is, APPROXIMATELY,
    A. 40%   B. 60%   C. 80%   D. 100%

31. With reference to vacuum tubes, if the amplification factor is divided by the plate resistance, the result will be a term called
    A. efficiency
    B. transconductance
    C. emission
    D. sensitivity
32. An amplifier in which the grid bias and alternating grid are such that plate current in a specific tube flows at all times with essentially linear amplification, is called a
    A. class A amplifier
    B. class B amplifier
    C. class C amplifier
    D. class AB_2 amplifier
33. Inverse feed back is used in audio amplifiers to
    A. magnify the amplification
    B. increase the power output
    C. increase the impedance of the loud speaker
    D. reduce distortion in the output stage
34. Constant-current inverse feedback is USUALLY obtained by
    A. increasing the value of the capacitor across the cathode resistor
    B. omitting the bypass capacitor across the cathode resistor
    C. increasing the gain of the output tube
    D. decreasing the plate resistance of the output tube
35. In order to make more natural the reproduction of music which has a very large volume range in a phonograph amplifier, it is BEST to use a(n)
    A. linear response amplifier
    B. volume suppressor
    C. volume expander
    D. output stage with two tubes in push-push
36. The limiter in FM receivers has the function of eliminating
    A. the second harmonic from the input to the detector
    B. the third harmonic from the input to the detector
    C. FM-Variations from the input to the detector
    D. amplitude variations from the input to the detector

Questions 37-39.
DIRECTIONS: Questions 37 to 39 inclusive are based on the diagram below.

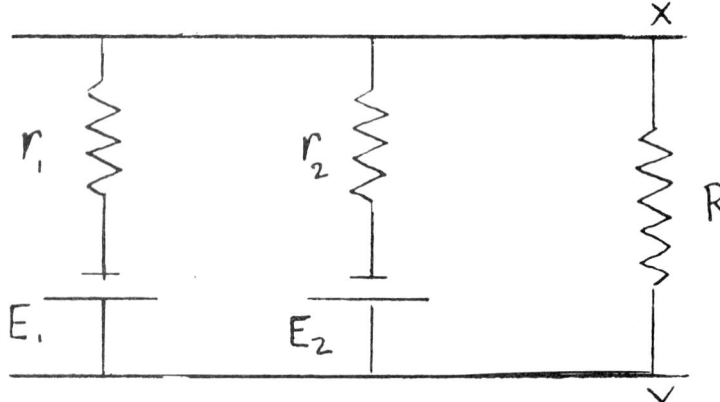

37. If r_1 = .01 ohm, r_2 = .01 ohm, E_1 = 1 volt, and R = infinity, the voltage across xy is, MOST NEARLY,
    A. 2 volts   B. 1 volt   C. .2 volt   D. .1 volt

38. If r_1 = .01 ohm, r_2 = .01 ohm, E_1= 1 volt, E_2 =2 volts, and   38. ...
    R = infinity, the voltage across xy is, MOST NEARLY,
    A. .5   B. 1   C. 1.5   D. 2
39. If r_1 = .01 ohm, r_2 = .01 ohm, E_1= 1 volt, E_2 =2 volts, and   39. ...
    R = 1 ohm, the voltage across xy is, MOST NEARLY,
    A. .5   B. 9   C. 1.1   D. 1.5

Question 40.
DIRECTIONS: Question 40 refers to the figure below.

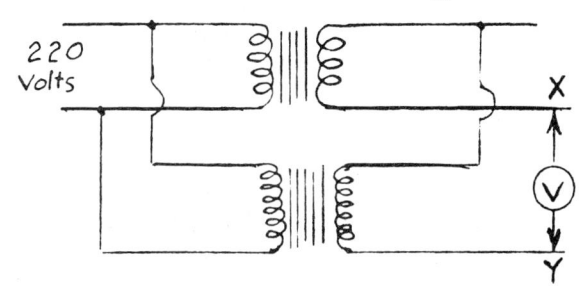

40. Two transformers with ratios of 2:1 are to be connected in   40. ...
    parallel. To test for proper connections, the circuit shown
    above is used. The transformers may be connected in parallel
    by connecting Lead "X" to Lead "Y" if the voltmeter shown
    reads
    A. zero   B. 120   C. 220   D. 340

Questions 41-42.
DIRECTIONS: Questions 41 and 42 refer to the figure below.

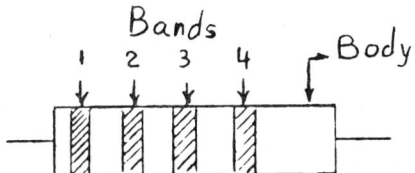

41. In the standard RMA color code chart for the value of re-   41. ...
    sistors, the band numbered 1 in the above figure represents
    the
    A. decimal multiplier   B. tolerance
    C. first significant figure   D. second significant figure
42. With reference to the RMA color code chart for the value   42. ...
    of resistors, if the 1st band is red, the 2nd band black,
    the 3rd band black, and the 4th band silver, the value of
    this resistor is
    A. 100 ohms 10%   B. 2000 ohms 5%
    C. 100 ohms 5%   D. 200 ohms 10%
43. A condenser having a capacitance of one microfarad is con-   43. ...
    nected across a 1000-volt D-C line. The energy stored by
    this condenser is
    A. 10 watts   B. 1/2 watt   C. 10 joules   D. 1/2 joule
44. If a powdered iron core is inserted into an inductance   44. ...
    coil, the coil
    A. resistance is increased   B. inductance is increased
    C. inductance is decreased   D. resistance is decreased
45. If a brass core is inserted into an inductance coil, the   45. ...
    coil
    A. resistance is increased   B. inductance is increased
    C. inductance is decreased   D. resistance is decreased

TEST 4

46. A disadvantage of the limiter commonly used in F.M. receivers 46. ....
is that it requires, for proper operation, a
    A. small signal amplitude
    B. low radio frequency amplification
    C. large signal amplitude
    D. high screen voltage
47. In the ratio detector the radio frequency is fed to the di- 47. ....
odes in the same manner as in the F-M discriminator except
that the diodes in the ratio detector are connected in
    A. parallel   B. push-push   C. push-pull   D. series
48. A general-purpose instrument that may be used for the measure- 48. ....
ment of the output frequency of an r-f oscillator within ac-
curacies of from .25% to 2% is known as a(n)
    A. absorption wave meter   B. Wien frequency bridge
    C. Maxwell bridge   D. Meteorograph bridge
49. The frequency of oscillation of a multivibrator is determined 49. ....
by the values of the
    A. resistance and inductance   B. inductance and capacity
    C. resistance and capacity   D. capacity alone
50. With reference to Radio-Frequency measurements, a primary   50. ....
standard of frequency is defined as one whose frequency is
determined
    A. directly in terms of time
    B. by comparison with another standard
    C. by the value of the RC constant
    D. by the values of L and C in the circuit
51. If a .75 Kw transmitter produces a field intensity of 10   51. ....
millivolts per meter at a distance of 5 miles and is received
by an antenna having an effective height of 10 meters, the
millivolts of signal induced in the antenna (neglecting
losses) will be, MOST NEARLY,
    A. 50   B. 75   C. 100   D. 125
52. With reference to directive microwave antennae, the parabol-   52. ....
ic reflector possesses the characteristic that
    A. the intensity of the reflected rays varies as the square
       of the distance
    B. all rays from the radiator striking the reflecting sur-
       face are reflected as parallel rays
    C. the intensity of the reflected rays varies inversely as
       the square of the distance
    D. all rays striking the reflecting surface are reflected
       as diverging rays
53. With reference to the oscilloscope, Lissajous curves are   53. ....
widely used for
    A. aligning radio I.F. transformers
    B. aligning television tuners
    C. obtaining a response curve of the I.F. stages in F.M.
       receivers
    D. frequency comparison
54. The one of the following oscillators which is used to deflect 54. ....
periodically the electron beam of a cathode-ray tube so as to
give a displacement that is a function of time is the
    A. sweep oscillator   B. beat oscillator
    C. jump oscillator   D. connecting oscillator

55. The impedance in ohms measured between the terminals of a   55. ...
    transmission line at the operating frequency is called
       A. patch impedance   B. lumped impedance
       C. surge impedance   D. sweep impedance
56. Decibels may be calculated by multiplying the common lo-   56. ...
    garithm of the power ratio by ten. Therefore, a power ra-
    tio of 100 corresponds to, MOST NEARLY,
       A. 10 db   B. 20 db   C. 30 db   D. 40 db
57. Power factor is defined as the ratio of active power to   57. ...
    apparent power, generally expressed in percent. In accord-
    ance with the definition given above, the power factor of
    a pure resistance is
       A. zero   B. unity   C. infinity   D. indeterminate

Questions 58-59.

DIRECTIONS: Questions 58 and 59 refer to the data given below.
    An L resistance attenuation network is required to match,
with minimum less, a 500-ohm source Z_S and a 250-ohm lead
Z_L; use the design data given below.

$$R_1 = \sqrt{Z_S(Z_S - Z_L)}$$
$$R_2 = \frac{Z_S Z_L}{R_1}$$

58. Using the above data and formula, the value of resistor R_1 58. ...
    for this network is, MOST NEARLY,
       A. 353   B. 305   C. 253   D. 75
59. With reference to the above L pad and formula, the value   59. ...
    of R_2 is, MOST NEARLY,
       A. 353   B. 305   C. 253   D. 75
60. In frequency modulation receivers, noise   60. ...
       A. causes an amplitude disturbance only
       B. is completely eliminated by the limiter
       C. causes some variation in the frequency swing of the
          desired signal
       D. has no effect
61. An open quarter-wave stub may be used as a   61. ...
       A. suppressor of even and odd harmonics
       B. suppressor of even harmonics only
       C. suppressor of odd harmonics only
       D. filter of odd harmonics only
62. A closed quarter-wave stub offers an infinite impedance at 62. ...
       A. low frequencies   B. high frequencies
       C. the resonant frequency D. all frequencies
63. The one of the following which is COMMONLY used as a stand- 63. ...
    ing wave detector operating as a current indicator is a
       A. one-turn pick-up loop with the ends connected to a r-f
          thermo galvanometer
       B. one-turn pick-up loop with the ends connected to a
          D'Arsonval galvanometer
       C. 1000-turn pick-up loop with the ends connected to a r-f
          thermo galvanometer
       D. 1000-turn pick-up loop with the ends connected to a
          D'Arsonval galvanometer

64. If a line having a characteristic impedance of 300 ohms is 64. ...
    terminated in a resistive load of 50 ohms, the standing-wave
    ratio is, MOST NEARLY,
    A. 1 to 12   B. 12 to 1   C. 1 to 6   D. 6 to 1
65. In aligning the sound discriminator of an F.M. receiver 65. ...
    with an oscilloscope, the pattern that should be obtained
    for proper adjustment is a(n)
    A. symmetrical "S" curve   B. asymmetrical "S" curve
    C. symmetrical parabolic curve D. asymmetrical parabolic curve
66. In A.M. radio telephone transmitters, negative feedback 66. ...
    A. is not used
    B. makes impractical the use of high-efficiency systems
    C. makes impractical the use of a power supply system
       with relatively inexpensive filtering
    D. decreases the amplitude distortion

Questions 67-70.
DIRECTIONS: Questions 67 to 70, inclusive, are based on the following
            description of a certain transmitter.

The radio transmitter is a frequency-modulated unit utilizing the phase-shift method of obtaining frequency deviations, and as such exhibits considerably different characteristics than the usual amplitude-modulated units.

Intelligence is conveyed in frequency variations of the constant-amplitude carrier wave. The use of the phase-shift method of frequency modulation allows direct crystal control of the mean carrier frequency, a necessity in unattended and mobile equipment. It necessitates, however, considerable frequency multiplication after the tubes are used for this function, and a total frequency multiplication of 48 times is effected. A twin triode acts as both crystal oscillator and phase modulator. The first half of the tube operates in a resistance coupled aperiodic oscillator circuit. The output frequency range is 152-162 mc.

The second half of the twin triode acts as a phase modulator. The r-f output of the crystal oscillator is impressed on the phase-modulator grid by means of a blocking condenser. The cathode circuit is provided with a large amount of degeneration by an unbypassed cathode resistor. Because of this degeneration feed-back, the transconductance of the triode is abnormally low - so low that the plate current is affected about as much by the direct grid-plate capacitance as by the transconductance. The two effects result in plate current Vectors almost 180° apart, and the total plate current is the resultant of the two components. In phase it will be about 90° removed from the phase of the voltage impressed on the grid. When audio is impressed on the grid thereby periodically changing the bias, and in consequence the transconductance, the plate current undergoes a periodic change in both amplitude and phase. The amplitude modulation is unimportant, and is removed in the frequency multipliers, but the phase modulation remains and is the essential element of the transmitted signal.

67. With reference to the above information, the crystal fre- 67. ...
    quency will be between
    A. 152 and 162 mc   B. 15.2 and 16.2 mc
    C. 3166.67 and 3375.0 Kc   D. 316.67 and 337.50 Kc

68. In the second part of the twin triode, the cathode resistor 68. ...
    A. is shunted by a large condenser
    B. has no condenser
    C. is shunted by a small condenser
    D. is in series with an electrolytic condenser
69. In this transmitter, frequency multiplication occurs 69. ...
    A. after modulation   B. before modulation
    C. in the phase modulator   D. in the oscillator circuit
70. With reference to the above information, when the audio is 70. ...
    impressed on the grid of the second triode of the twin triode,
    A. the plate current undergoes a change in amplitude only
    B. the plate current undergoes a change in amplitude and phase
    C. any amplitude modulation is cut off by the transconductance
    D. any phase modulation is eliminated

TEST 5

1. The unit of measure of magnetomotive force is the 1. ...
   A. gilbert   B. gauss   C. henry   D. mho
2. The figure of merit of a coil or circuit is 2. ...
   A. $\frac{R}{Z}$ B. $\frac{X_L}{R}$ C. $X_c X_L$ D. $Z = R$
3. The molecular friction produced by the alternating current 3. ...
   reversals in a magnetic core material is known as
   A. retentivity   B. hysteresis
   C. eddy current   D. counter M.M.F.
4. One horsepower is equal to 4. ...
   A. 467 watts B. 647 watts C. 1646 watts D. 746 watts
5. The ability of a magnetic material to conduct magnetic lines 5. ...
   of force is called
   A. reluctance   B. conductance
   C. permeability   D. admittance
6. A small mica condenser marked with three dots as follows, 6. ...
   has a capacitance of what value? 1.Red;2.green;3.brown:
   A. 250 mmf.   B. 2500 mmf.   C. 25 mmf.   D. 2.5 mmf.
7. If the current through the windings of an electromagnet is 7. ...
   constantly increased, the field strength will increase in proportion to the current, up to a certain point, beyond which
   the field strength will increase only slightly for a further
   increase in current. This point is called
   A. permeability   B. saturation
   C. BH curve   D. phase point
8. Gold band on a resistor indicates a tolerance of 8. ...
   A. 10%   B. 20%   C. 5%   D. 15%
9. Placing a "permeability slug" into an rf transformer will 9. ...
   A. decrease the frequency of the ckt.
   B. increase the frequency of the ckt.
   C. decrease the inductance
   D. none of the above

10. What law states that the total current entering a junction in a circuit is equal to the total current leaving that junction?
   A. Lenz's   B. Coulomb's   C. Ohm's   D. Kirchhoff's

11. The MAXIMUM current carrying capacity of a resistor marked "5000 Ohms-200 Watts" is
   A. 25 amperes   B. .2 amperes   C. 2 amperes   D. 2.5 amperes

12. Three condensers of 2 uF., 2 uF., and 4 uF. are connected in series. The resulting capacitance of this combination will be
   A. 0.8 uF   B. 8.0 uF.   C. 1.6 uF   D. 16 uF

13. In order to obtain the maximum short circuit current from a group of similar cells in a storage battery, they should be connected in
   A. parallel   B. series-parallel
   C. series   D. parallel-series

14.

   I_T equals
   A. .5 amp.   B. 5½ amp.   C. 2 amp.   D. 0 amp.

15. A resistor marked as follows, has a value of how many ohms? Body: red; Tip: green; Band or dot: orange.
   A. 1400 ohms   B. 36,000 ohms   C. 25,000 ohms   D. .25 MEG

16. A 10W, 1000 ohm resistor is in parallel with a 100W, 10,000 ohm resistor and a 50W, 20,000 ohm resistor. The HIGHEST permissible line voltage for this combination without exceeding the power ratings of these resistors is
   A. 1,000 volts   B. 10 volts   C. 100 volts   D. 500 volts

17. The fully charged condition of a lead acid storage cell is indicated when a hydrometer reads
   A. 1.080   B. 1.280   C. 1.150   D. 1.500

18. You are called upon to repair, if possible, a storage battery which is discharged and in which the cells are only half full of electrolyte. You should FIRST
   A. fill with a solution of acid and water to 1200 S.G.
   B. fill with plain distilled water and charge
   C. pour out remaining electrolyte and refill with a new solution of water and acid to 1200 S.G.
   D. none of the above - the battery is beyond repair

19. The voltmeter connected as shown will read the voltage drop across

   A. R_1 B. R_2 C. R_1 and R_2 D. R_2 and R_3

20. A radio receiver has a power transformer designed to supply 20. ...
    250 volts when operating from a 110-volt 60-cycle supply
    line. When the primary is connected to a 110-volt D.C. source,
    the
    A. secondary voltage will decrease
    B. secondary voltage will increase
    C. primary current will decrease
    D. primary current will increase
21. A coupling system that passes certain frequencies and at 21. ...
    the same time rejects other frequencies, is called
    A. choke   B. phase shifter C. filter   D. bypass condenser
22. Audio frequencies lie between 22. ...
    A. 200 to 200,000 cps   B. 20 to 20,000 cps
    C. 60 to 120 cps   D. 5 to 4,000 cps
23. Vertical sweep circuits may be distinguished from horizon- 23. ...
    tal by their
    A. higher plate voltages
    B. larger capacity condensers
    C. greater power ratings on controls
    D. lower plate voltages
24. In an inverted amplifier, output is taken from the 24. ...
    A. plate circuit   B. cathode circuit
    C. control grid circuit D. shield grid circuit
25. Poor reception on a newly installed commercial television 25. ...
    receiver GENERALLY indicates
    A. improper adjustment of I.F. stages
    B. improper adjustment of 8.25 Mc trap
    C. wrong value R-C components in sweep circuits
    D. poor antenna installation
26. The voltage across the output of the discriminator at re- 26. ...
    sonance should
    A. be a maximum   B. be a minimum
    C. vary between a maximum and a minimum
    D. be a value depending on the signal voltage
27. For optimum operation of an A.F. resistance coupled vol- 27. ...
    tage amplifier using a triode (not considering frequency
    restrictions), the plate resistor should be
    A. equal to the plate resistance of the tube
    B. equal to the transconductance of the tube
    C. twice the plate resistance of the tube
    D. equal to plate voltage divided by plate current of tube
28. Peak inverse voltage being delivered to a full wave recti- 28. ...
    fier with condenser input is equal to r.m.s. of total se-
    condary
    A. X 1.414   B. X .707   C. X.636
    D. plus voltage on condenser
29. In performing a visual alignment, the voltage fed into the 29. ...
    stages to be aligned MUST be
    A. amplitude modulated   B. unmodulated
    C. frequency modulated   D. demodulated
30. The discriminator in an FM receiver corresponds to the 30. ...
    stage in an AM receiver known as the
    A. converter   B. second detector
    C. output amplifier   D. preselector

31. A 200 mmfd padder is connected in series with a 400 mmfd   31. ...
    tuning condenser. The total MAXIMUM capacity will be
       A. 600 mmfd B. 300 mmfd C. 133 mmfd D. 266 mmfd
32. Shunting a "tank circuit" with an inductance will make it   32. ...
       A. respond to a higher frequency
       B. respond to a lower frequency
       C. destroy its oscillatory action
       D. decrease its resistive component
33. Video frequencies in modern television service range from   33. ...
       A. 15-15,000 cps B. 30-3,500,000 cps C. 44-71 mcs
       D. 4.3-12 mcs
34. A superheterodyne is tuned to a desired signal at 1000 KC.   34. ...
    Its conversion oscillator is operating at 1300 KC. A signal
    at _____ may cause an image interference.
       A. 300 KC   B. 900 KC   C. 1600 KC   D. 100 KC
35. The plate E of an RF or IF stage is above normal. The screen 35. ...
    grid E is above normal. The cathode E is above normal. Trouble
    PROBABLY is   (E = voltage.)
       A. open screen dropping resistor
       B. shorted plate loud resistor
       C. open cathode resistor
       D. shorted screen bi-pass condenser
36. Low output voltage from AC/DC power supply may be caused by   36. ...
    open
       A. output filter condenser
       B. condenser in power amplifier cathode circuit
       C. condenser on input side of filter
       D. coupling condenser to power amplifier
37. Adjustments in Lecher-Wires are GENERALLY accomplished by   37. ...
       A. sliding a shorting-bar along the line
       B. trimming off the ends of the line
       C. placing a variable condenser across the lines
       D. varying the spacing between the lines
38. Local oscillators in FM receivers often have a mica and a   38. ...
    ceramic condenser in parallel across the tank. The purpose
    of this combination is to
       A. increase the "Q" of the circuit
       B. operate the tank at a greater C/L ratio
       C. prevent temperature co-efficient drift
       D. prevent breakdown of condensers
39. A signal reaching the grid of a grid-leak type of Limiter,   39. ...
    at a peak value greater than the bias on the tube, will
    PROBABLY cause
       A. lack of linearity in discriminator output
       B. second-harmonic distortion in A.F. output
       C. saturation in the discriminator "S" curve
       D. normal operation of the stage
40. Frequency adjustments in Klystron tubes are GENERALLY made   40. ...
    by
       A. sliding a shorting-bar along the lines
       B. mechanically compressing the tube along its length
       C. tuning the pickup loop
       D. changing the grid-bias

TEST 5

41. The second harmonic of 200 meters is   41. ...
    A. 400 meters B. 100 meters C. 800 meters D. 50 meters
42. To reduce the natural resonant frequency of a Marconi an-   42. ...
    tenna, we may
      A. place an inductance in series with the antenna
      B. place a condenser in series with the antenna
      C. operate the antenna on a harmonic
      D. reduce the physical length of the antenna
43. The length of a ¼ wave vertical radiator for 800 KC opera-   43. ...
    tion should be ABOUT
      A. 200 meters B. 94 meters C. 400 meters D. 367 meters
44. Alignment of a Discriminator is BEST checked   44. ...
      A. by use of an output meter
      B. by use of an audio analyzer
      C. by use of a vacuum tube voltmeter
      D. by ear
45. A line may be kept non-resonant by   45. ...
      A. terminating the line at its natural impedance
      B. keeping it an even number of ¼ waves long
      C. twisting or transposing the wires
      D. running one conductor inside the other
46. Placing a reflector behind a di-pole antenna makes it   46. ...
      A. non-directional
      B. directional away from the reflector
      C. directional toward the side on which the reflector is
         placed
      D. directional toward its end
47. Klystron tubes depend for their action upon   47. ...
      A. parallel-line tanks connected to the grids
      B. class "C" operation with a TPTG circuit
      C. bunching of electrons in a velocity-electron stream
      D. circular rotation of electrons under a strong magnetic
         influence
48. Ordinary vacuum tubes are ineffective in UHF circuits be-   48. ...
    cause
      A. their plate currents are too high
      B. heater voltages of 6.3v ac are impractical at ultra-
         high frequencies
      C. socket terminals will arc over at UHF
      D. inter-electrode capacities are too high for ultra-
         high frequencies
49. Wave-guides are NOT used at low frequencies because   49. ...
      A. long waves cannot be guided
      B. power is too great at low frequencies
      C. their physical size would be impractical
      D. the wave length of low frequencies is too short
50. The hum frequency of a full wave rectifier is _____   50. ...
    the frequency of the line voltage frequency.
      A. once   B. twice   C. three times
      D. four times

KEYS (CORRECT ANSWERS)

TEST 1	TEST 2	TEST 3	TEST 4		TEST 5
1. A	1. C	1. C	1. C	36. D	1. A
2. B	2. D	2. A	2. C	37. B	2. B
3. D	3. B	3. B	3. C	38. C	3. B
4. C	4. D	4. A	4. C	39. D	4. D
5. C	5. A	5. C	5. B	40. A	5. C
6. A	6. A	6. D	6. A	41. C	6. A
7. C	7. C	7. D	7. C	42. D	7. B
8. D	8. B	8. D	8. A	43. D	8. C
9. C	9. C	9. C	9. A	44. B	9. A
10. C	10. D	10. B	10. C	45. C	10. D
11. B	11. B	11. A	11. B	46. C	11. B
12. B	12. B	12. C	12. B	47. D	12. A
13. C	13. D	13. D	13. A	48. A	13. A
14. D	14. C	14. C	14. C	49. C	14. B
15. B	15. A	15. B	15. B	50. A	15. C
16. A	16. D	16. D	16. D	51. C	16. C
17. C	17. B	17. C	17. A	52. B	17. B
18. D	18. B	18. A	18. C	53. D	18. B
19. C	19. C	19. D	19. B	54. A	19. D
20. B	20. C	20. B	20. D	55. C	20. D
21. C	21. B	21. C	21. C	56. B	21. C
22. C	22. D	22. B	22. D	57. B	22. B
23. C	23. C	23. D	23. A	58. A	23. B
24. C	24. B	24. B	24. D	59. A	24. B
25. C	25. D	25. A	25. B	60. C	25. D
26. D	26. A	26. B	26. C	61. B	26. B
27. D	27. C	27. D	27. C	62. C	27. C
28. B	28. D	28. C	28. C	63. A	28. A
29. B	29. B	29. C	39. D	64. D	29. C
30. D	30. B	30. D	30. D	65. A	30. B
31. D	31. B	31. B	31. B	66. D	31. C
32. B	32. C	32. A	32. A	67. C	32. A
33. C	33. A	33. C	33. D	68. B	33. B
34. B	34. B	34. B	34. B	69. A	34. C
35. C	35. B	35. C	35. C	70. B	35. C
36. A	36. B	36. D			36. C
37. B	37. C	37. D			37. A
38. B	38. D	38. C			38. C
39. B	39. A	39. C			39. D
40. A	40. B	40. A			40. B
		41. A			41. B
		42. B			42. A
		43. B			43. B
		44. D			44. C
		45. C			45. A
		46. D			46. B
		47. A			47. C
		48. B			48. D
		49. D			49. C
		50. A			50. B

ANSWER SHEET

TEST NO. _____ PART _____ TITLE OF POSITION _____
(AS GIVEN IN EXAMINATION ANNOUNCEMENT - INCLUDE OPTION, IF ANY)

PLACE OF EXAMINATION _____ DATE _____
(CITY OR TOWN)   (STATE)

RATING

USE THE SPECIAL PENCIL.   MAKE GLOSSY BLACK MARKS.

Make only ONE mark for each answer. Additional and stray marks may be counted as mistakes. In making corrections, erase errors COMPLETELY.

ANSWER SHEET

TEST NO. _____ PART _____ TITLE OF POSITION _____
(AS GIVEN IN EXAMINATION ANNOUNCEMENT - INCLUDE OPTION, IF ANY)

PLACE OF EXAMINATION _____ DATE _____
(CITY OR TOWN) (STATE)

RATING

USE THE SPECIAL PENCIL. MAKE GLOSSY BLACK MARKS.

	A	B	C	D	E		A	B	C	D	E		A	B	C	D	E		A	B	C	D	E		A	B	C	D	E
1	⋮	⋮	⋮	⋮	⋮	26	⋮	⋮	⋮	⋮	⋮	51	⋮	⋮	⋮	⋮	⋮	76	⋮	⋮	⋮	⋮	⋮	101	⋮	⋮	⋮	⋮	⋮
2	⋮	⋮	⋮	⋮	⋮	27	⋮	⋮	⋮	⋮	⋮	52	⋮	⋮	⋮	⋮	⋮	77	⋮	⋮	⋮	⋮	⋮	102	⋮	⋮	⋮	⋮	⋮
3	⋮	⋮	⋮	⋮	⋮	28	⋮	⋮	⋮	⋮	⋮	53	⋮	⋮	⋮	⋮	⋮	78	⋮	⋮	⋮	⋮	⋮	103	⋮	⋮	⋮	⋮	⋮
4	⋮	⋮	⋮	⋮	⋮	29	⋮	⋮	⋮	⋮	⋮	54	⋮	⋮	⋮	⋮	⋮	79	⋮	⋮	⋮	⋮	⋮	104	⋮	⋮	⋮	⋮	⋮
5	⋮	⋮	⋮	⋮	⋮	30	⋮	⋮	⋮	⋮	⋮	55	⋮	⋮	⋮	⋮	⋮	80	⋮	⋮	⋮	⋮	⋮	105	⋮	⋮	⋮	⋮	⋮
6	⋮	⋮	⋮	⋮	⋮	31	⋮	⋮	⋮	⋮	⋮	56	⋮	⋮	⋮	⋮	⋮	81	⋮	⋮	⋮	⋮	⋮	106	⋮	⋮	⋮	⋮	⋮
7	⋮	⋮	⋮	⋮	⋮	32	⋮	⋮	⋮	⋮	⋮	57	⋮	⋮	⋮	⋮	⋮	82	⋮	⋮	⋮	⋮	⋮	107	⋮	⋮	⋮	⋮	⋮
8	⋮	⋮	⋮	⋮	⋮	33	⋮	⋮	⋮	⋮	⋮	58	⋮	⋮	⋮	⋮	⋮	83	⋮	⋮	⋮	⋮	⋮	108	⋮	⋮	⋮	⋮	⋮
9	⋮	⋮	⋮	⋮	⋮	34	⋮	⋮	⋮	⋮	⋮	59	⋮	⋮	⋮	⋮	⋮	84	⋮	⋮	⋮	⋮	⋮	109	⋮	⋮	⋮	⋮	⋮
10	⋮	⋮	⋮	⋮	⋮	35	⋮	⋮	⋮	⋮	⋮	60	⋮	⋮	⋮	⋮	⋮	85	⋮	⋮	⋮	⋮	⋮	110	⋮	⋮	⋮	⋮	⋮

Make only ONE mark for each answer. Additional and stray marks may be counted as mistakes. In making corrections, erase errors COMPLETELY.

	A	B	C	D	E		A	B	C	D	E		A	B	C	D	E		A	B	C	D	E		A	B	C	D	E
11	⋮	⋮	⋮	⋮	⋮	36	⋮	⋮	⋮	⋮	⋮	61	⋮	⋮	⋮	⋮	⋮	86	⋮	⋮	⋮	⋮	⋮	111	⋮	⋮	⋮	⋮	⋮
12	⋮	⋮	⋮	⋮	⋮	37	⋮	⋮	⋮	⋮	⋮	62	⋮	⋮	⋮	⋮	⋮	87	⋮	⋮	⋮	⋮	⋮	112	⋮	⋮	⋮	⋮	⋮
13	⋮	⋮	⋮	⋮	⋮	38	⋮	⋮	⋮	⋮	⋮	63	⋮	⋮	⋮	⋮	⋮	88	⋮	⋮	⋮	⋮	⋮	113	⋮	⋮	⋮	⋮	⋮
14	⋮	⋮	⋮	⋮	⋮	39	⋮	⋮	⋮	⋮	⋮	64	⋮	⋮	⋮	⋮	⋮	89	⋮	⋮	⋮	⋮	⋮	114	⋮	⋮	⋮	⋮	⋮
15	⋮	⋮	⋮	⋮	⋮	40	⋮	⋮	⋮	⋮	⋮	65	⋮	⋮	⋮	⋮	⋮	90	⋮	⋮	⋮	⋮	⋮	115	⋮	⋮	⋮	⋮	⋮
16	⋮	⋮	⋮	⋮	⋮	41	⋮	⋮	⋮	⋮	⋮	66	⋮	⋮	⋮	⋮	⋮	91	⋮	⋮	⋮	⋮	⋮	116	⋮	⋮	⋮	⋮	⋮
17	⋮	⋮	⋮	⋮	⋮	42	⋮	⋮	⋮	⋮	⋮	67	⋮	⋮	⋮	⋮	⋮	92	⋮	⋮	⋮	⋮	⋮	117	⋮	⋮	⋮	⋮	⋮
18	⋮	⋮	⋮	⋮	⋮	43	⋮	⋮	⋮	⋮	⋮	68	⋮	⋮	⋮	⋮	⋮	93	⋮	⋮	⋮	⋮	⋮	118	⋮	⋮	⋮	⋮	⋮
19	⋮	⋮	⋮	⋮	⋮	44	⋮	⋮	⋮	⋮	⋮	69	⋮	⋮	⋮	⋮	⋮	94	⋮	⋮	⋮	⋮	⋮	119	⋮	⋮	⋮	⋮	⋮
20	⋮	⋮	⋮	⋮	⋮	45	⋮	⋮	⋮	⋮	⋮	70	⋮	⋮	⋮	⋮	⋮	95	⋮	⋮	⋮	⋮	⋮	120	⋮	⋮	⋮	⋮	⋮
21	⋮	⋮	⋮	⋮	⋮	46	⋮	⋮	⋮	⋮	⋮	71	⋮	⋮	⋮	⋮	⋮	96	⋮	⋮	⋮	⋮	⋮	121	⋮	⋮	⋮	⋮	⋮
22	⋮	⋮	⋮	⋮	⋮	47	⋮	⋮	⋮	⋮	⋮	72	⋮	⋮	⋮	⋮	⋮	97	⋮	⋮	⋮	⋮	⋮	122	⋮	⋮	⋮	⋮	⋮
23	⋮	⋮	⋮	⋮	⋮	48	⋮	⋮	⋮	⋮	⋮	73	⋮	⋮	⋮	⋮	⋮	98	⋮	⋮	⋮	⋮	⋮	123	⋮	⋮	⋮	⋮	⋮
24	⋮	⋮	⋮	⋮	⋮	49	⋮	⋮	⋮	⋮	⋮	74	⋮	⋮	⋮	⋮	⋮	99	⋮	⋮	⋮	⋮	⋮	124	⋮	⋮	⋮	⋮	⋮
25	⋮	⋮	⋮	⋮	⋮	50	⋮	⋮	⋮	⋮	⋮	75	⋮	⋮	⋮	⋮	⋮	100	⋮	⋮	⋮	⋮	⋮	125	⋮	⋮	⋮	⋮	⋮

EXAMINATION SECTION

DIRECTIONS FOR THIS SECTION:
Each question or incomplete statement is followed by several suggested answers or completions. Select the one that BEST answers the question or completes the statement. *PRINT THE LETTER OF THE CORRECT ANSWER IN THE SPACE AT THE RIGHT.*

TEST 1

1. A voice grade line is a line which
    A. is directly connected from point to point
    B. has a speed of 600-4800 bits per second
    C. is used for voice transmission only
    D. does not have signaling capability

2. A half-duplex line is one which
    A. transmits in one direction only
    B. transmits in both directions simultaneously
    C. requires four wires for transmission
    D. transmits in both directions, but only in one direction at a time

3. The CHIEF advantage of a switched line as compared to a private line is that a switched line has
    A. low cost if the line has low usage
    B. higher line capacity
    C. ability to compensate for distortion
    D. greater signal-to-noise ratio

4. A telephone line of 3000 hz. bandwidth with a signal-to-noise ratio of 20 db. has a *theoretical maximum* capacity of
    A. 17,300 bits per second   B. 19,900 bits per second
    C. 23,100 bits per second   D. 27,600 bits per second

5. A conditioned line is defined as one which
    A. is available in a switched network
    B. is used only on a part-time basis
    C. has rigid specifications on amplitude variation and envelope delay
    D. is available as a simplex line

6. A factor that distinguishes a coaxial cable line from wire pairs is that a coaxial cable line has
    A. a smaller bandwidth than wire pairs
    B. more crosstalk between cables than wire pairs
    C. lower propagation speeds than wire pairs
    D. less delay distortion than wire pairs

7. A microwave relay line does NOT
    A. require fewer amplifiers per mile than a coaxial line
    B. require a line of sight path
    C. react to adverse weather conditions
    D. cost more per mile than comparable coaxial line

8. In the absence of any noise, a telegraph type line of 300 hz. bandwidth with two voltage sending levels is *theoretically* capable of transmitting
    A. 600 bits per second   B. 300 bits per second
    C. 150 bits per second   D. 75 bits per second

1. ...
2. ...
3. ...
4. ...
5. ...
6. ...
7. ...
8. ...

TEST 1

9. The speed of a transmission line is often quoted as being   9. ...
a certain number of "bauds." If the line can be in any of
four possible states at any given time, the number of bits
per second transmitted will be
   A. equal to the number of "bauds"
   B. twice the number of "bauds"
   C. half the number of "bauds"
   D. four times the number of "bauds"

10. If a rectangular pulse is passed through a band limited   10. ...
line (0-3000 hz), the output of the line will have
   A. the vertical sides of the pulse with finite slope
   B. the flat top of the pulse tilted
   C. both the flat top of the pulse tilted and the vertical sides of the pulse with finite slope
   D. no distortion in the pulse

11. "Systematic Distortion" is defined as distortion which   11. ...
   A. is produced from input to output
   B. can be predicted and thus compensated for
   C. is characteristic only of a single component of the system
   D. can include noise and switch chatter as one of its components

12. Distortion on a line due to a non-linear phase shift with   12. ...
frequency is
   A. *unimportant* for voice transmission, since understanding of speech is unaffected by it
   B. *unimportant* for data transmission, since only rms values of voltage are detected
   C. *necessary* for proper voice and data transmission
   D. *necessary* only for proper voice transmission

13. "Gaussian" noise is noise which   13. ...
   A. is caused by magnetic circuits
   B. varies about a signal level in a purely random fashion
   C. is caused by rhythmic phenomena
   D. is caused by lightning

14. "White" noise is NOT noise which   14. ...
   A. on the average contains all spectral frequencies equally
   B. is due to thermal effects
   C. can be eliminated by cooling equipment to absolute zero
   D. is caused by switch chatter

15. If the bandwidth of a system is increased, the noise   15. ...
power generated in an electrical conductor will
   A. increase proportionately with the bandwidth
   B. decrease inversely with the bandwidth
   C. be unaffected by the bandwidth
   D. vary only slightly with the bandwidth

Questions 16-18.
DIRECTIONS: For Questions 16 through 18 inclusive, reference should be made to the following generalized expression for a modulated signal:
$$a_c = A_c \sin(2\pi f_c t + \theta_c)$$

16. If the signal information is contained as part of the A_c 16. ...
term, the modulation is called
   A. amplitude modulation   B. frequency modulation
   C. phase modulation   D. pulse code modulation

2

17. If the signal is contained in the θ_c term, the modulation is called
    A. amplitude modulation B. frequency modulation
    C. phase modulation   D. pulse code modulation
18. If the signal is contained in the f_c term, the modulation is called
    A. amplitude modulation B. frequency modulation
    C. phase modulation   D. pulse code modulation
19. If the pulse train shown below is modulating a sine wave carrier and the result is as shown below, then the modulation is

    PULSE TRAIN
    RESULT

    A. amplitude modulation B. frequency modulation
    C. phase modulation   D. pulse code modulation
20. If the pulse train shown below is modulating a sine wave carrier and the result is as shown below, then the modulation is

    PULSE TRAIN
    RESULT

    A. amplitude modulation B. frequency modulation
    C. phase modulation   D. pulse code modulation
21. If a carrier of 60,000 hz is amplitude modulated by a 1500 hz sine wave, the modulated signal will contain frequencies only of
    A. 60,000 and 1500 hz   B. 60,000 and 61,500 hz
    C. 60,000, 61,500 and 58,500 hz
    D. 61,500 and 58,500 hz
22. The modulation index of an AM signal is defined as the
    A. relative power of the carrier
    B. relative power of the modulating signal
    C. ratio of the modulation amplitude to the carrier amplitude
    D. absolute power of the total signal
23. If the value of the modulation index were to exceed unity in an AM system, the
    A. modulation would be more efficient
    B. carrier wave's amplitude would be less than the modulating wave's amplitude
    C. signal could not be recovered without distortion
    D. transmitter would pulse on and off

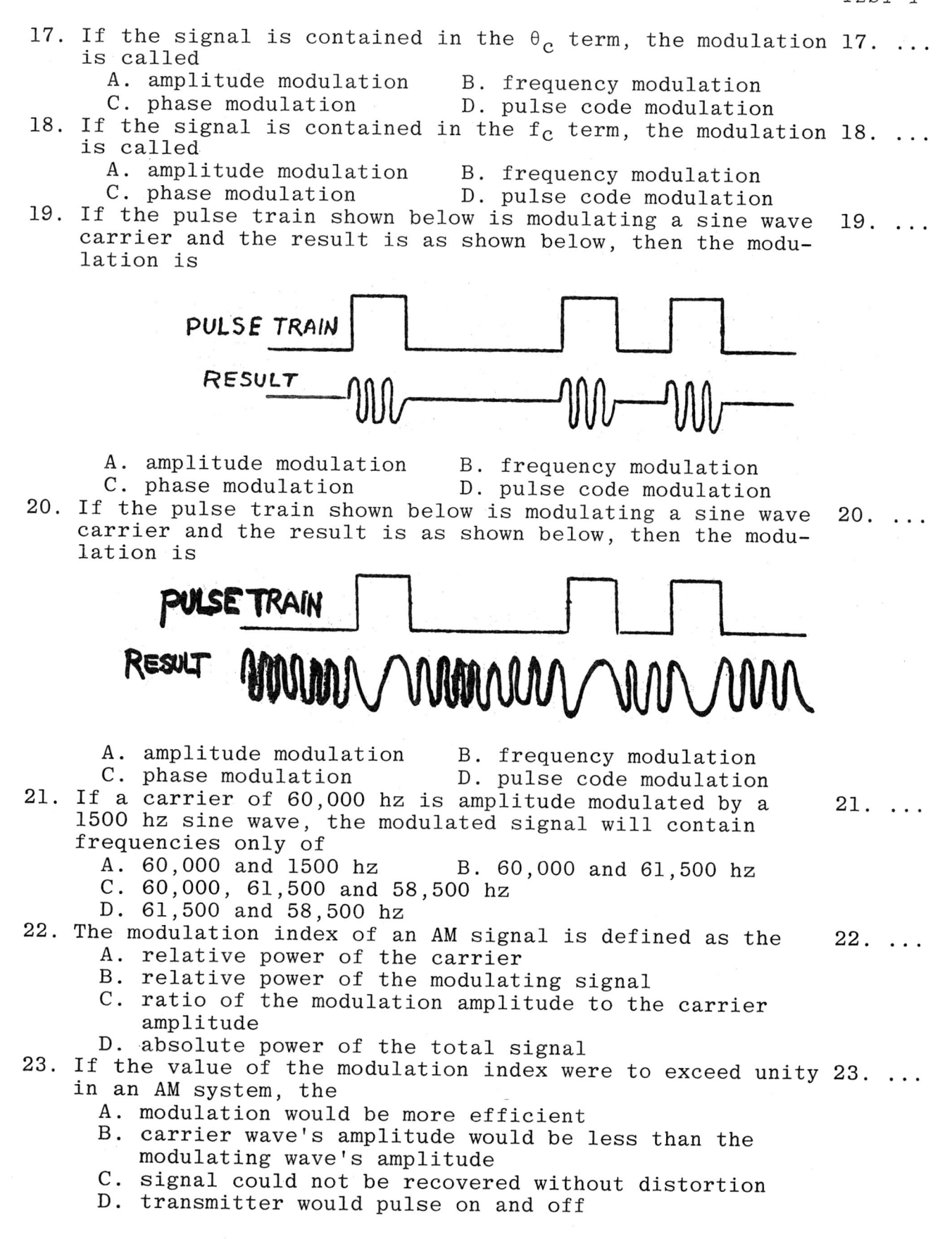

24. If the modulating signal is not sinusoidal in an AM   24. ...
    system, the one of the following results which is MOST
    likely to occur is that
       A. the output will be distorted
       B. a band of frequencies will be generated rather than
          a single set of sidebands
       C. the frequency of the carrier will shift
       D. linear analysis will not apply
25. The one of the following statements which is *true* of   25. ...
    single sideband amplitude modulation is that it *usually*
       A. requires greater bandwidth than full AM
       B. improves the signal-to-noise ratio over full AM
       C. loses information content
       D. requires greater transmitting power than full AM
26. Envelope detection of an AM signal will   26. ...
       A. not require a reference signal
       B. not require both sidebands
       C. be more expensive than "synchronous detection"
       D. require less bandwidth than "synchronous detection"
27. "Synchronous, coherent, or homodyne" detection of an AM   27. ...
    signal will
       A. not require a reference signal
       B. not require filtering
       C. be less expensive than envelope detection
       D. require less bandwidth than envelope detection
28. When a sine wave is frequency modulated by a low fre-   28. ...
    quency sine wave,
       A. only three sidebands are generated
       B. the number of sidebands depends on the modulating
          frequency
       C. the carrier is suppressed
       D. an infinite number of sidebands is theoretically
          generated
29. If a pulse signal is used to modulate a carrier, the   29. ...
       A. carrier can only be amplitude modulated
       B. carrier can only be frequency modulated
       C. modulation to be chosen depends on the particular
          code
       D. carrier can be either amplitude modulated or frequen-
          cy modulated
30. Of the following, the maximum sampling interval which   30. ...
    permits complete reconstruction of a band-limited signal
    in the range 0-3,000 hz is, *most nearly*,
       A. 0.1 milliseconds   B. 0.3 milliseconds
       C. 1.0 milliseconds   D. 10.0 milliseconds

TEST 2

1. The MAIN disadvantage of pulse code transmission as com-   1. ...
   pared to analog transmission is that in pulse code transmission
      A. the signal-to-noise ratio is low
      B. repeater stations add noise to the system

C. a greater bandwidth is required
D. it is more expensive than frequency division multiplexing
2. In a pulse amplitude modulation system, the analog signal is converted to a series of pulses which 2. ...
    A. are unequally spaced according to the analog signal amplitude
    B. start at equal time increments but are of unequal duration according to the amplitude of the analog signal
    C. are of equal spacing and duration but whose amplitude varies with the analog signal
    D. are of equal duration but whose spacing depends on the analog signal
3. In a pulse duration (width) modulation system, the analog signal is converted to a series of pulses which 3. ...
    A. start at equal time increments but whose durations are proportional to the amplitude of the analog signal
    B. are unequally spaced in time in accordance with the amplitude of the analog signal
    C. are of equal spacing and duration but whose amplitude varies with the analog signal
    D. are of equal duration but whose spacing depends on the analog frequency
4. Before an analog signal can be sent by pulse code modulation it must be quantized. This means that the 4. ...
    A. frequency must be determined
    B. zero crossings must be counted
    C. signal must be passed through a band pass filter
    D. analog values must be selected so that they fall into discrete values
5. When an analog signal to be sent by pulse code modulation is quantized and sampled, the result that is transmitted is a 5. ...
    A. pulse of amplitude approximately equal to the amplitude of the analog signal
    B. pulse of duration approximately proportional to the amplitude of the analog signal
    C. series of pulses equal to a binary representation of the amplitude of the sampled signal
    D. sequence of pulses generated at the zero crossings of the analog signal
6. When several different signals are sent on a single cable by modulating several different carriers, the process is known as 6. ...
    A. time division multiplexing   B. time slice multiplexing
    C. single sideband transmission
    D. frequency division multiplexing
7. Space division multiplexing involves 7. ...
    A. several signals at different center frequencies in a cable
    B. sampled signals sent in a time sequential manner
    C. several coaxial units grouped into a single cable
    D. multiplexing of signals by microwaves

8. When signals are multiplexed using frequency division   8. ...
   multiplexing, they are usually passed through a low pass
   filter first. This is done PRIMARILY because
     A. higher frequencies need more power
     B. low frequencies have more power
     C. the filters cannot be ideal
     D. it prevents crosstalk between channels
9. "Guard Bands" in a frequency division multiplexer are   9. ...
   necessary MAINLY because
     A. better use can be made of the available bandwidth
     B. filters cannot have infinitely steep sides
     C. carrier frequencies must be identified
     D. the sidebands are equal
10. The MAIN disadvantage of frequency division multiplexing 10. ...
    as compared with time division multiplexing is that
      A. less efficient use is made of the band
      B. with current technology the expense of building filters
         is greater than the expense of building logic circuits
      C. signals cannot be continuous
      D. the transmission quality is lower
11. In a time division multiplexing system,   11. ...
      A. complete messages are transmitted over frequency
         bands that are separated from each other
      B. several messages are sampled and the samples are
         transmitted sequentially
      C. complete messages are transmitted sequentially
      D. sampled messages are transmitted over "guarded"
         frequency bands
12. A time division multiplexed system   12. ...
      A. requires a means of accurately synchronizing trans-
         mitter and receiver
      B. allows samples to be packed tightly together
      C. cannot be used with binary coding
      D. cannot be used to transmit computer data
13. A Time Assignment Speech Interpolation (TASI) system is 13. ...
    one which
      A. completes messages before transmitting them
      B. combines time division multiplexing and frequency
         division multiplexing
      C. is a method of pulse position modulation for speech
      D. is useful for transmission of large amounts of con-
         tinuous data
14. Pulse code modulation is to be used to transmit an analog 14. ...
    signal below 3000 hz. Each sample is coded at one of 64
    levels.
    Of the following, the number of bits per second that must
    be transmitted is, *most nearly*,
      A. 3000   B. 6000   C. 18,000   D. 36,000
15. In order to decrease the bandwidth needed for pulse code 15. ...
    modulation, one should
      A. *increase* the number of quantizing levels
      B. *decrease* the number of quantizing levels
      C. *increase* the bandwidth of the modulating signal
      D. *decrease* the sampling time

TEST 2

16. Of the following, the MAIN purpose of a "modem" or "data set" in a computer-terminal system is to
    A. provide an interface between the terminal and the computer
    B. convert terminal (computer) signals to modulated signals for transmission by common carrier and vice versa
    C. standardize codes
    D. provide the means for voice communication on a data line

17. The one of the following which is a *correct* statement regarding modems or "data sets" is that they
    A. are necessary on all terminal-computer combinations
    B. are necessary if communication lines are frequency multiplexed
    C. do not improve the speed of transmission
    D. must be used only if the distance between terminal and computer is greater than 150 feet.

18. In order to convert an analog signal to a digital signal,
    A. the signal first must be differentiated
    B. the signal first must be integrated
    C. a precise reference level is necessary
    D. a clock pulse must be accumulated

19. One scheme for analog-to-digital conversion is shown below:

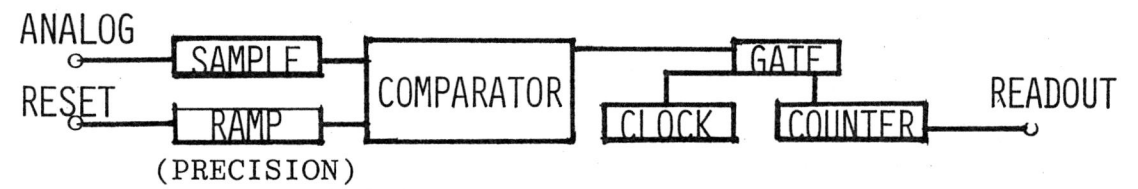

    The CHIEF asset of such a scheme is
    A. high speed   B. accuracy
    C. low cost   D. high sampling rate

20. The HIGHEST rate of analog-to-digital conversion consistent with the present level of technology is, *most nearly*,
    A. 200 /sec   B. 50,000 /sec   C. 10^6 /sec   D. 10^9 /sec

21. A three-bit binary parallel signal is to be converted to an analog signal by means of the following circuit:

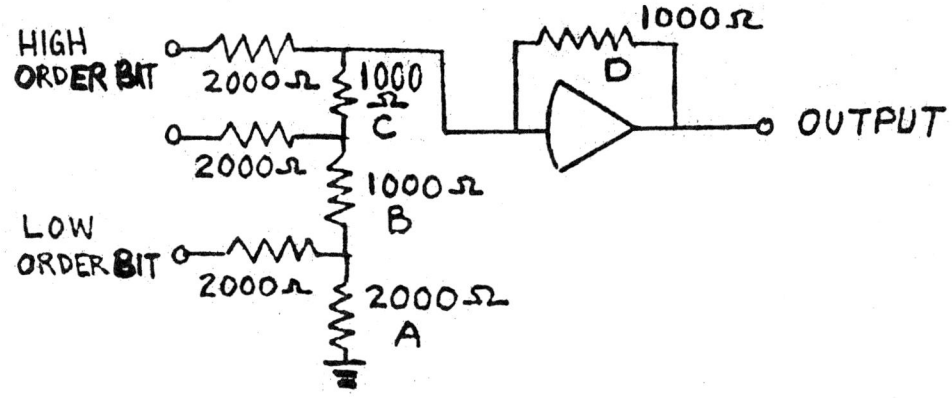

    In this circuit the resistor whose accuracy is of LEAST importance is
    A. A   B. B   C. C   D. D

22. A three-bit binary parallel signal is to be converted to an analog signal by means of the following circuit:

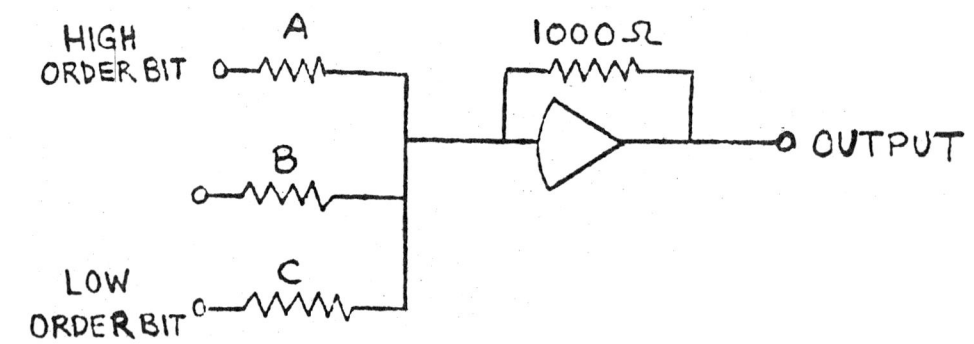

In this circuit, resistors A, B, C should have the values, in ohms, of
   A. A=1000 B=500   C=250   B. A=250 B=500   C=1000
   C. A=1000 B=1000 C=1000   D. A=1000 B=2000 C=3000

23. In order to convert a serial binary number into an analog signal,
   A. bits must not be sampled
   B. only the most significant bit can be used
   C. serial bits must be stored in a shift register and presented in parallel
   D. analog signals must be converted to DC

24. Of the following, the type of error MOST likely to occur in a process involving conversion from analog-to-digital and then back to analog, is
   A. noise in the transmission system
   B. phase delay
   C. frequency distortion
   D. quantization distortion

25. "Error correcting codes" are codes
   A. whose information can be retrieved even though some bits are lost
   B. that cannot be "broken" by outsiders
   C. that contain odd parity bits
   D. that do not contain parity bits

26. The Baudot code is *normally* used
   A. in transmitting between computers
   B. as an error correcting code
   C. as a code in telegraph and teletype
   D. only on computer terminals

27. The ASCII code is
   A. the US standard code for information exchange
   B. the only code permitted as computer input
   C. limited to computer use
   D. a six-bit code

28. A parity bit in a code is
   A. a bit added to an array of bits to insure that the sum of all the bits is either always odd or always even
   B. never sent along a transmission line
   C. sent or not sent as directed
   D. only used for local error checking

29. The AT&T #33 ASR teletype operates using the 29. ...
    A. Baudot code   B. five-channel teletype code
    C. ASCII code   D. parity checking feature
30. In order to send the sequence of characters A3C2 in 30. ...
    ASCII code, the *number* of 7 bit characters that must be
    sent is
    A. 8   B. 7   C. 6   D. 4

TEST 3

1. The CHIEF asset of a magnetic core memory system is the 1. ...
    A. low cost of the system
    B. quantity of data that can be stored
    C. speed with which a fetch or a store of data can be
       executed
    D. volatility of the storage
2. The disc storage memory unit is used PRIMARILY when 2. ...
    A. large amounts of data must be accessed randomly and
       fairly fast
    B. the expense of storage is the chief concern
    C. data must be accessed rapidly and very often
    D. long term storage is needed with only occasional access
3. When data is stored on magnetic tape, it is normally 3. ...
    "blocked." This means
    A. the tape cannot be erased
    B. a large amount of data is recorded between unrecorded
       gaps
    C. the tape cannot be written over
    D. the data items are individually accessible
4. In a multiterminal computer system, terminals are "polled" 4. ...
    sequentially. This means that
    A. each terminal is connected for its own "time slot"
    B. each terminal transmits when ready
    C. a signal is sent inquiring if a particular terminal
       is ready to transmit
    D. terminals "seize" the input on an interrupt basis
5. Terminal devices can operate in different codes. The 5. ...
    means of conversion from one code to another which is
    MOST efficient *timewise* is
    A. hardware   B. memory table
    C. program manipulation D. commutation
6. The number 15 (decimal) is equivalent to the binary number, 6. ...
    A. 1111   B. 1050   C. 1010   D. 0017
7. The number 10110 (binary) is equivalent to the decimal 7. ...
    number,
    A. 111   B. 22   C. 26   D. 19
8. The number 110101 (binary) is equivalent to the octal 8. ...
    number,
    A. 53   B. 37   C. 46   D. 65
9. The number 73 (octal) is equivalent to the binary number, 9. ...
    A. 101101   B. 59   C. 111011   D. 55
10. The number 27 (decimal) is equivalent to the octal number, 10. ...
    A. 17   B. 10111   C. 11011   D. 33

11. The following is a list of current addresses and locations to be addressed, in a DEC PDP/8 computer:

	Current addresses	Location to be addressed
1.	0050	0120
2.	1230	1377
3.	2742	2450
4.	6555	6600

Of the following statements pertaining to this list, the one which is *correct* is that
- A. all the second locations must be addressed directly
- B. all the second locations must be addressed indirectly
- C. the second locations for 1 and 2 can be addressed directly and for 3 and 4 must be addressed indirectly
- D. the second location for 1 and 4 must be addressed directly and for 2 and 3 must be addressed indirectly

11. ...

12. The following is a DEC PDP/8 program:

```
*200
START,      CLA CLL
            TAD A
            CIA
            DCA TALLY
MULT ,      TAD B
            ISZ TALLY
            JMP MULT
            HLT
A,          0022
B,          0044
TALLY,      0000
$
```

When the program stops, the one of the following which will be stored in location B is
A. 0022_8 B. 1210_8 C. 0044_8 D. 648_8

12. ...

13. The following is a DEC PDP/8 program:

```
*200
START,      CLA CLL
            TAD COUNT
            CIA
            DCA TALLY
ADD,        TAD 300
            ISZ ADD
            ISZ TALLY
            JMP ADD
            DCA SUM
            HLT
COUNT,      0100
TALLY,      0000
SUM,        0000
$
```

This program sums 100_8 numbers in locations
- A. 100_8 to 177_8 and stores the sum in the location SUM
- B. 100_8 to 177_8 and displays the sum in the accumulator
- C. 300_8 to 377_8 and stores the sum in the location SUM
- D. 300_8 to 377_8 and displays the sum in the accumulator

13. ...

14. The following is a DEC PDP/8 program:
```
*200
    TEST,       CLA CLL
                TAD B
                CIA
                TAD A
                SMA CLA
                HLT
                TAD A
                DCA TEMP
                TAD B
                DCA A
                TAD TEMP
                DCA B
                HLT
    A,          1234
    B,          2460
    TEMP,
$
```
   At the end of program execution, the content of location
   A. A and location B are the same
   B. A is larger than that of location B
   C. A is smaller than that of location B
   D. A is zero

15. The following is an incomplete DEC PDP/8 program to print one ASCII character stored in a memory location:
```
*200
    START,      CLA CLL
                TLS
                TAD HOLD
                missing instruction
                HLT
    TYPE,       0
                TSF
                JMP,-1
                TLS
                CLA CLL
                JMP I TYPE
    HOLD,       301
$
```
   The instruction missing from this program is
   A. JMP TYPE   B. JMS TYPE   C. SKP   D. SPA

16. In FORTRAN, the statement involving "WRITE" in conjunction with the FORMAT statement will
   A. control the input of the data
   B. control the way data is stored in memory
   C. alter the form of stored numbers
   D. control the manner in which output is printed

17. A portion of a FORTRAN program is shown below:
```
            A=6.0
            B=4.0
            C=2.0
            E=3.0
            D=A + B/C + E
```
   The result stored in D after these steps, will be
   A. 2.0   B. 11.0   C. 6.8   D. 8.0

18. A portion of a FORTRAN program is shown below:
       C=6.0
       D=2.0
       E=2.0
       F=1.0
       A=C/D**E*(F + 1.0)
    The result stored in A after these steps, will be
       A. 0.75   B. 3.0   C. 0.375   D. 18.0
19. A portion of a FORTRAN program is shown below:
           M=0
       8   DO 17,N=1,3
       17 M=M+N
           K=M
    The result stored in K after these steps, will be
       A. 1   B. 3   C. 6   D. 10
20. A portion of a FORTRAN program is shown below:
           T=-3.0
       15 IF(T)10,20,30
       10 S=5.0
           GO TO 50
       20 S=10.0
           GO TO 50
       30 S=15.0
       50 V=S
    The result stored in V after these steps, will be
       A. 5.0   B. -3.0   C. 10.0   D. 15.0
21. The time average of a measured quantity can be *approximated* by
    A. sampling more than twice per cycle
    B. differentiating and sampling more than twice per cycle
    C. integrating for a fixed length of time
    D. integrating for a variable length of time
22. When a signal tends to be "noisy," the effect of integrating the signal will be to
    A. accentuate the high frequency noise
    B. eliminate the high frequency noise
    C. increase the effective bandwidth of the system
    D. make the output respond more readily to fast input changes
23. Integrators, unless carefully designed and constructed, have a tendency to
    A. reduce the gain of the system
    B. be noisy
    C. have their DC level drift
    D. stretch the frequency band
24. For telemetry purposes, high level radioactivity can be measured BEST by means of a(n)
    A. electroscope   B. manometer
    C. film gauge   D. geiger counter
25. Sulfur dioxide content in an air sample can be measured BEST by passing
    A. the air through water and measuring the conductivity change
    B. ultraviolet light through the air sample and measuring the diffraction

TEST 3/4

    C. infrared light through the air sample and measuring the absorption
    D. the air sample through a filter paper and measuring the change in reflectance

26. Carbon monoxide content in an air sample can be measured BEST by passing 26. ...
    A. the air through water and measuring the conductivity change
    B. ultraviolet light through the air sample and measuring the diffraction
    C. infrared light through the sample and measuring the absorption
    D. the air sample through a filter paper and measuring the change in reflectance

27. "Smoke shade" information for air pollution monitoring is obtained by passing 27. ...
    A. the air through water and measuring the conductivity change
    B. ultraviolet light through the sample and measuring the diffraction
    C. infrared light through the sample and measuring the absorption
    D. the air sample through a filter paper and measuring the change in reflectance

28. Wind direction can be telemetered by data from a 28. ...
    A. manoscope connected to a weathervane
    B. wind vane connected to a synchro system
    C. wind vane connected to a hygrometer
    D. propeller connected to a magneto

29. Wind speed can BEST be telemetered by data from a 29. ...
    A. pitot tube   B. manometer
    C. propeller-driven magneto   D. evaporative cooling effect

30. Of the following, the BEST description of a telemetered sensor for temperature measurement is a 30. ...
    A. conductivity change of water measured by a conductance cell
    B. temperature sensitive resistor measured by an ohmmeter
    C. temperature sensitive resistor measured by a self-balancing Wheatstone bridge
    D. frequency shift oscillator

TEST 4

1. Assuming the velocity of light to be 3×10^8 meters per second, the frequency of electromagnetic energy having a wave length of 1×10^{-5} centimeters, is (in cycles per second) 1. ...
    A. 3×10^5 B. 1×10^{13} C. 1×10^{14} D. 3×10^{15}

2. Two metal spheres are suspended by insulating threads so that they are touching. A charged body is then brought NEAR one of the spheres and away from the other and held there while the spheres are moved apart. After the rod is removed, the spheres will 2. ...
    A. *repel each other* because of equal negative charges on each

B. *repel each other* because of equal positive charges on each
C. *attract each other* because opposite charges were induced on each
D. *have no mutual electrostatic effect* because no charge was transferred

3. Of the following, when an atom emits an alpha particle, its MASS NUMBER is   3. ...
   A. *decreased* by 4 and its ATOMIC NUMBER is *increased* by 2
   B. *increased* by 4 and its ATOMIC NUMBER is *decreased* by 2
   C. *increased* by 4 and its ATOMIC NUMBER is *increased* by 2
   D. *decreased* by 4 and its ATOMIC NUMBER is *decreased* by 2

4. The Doppler effect is associated *most closely* with that property of sound or light known as   4. ...
   A. amplitude B. velocity C. frequency D. intensity

5. Of the following, the TRUE statement about X-rays is that they are   5. ...
   A. electromagnetic rays having a smaller wave length than gamma rays
   B. longitudinal waves having a frequency range above 12,000 v.p.s.
   C. transverse waves having a smaller wave length than ultra-violet waves
   D. transverse waves having a wave length range of 4000 to 8000 Angstroms

6. Which *one* of the following is a CHARACTERISTIC of a parallel electrical circuit?   6. ...
   A. The current is the same in all parts of the circuit.
   B. The voltage across all the branches is the same.
   C. A break through any part of the circuit will stop the flow of current throughout the circuit.
   D. The total resistance is equal to the sum of the resistances of the component parts.

7. Quasi-stellar radio sources have been found which radiate energy at the rate of 10^{44} ergs per second. This power, when converted into watts, is CLOSEST to *which one* of the following?   7. ...
   A. 10^6 B. 10^7 C. 10^{37} D. 10^{51}

8. If the molecules in a cylinder of oxygen and those in a cylinder of hydrogen have the *same* average speed, *then*   8. ...
   A. both gases have the *same* temperature
   B. both gases have the *same* pressure
   C. the hydrogen has the *higher* temperature
   D. the oxygen has the *higher* temperature

9. Just as the photon is a *quantum* in electromagnetic field theory, *which one* of the following is considered to be the *quantum* in the nuclear field?   9. ...
   A. Neutrino   B. Electron   C. Meson   D. Neutron

10. When an electron moves with a speed equal to 4/5 that of light, the *ratio* of the mass to its rest mass is   10. ...
    A. 5/4   B. 5/3   C. 25/9   D. 25/16

11. When accelerating a proton, a synchrotron subjects the proton to an electric field whose frequency   11. ...
    A. *varies*, and to a *varying* magnetic field intensity
    B. *varies*, and to a *constant* magnetic field intensity
    C. *is constant*, and to a *constant* magnetic field intensity
    D. *is constant*, and to a *varying* magnetic field intensity

TEST 4

12. Under optimum conditions of irradiation, photoelectrons of HIGHEST energy will be ejected by *which one* of the following?
    A. Ultraviolet radiation   B. Infrared radiation
    C. Monochromatic yellow light D. Gamma rays

13. Assume that a particle is moving at a speed near that of light. In order to halve its Einstein energy equivalence, the particle's speed must be *reduced*
    A. to $\frac{1}{2}$ of its original value   B. to $\frac{1}{4}$ of its original value
    C. to $\sqrt{\frac{1}{2}}$ of its original value
    D. until its relativistic mass is halved

14. The frequency of a wave motion is doubled while the amplitude is held constant. The intensity of the wave motion *now* will be
    A. the same as that of the former wave motion
    B. multiplied by 2   C. divided by 2
    D. multiplied by 4

15. Three ideal components -- a resistor, an inductor, and a capacitor -- are connected in series to a source of a-c. The potential difference across each component is 40 volts. The *total voltage* across the three components is
    A. zero   B. $40\sqrt{2}$v   C. 40v   D. 120v

16. The potential difference across a 6-ohm resistor is 6 volts. The *power* used by the resistor is, in watts,
    A. 6   B. 12   C. 18   D. 24

17. Of the following, the *one* that is NOT normally used as a component of some electronic oscillator circuits is the
    A. lighthouse tube   B. pitot tube
    C. klystron   D. magnetron

18. If a charged capacitor loses one-half its charge by leakage, it has lost what fraction of its store of energy?
    A. 1/8   B. 1/4   C. 1/2   D. 3/4

19. The force, in newtons, required to stop a bullet that has a mass of 15g and a velocity of 400 m/sec in a distance of 20 cm, will be
    A. 4,000   B. 5,000   C. 6,000   D. 8,000

20. Of the following, the *unit* that is NOT used to measure the torque of a rotating body is
    A. lb-ft   B. m-newton C. slug-ft   D. cm-dyne

21. A 2 lb body vibrates in simple harmonic motion with an amplitude of 3 in and a period of 5 sec. The acceleration at the mid-point will be, in in/sec, CLOSEST to *which one* of the following?
    A. 0   B. 0.6   C. 1.2   D. 3.8

22. In connection with the molecular theory of matter, which one of the following is NOT assumed to be *accurate*?
    A. Effects of individual molecules are easily observed
    B. Law of conservation of kinetic energy
    C. Newton's laws of motion
    D. Law of conservation of momentum

23. Of the following, the force which to the LEAST extent follows an inverse-square law is
    A. electrical   B. nuclear   C. magnetic   D. gravitational

24. In a nuclear pile, boron rods are used for
    A. fuel   B. shielding   C. control   D. moderation

25. Antimatter consists of atoms containing
    A. protons, neutrons, and electrons
    B. protons, meutrons, and positrons
    C. antiprotons, antineutrons, and positrons
    D. antiprotons, antineutrons, and electrons
26. A high-energy gamma ray may materialize into a(n)
    A. meson   B. electron and a proton
    C. proton and a neutron D. electron and a positron
27. The usefulness of the early cyclotron was LIMITED by the fact that
    A. the supply of electrical power was limited
    B. magnetic fields could not be sufficiently increased
    C. the mass of electrons increases at high velocities
    D. it was too expensive
28. The Wimshurst Machine is used to study
    A. electrostatic charges   B. radioactivity
    C. electrolysis   D. the electric motor
29. Light can be polarized by the use of
    A. an electric current through a wire
    B. a calcite crystal
    C. powerful magnets
    D. an electrostatic field
30. If $_{84}Po^{210}$ emits a beta particle, the resulting nucleus will have an atomic number of
    A. 82   B. 83   C. 84   D. 85

KEYS (CORRECT ANSWERS)

TEST 1		TEST 2		TEST 3		TEST 4	
1. B	16. A	1. C	16. B	1. C	16. D	1. D	16. A
2. D	17. C	2. C	17. B	2. A	17. B	2. C	17. B
3. A	18. B	3. A	18. C	3. B	18. B	3. D	18. D
4. B	19. A	4. D	19. C	4. C	19. C	4. C	19. C
5. C	20. B	5. C	20. C	5. A	20. A	5. C	20. C
6. D	21. C	6. D	21. A	6. A	21. C	6. B	21. A
7. D	22. C	7. C	22. B	7. B	22. B	7. C	22. A
8. A	23. C	8. D	23. C	8. D	23. C	8. D	23. B
9. B	24. B	9. B	24. D	9. C	24. D	9. C	24. C
10. A	25. B	10. B	25. A	10. D	25. A	10. B	25. C
					26. C		
11. B	26. A	11. B	26. C	11. C	27. D	11. A	26. D
12. A	27. D	12. A	27. A	12. C	28. B	12. D	27. C
13. B	28. D	13. B	28. A	13. C	29. C	13. D	28. A
14. D	29. D	14. D	29. C	14. B	30. C	14. D	29. B
15. A	30. A	15. B	30. D	15. B		15. C	30. D

EXAMINATION SECTION
TEST 1

DIRECTIONS: Each question or incomplete statement is followed by several suggested answers or completions. Select the one that BEST answers the question or completes the statement. *PRINT THE LETTER OF THE CORRECT ANSWER IN THE SPACE AT THE RIGHT.*

1. Which of the following capacitors could be damaged by a reversal in polarity? A(n) _____ capacitor.

    A. ceramic B. paper C. mica
    D. electrolytic E. vacuum

    1._____

2. If the current through a resistor is 6 amperes and the voltage drop across it is 100 volts, what is the approximate value of the resistor in ohm(s)?

    A. 1660 B. 166 C. 16.6 D. 1.66 E. 0.0166

    2._____

3. What is the CORRECT use for an arbor press?

    A. Bending sheet metal B. Driving self-tapping screws
    C. Removing screws D. Removing "C" rings
    E. Removing bearings from shafts

    3._____

4. Which one of the following is a tensioning device in bulk-belt-type conveyor systems?
   _____ take-up.

    A. Spring B. Power C. Hydraulic
    D. Fluid coupled E. Flexible coupled

    4._____

5. When $X_L = X_C$ in a series circuit, what condition exists?

    A. The circuit impedance is increasing
    B. The circuit is at resonant frequency
    C. The circuit current is minimum
    D. The circuit has no e.m.f. at this time
    E. None of the above

    5._____

6. Which of the following pieces of information is NOT normally found on a schematic diagram?

    A. Functional stage name B. Supply voltages
    C. Part symbols D. Part values
    E. Physical location of parts

    6._____

7. When a single-phase induction motor drawing 24 amps at 120 VAC is reconnected to 240 VAC, what will be the amperage at 240 VAC? _____ amps.

    A. 6 B. 8 C. 12 D. 24 E. 36

    7._____

8. Which one of the following meters measures the SMALLEST current?

    A. Kilometer   B. Milliammeter   C. Microvoltmeter
    D. Millivoltmeter   E. Kilovoltmeter

9. If the current through a 1000-ohm resistor is 3 milliamperes, the voltage drop across the resistor is _____ volt(s).

    A. 1   B. 2.5   C. 3   D. 30   E. 300

10. The normally closed contacts of a relay are open when its solenoid is energized with VDC. The voltage at which the contacts re-close will be

    A. dependent upon the current through the contacts
    B. dependent upon the voltage applied to the contacts
    C. 24 VDC through the coil
    D. more than 24 VDC through the contacts
    E. less than 24 VDC through the coil

11. Electrical energy is converted to mechanical rotation by what component in the electric motor?

    A. Armature   B. Commutator   C. Field
    D. Start windings   E. Stator

12. Ohm's Law expresses the basic relationship of

    A. current, voltage, and resistance
    B. current, voltage, and power
    C. current, power, and resistance
    D. resistance, impedance, and voltage
    E. resistance, power, and impedance

13. In parallel circuits, the voltage is *always*

    A. variable   B. constant   C. alternating
    D. fluctuating   E. sporadic

14. Which one of the following is used as a voltage divider?

    A. Rotary converter   B. Potentiometer   C. Relay
    D. Circuit breaker   E. Voltmeter

Question 15.

Question 15 is based on the following diagram.

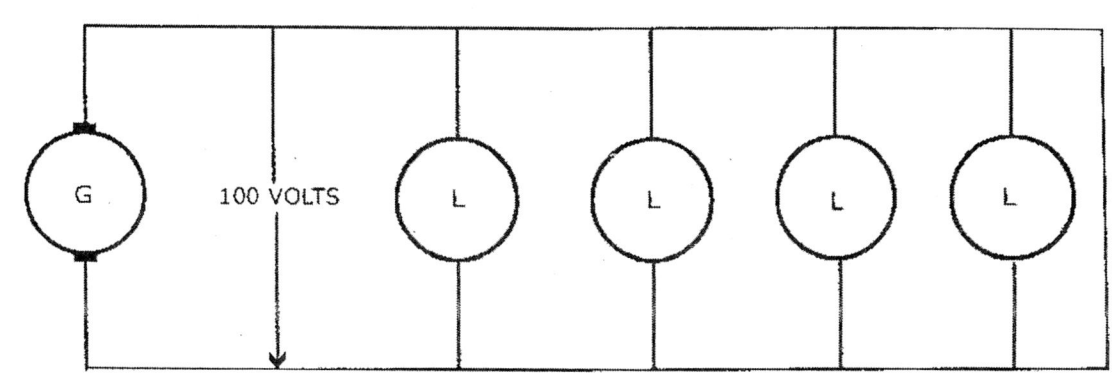

CURRENT IN EACH LAMP 1/2 AMPERE

15. What is the resistance of the entire circuit? _____ ohms. 15.____

    A. 15   B. 25   C. 35   D. 45   E. 50

16. Which one of the following tools is used to bring a bore to a specified tolerance? 16.____

    A. Tap   B. Reamer   C. Countersink
    D. Counterbore E. Center drill

17. The primary function of a take-up pulley in a belt conveyor is to 17.____

    A. carry the belt on the return trip
    B. track the belt
    C. maintain the proper belt tension
    D. change the direction of the belt
    E. regulate the speed of the belt

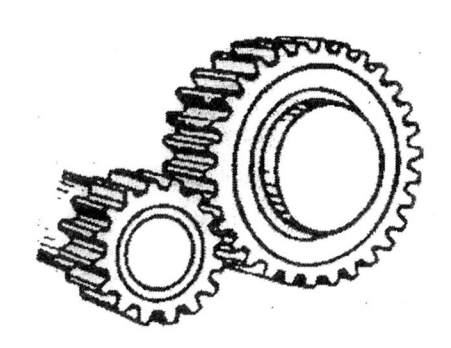

Question 18.

Question 18 is based on the following diagram.

18. What is the name of the gears? 18.____

    A. Spur external   B. Spur internal   C. Helical
    D. Herringbone   D. Worm

Question 19.

Question 19 is based on the following diagram.

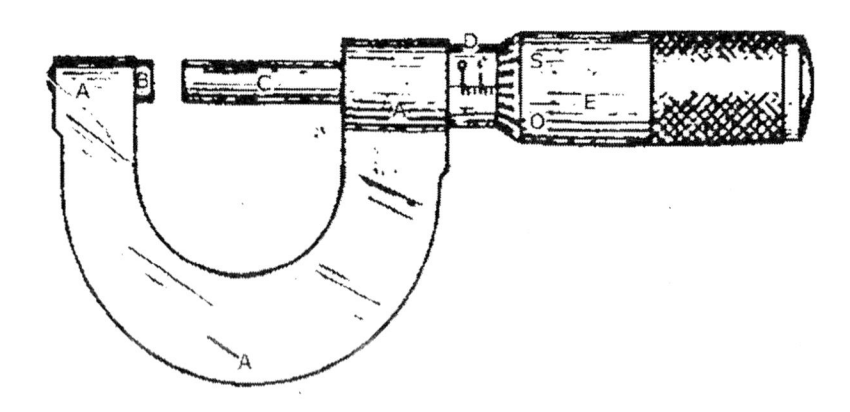

19. The part labeled D is the

    A. sleeve   B. thimble   C. frame
    D. anvil   E. pindle

19.____

Question 20.

Question 20 is based on the following symbol.

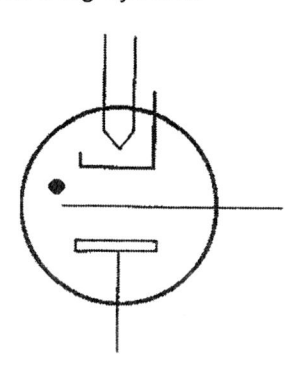

20. This symbol represents a _____ tube.

    A. thyratron vacuum   B. thyratron gas
    C. variable-mu vacuum   D. variable-mu gas
    E. vacuum photo

20.____

21. A diode can be substituted for which one of the following?

    A. Transformer   B. Relay   C. Rectifier
    D. Condenser   E. Rheostat

21.____

5 (#1)

Question 22.

Question 22 is based on the following diagram.

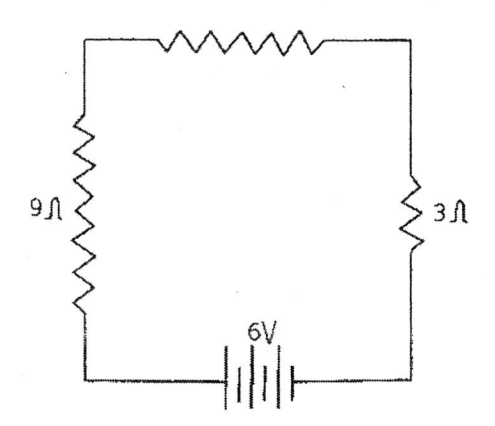

22. The rate of amperes flowing in the circuit is: 22.____
    A. .03 1/3   B. .18   C. .24
    D. .30 1/3   E. .33 1/3

23. The firing point in a thyratron tube is *most usually* controlled by the   23.____
    A. cathode   B. grid   C. plate
    D. heater   E. envelope

Questions 24-25.

Questions 24 and 25 shall be answered in accordance with the diagram below.

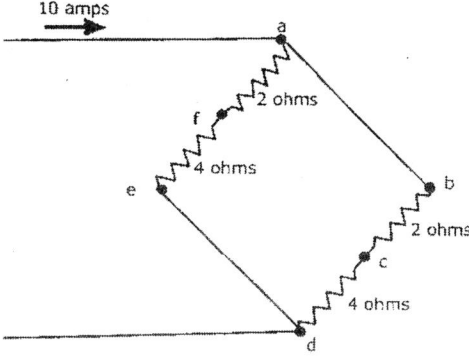

24. With reference to the above diagram, the voltage difference between   24.____
    points c and f is, *most nearly*, in volts,
    A. 40   B. 20   C. 10   D. 5   E. 0

25. With reference to the above diagram, the current flowing through the resistance   25.____
    c d is, *most nearly*, in amperes,
    A. 10   B. 5   C. 4   D. 2   E. 1

KEY (CORRECT ANSWERS)

1. D	6. E	11. A	16. B	21. C
2. C	7. C	12. A	17. C	22. E
3. E	8. B	13. B	18. A	23. B
4. A	9. C	14. B	19. A	24. E
5. B	10. E	15. E	20. B	25. B

EXAMINATION SECTION
TEST 1

DIRECTIONS: Each question or incomplete statement is followed by several suggested answers or completions. Select the one that BEST answers the question or completes the statement. *PRINT THE LETTER OF THE CORRECT ANSWER IN THE SPACE AT THE RIGHT.*

1. Two gears are meshed. The first gear has 20 teeth per inch and is rotating at 500 rpms. What is the speed of the second gear if it has 40 teeth per inch? _____ rpms.   1.____
   A. 500   B. 400   C. 250   D. 200

2. With two meshed gears, the first gear rotates at 100 rpms, the second gear rotates at 2000 rpms and has 10 teeth per inch.
   The first gear has _____ number of teeth per inch.   2.____
   A. 200   B. 100   C. 50   D. 150

3. Two pulleys are connected. The first pulley has a diameter of 5 inches; the second pulley has a diameter of 15 inches and rotates at 25 rpms.
   The speed of the first pulley is _____ rpms.   3.____
   A. 30   B. 75   C. 200   D. 400

4. Of two connected pulleys, the first has a radius of 10 inches and rotates at 50 rpms; the second rotates at 25 rpms.
   The diameter of the second pulley is _____ inches.   4.____
   A. 40   B. 30   C. 20   D. 10

5. Two pulleys are connected. The first pulley rotates at 75 rpms; the second pulley rotates at 100 rpms and has a diameter of 9 inches.
   The diameter of the first pulley is _____ inches.   5.____
   A. 10   B. 12   C. 15   D. 20

6. Of two connected pulleys, the first pulley has a radius of 12 inches and rotates at 60 rpms; the second pulley has a diameter of 16 inches.
   The speed of the second pulley is _____ rpms.   6.____
   A. 1000   B. 1020   C. 1040   D. 1080

7. If 16_{10} were converted to base 2, 8, and 16, the results would be _____ base 2, _____ base 8, and _____ base 16, respectively.   7.____
   A. 10000; 20; 10
   B. 1000; 2000; 20
   C. 20000; 200; 20
   D. 2000; 100; 10

8. Converting CAF_{16} to base 10 and base 8, the results would be _____ base 10 and _____ base 8, respectively.   8.____
   A. 2437; 2567
   B. 3247; 6257
   C. 4327; 5267
   D. 3427; 2657

9. Converting 101011001_2 to base 8, 10, and 16, the results would be _____ base 8, _____ base 10, and _____ base 16, respectively.

   A. 135; 45; 59
   B. 567; 435; 259
   C. 315; 245; 135
   D. 531; 345; 159

10. If 136_8 were converted to base 2, 10, and 16, the results would be _____ base 2, _____ base 10, and _____ base 16, respectively.

    A. 001011110; 94, 5E
    B. 010100110; 92; 10E
    C. 00100000; 90; 15E
    D. 011001110; 96; 20E

11. It may be correctly stated that 1000 picofarads are equal to _____ microfarads.

    A. .0001   B. .001   C. .01   D. .1

12. If 5 megohms were converted to kohms, the result would be _____ kohms.

    A. 1000   B. 2000   C. 4000   D. 5000

13. 1 nanohenry would convert to _____ millihenries.

    A. .001   B. .0001   C. .00001   D. .0000001

14. If 7 milliamps were converted to microamps, the answer would be _____ microamps.

    A. 7000   B. 700   C. 70   D. 7

15. If two resistors are in parallel and are 100 ohms each, the total resistance is

    A. 100   B. 150   C. 50   D. 10

16. In reference to the circuit in Question 15, if the first resistor has 25 volts DC, (VDC) across it, the second resistor also has 25 VDC across it, and there are no other components in the circuit except for the power source, the total circuit voltage is _____ VDC.

    A. 25   B. 50   C. 250   D. 500

17. In reference to the circuit in Question 15, if the first resistor has 1 amp on it, and the second resistor also has 1 amp on it, the total circuit amperage is _____ amps.

    A. 1   B. 2   C. 3   D. 4

18. If two resistors are in series and are 100 ohms each, the total resistance is

    A. 50   B. 100   C. 150   D. 200

19. In reference to the circuit in Question 18, if the first resistor has 25 VDC across it and the second resistor also has 25 VDC across it, the total circuit voltage is

    A. 50   B. 100   C. 200   D. 500

20. In reference to the circuit in Question 18, if the first resistor has 1 amp across it and the second resistor also has 1 amp on it, the total circuit amperage is

    A. 1   B. 5   C. 10   D. 15

21. Where two resistors are in parallel, one is 100 ohms and the other is 300 ohms. 21.____
    The total resistance is _____ ohms.

    A. 25　　　　B. 35　　　　C. 55　　　　D. 75

22. Three resistors in series are 25 ohms, 50 ohms, and 75 ohms, respectively. 22.____
    The total resistance is _____ ohms.

    A. 25　　　　B. 50　　　　C. 100　　　　D. 150

23. Two inductors are in parallel; the first is 50 henries and the second is also 50 henries. 23.____
    The total inductance is _____ henries.

    A. 25　　　　B. 50　　　　C. 55　　　　D. 60

24. Two inductors are in series and the first is 50 henries; the second is 50 henries. 24.____
    The total inductance is _____ henries.

    A. 25　　　　B. 50　　　　C. 75　　　　D. 100

25. Where two inductors are in parallel, the first is 100 henries and the second is 200 henries. 25.____
    The total inductance is _____ henries.

    A. 50　　　　B. 75　　　　C. 65　　　　D. 100

KEY (CORRECT ANSWERS)

1. C	6. D	11. B	16. A	21. D
2. A	7. A	12. D	17. B	22. D
3. B	8. B	13. D	18. D	23. A
4. A	9. D	14. A	19. A	24. D
5. B	10. A	15. C	20. A	25. B

TEST 2

DIRECTIONS: Each question or incomplete statement is followed by several suggested answers or completions. Select the one that BEST answers the question or completes the statement. *PRINT THE LETTER OF THE CORRECT ANSWER IN THE SPACE AT THE RIGHT.*

1. Two inductors are in series; the first inductor is 100 henries and the second is 200 henries.
   The total inductance is _____ henries.
   A. 200 B. 300 C. 400 D. 500

2. Two capacitors are in parallel; each capacitor is 30 farads.
   The total capacitance is _____ farads.
   A. 60 B. 80 C. 100 D. 200

3. Two capacitors are in series; each capacitor is 30 farads. The total capacitance is _____ farads.
   A. 10 B. 15 C. 20 D. 25

4. Two capacitors are in parallel; the first is 50 farads and the second is 100 farads.
   The total capacitance is _____ farads.
   A. 50 B. 100 C. 125 D. 150

5. Two capacitors are in series; the first is 50 farads and the second is 100 farads.
   The total capacitance is _____ farads.
   A. 33.333 B. 49.999 C. 13.333 D. 25.555

6. A resistor's color codes are orange, blue, yellow, and gold, in that order.
   The value of the resistor is _____ kohms ± _____ %.
   A. 200; 2 B. 300; 4 C. 360; 5 D. 400; 7

7. If a resistors color codes are red, black, and blue, the value of this resistor is _____ megohms ± _____ %.
   A. 20; 20 B. 40; 80 C. 30; 30 D. 50; 50

8. If a resistor's color codes are gray, green, black, and silver, the resistor's value is _____ ohms ± _____ %.
   A. 55; 5 B. 75; 15 C. 85; 10 D. 100; 25

9. One complete cycle of a sinewave takes 1000 microseconds. Its frequency is _____ hertz.
   A. 500 B. 1000 C. 2000 D. 5000

10. If one complete cycle of a squarewave takes 5 microseconds, its frequency is _____ khertz.
    A. 200 B. 500 C. 700 D. 1000

11. What is the PRT (pulse repetition time) of a 50 hertz (hz) sinewave? _____ milliseconds. 11._____

    A. 10   B. 20   C. 40   D. 60

12. The PRT of a 20 khz sawtooth signal is _____ megahertz. 12._____

    A. 50   B. 100   C. 200   D. 500

13. If a resistor measures 10 volts and 2 amps across it, the resistance is _____ ohms. 13._____

    A. 0   B. 2   C. 5   D. 10

14. If a 30 ohm resistor measures 10 volts, the power consumed by the resistor is _____ watts. 14._____

    A. 3000   B. 5000   C. 6500   D. 7000

15. If a 50 ohm resistor measures 4 amps across, the power consumed by it is _____ watts. 15._____

    A. 200   B. 400   C. 600   D. 800

16. If a 100 ohm resistor measures 25 volts across, the current on it is _____ amps. 16._____

    A. .15   B. .25   C. .55   D. .65

Questions 17-23.

DIRECTIONS: Questions 17 through 23 are to be answered on the basis of the following diagram.

SERIES CIRCUIT

$V_{supply} = V_A + V_B + V_C$
$I_{total} = I_A = I_B = I_C$

PARALLEL CIRCUIT

$V_{supply} = V_A = V_B = V_C$
$I_{total} = I_A + I_B + I_C$

17. In the series circuit above, if Vsupply = 100 VDC, resistor A is 10 ohms, resistor B is 50 ohms, and resistor C is 5 ohms, the total circuit current is _____ amps. 17._____

    A. 1.538   B. 1.267   C. 1.358   D. 1.823

18. In the series circuit shown above, the current across each individual resistor is _____ amps. 18._____

    A. .5   B. 1.5   C. 2.5   D. 3.5

19. In the series circuit shown above, the total power drawn by the circuit is _____ watts.

    A. 140.25   B. 150.75   C. 153.38   D. 173.38

20. In the series circuit shown above, the power drawn from each individual resistor is _____, _____, and _____ watts, respectively.

    A. 23.65; 118.27; 11.827
    B. 17.567; 123.27; 11.27
    C. 18.627; 145.27; 12.27
    D. 21.735; 116.87; 11.83

21. In the parallel circuit shown above, if Vsupply = 100 VDC, resistor A is 10 ohms, resistor B is 50 ohms, and resistor C is 5 ohms, the total circuit current is _____ amps.

    A. 21   B. 27   C. 32   D. 45

22. In the parallel circuit shown above, the total power drawn by the circuit is _____ watts.

    A. 1200   B. 2300   C. 2700   D. 3200

23. In the parallel circuit above, the power drawn by each individual resistor is _____ watts, respectively.

    A. 100; 200; 2000
    B. 200; 400; 5000
    C. 300; 500; 750
    D. 450; 600; 1500

24. On an 0-scope display, one cycle of a signal takes up 4 1/2 divisions and the peak-to-peak amplitude of the signal takes up 3 3/4 divisions.
    With the volts/division knob set on 5 volts and the time/division knob set to 5 microseconds, the peak-to-peak amplitude and the frequency of the signal are _____ volts and _____ khz, respectively.

    A. 15.75; 100
    B. 22.5; 200
    C. 37.5; 350
    D. 45.75; 570

25. If a signal that has a peak-to-peak amplitude of 15 volts and a frequency of 5 megaherz is to be observed on an 0-scope with one complete cycle shown, the time/division knob and volts/division knob should be set on _____ microseconds and _____ volts per division, respectively.

    A. .02; 2   B. .05; 4   C. .07; 3.5   D. 10; 7.5

KEY (CORRECT ANSWERS)

1. B	6. C	11. B	16. B	21. C
2. A	7. A	12. A	17. A	22. D
3. B	8. C	13. C	18. B	23. A
4. D	9. B	14. A	19. C	24. B
5. A	10. A	15. D	20. A	25. A

MECHANICAL APTITUDE

EXAMINATION SECTION
TEST 1

MECHANICAL COMPREHENSION

DIRECTIONS: Questions 1 to 4 test your ability to understand general mechanical devices. Pictures are shown and questions asked about the mechanical devices shown in the picture. Read each question and study the picture. Each question is followed by four choices. For each question, choose the one BEST answer (A, B, C, or D). Then *PRINT THE LETTER OF THE CORRECT ANSWER IN THE SPACE AT THE RIGHT.*

1. The reason for crossing the belt connecting these wheels is to 1.____

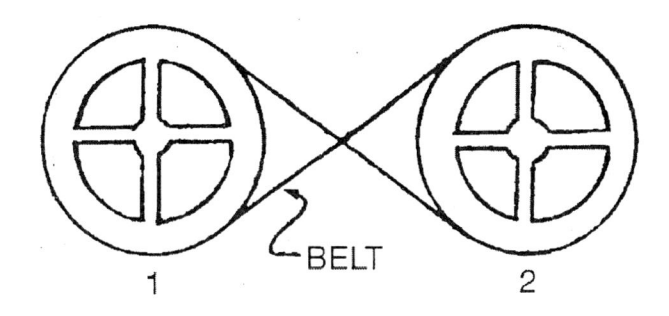

    A. make the wheels turn in opposite directions
    B. make wheel 2 turn faster than wheel 1
    C. save wear on the belt
    D. take up slack in the belt

2. The purpose of the small gear between the two large gears is to 2.____

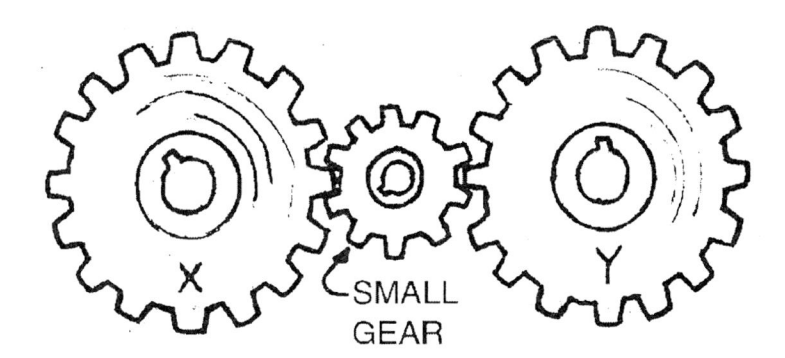

    A. increase the speed of the larger gears
    B. allow the larger gears to turn in different directions
    C. decrease the speed of the larger gears
    D. make the larger gears turn in the same direction

3. Each of these three-foot-high water cans have a bottom with an area of one square foot. The pressure on the bottom of the cans is

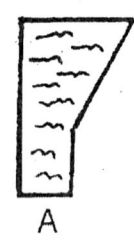

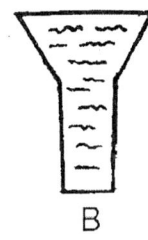

3._____

A.   least in A
C.   least in C
B.   least in B
D.   the same in all

4. The reading on the scale should be

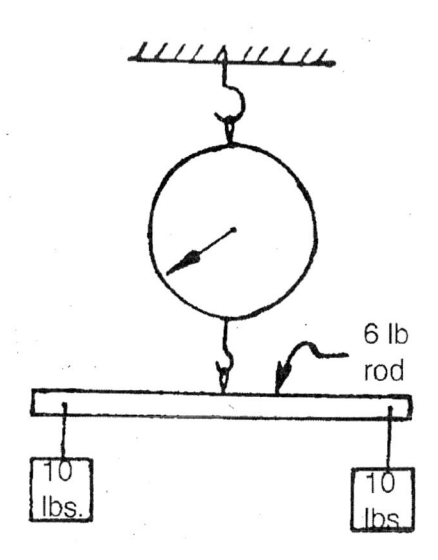

4._____

A.   zero
B.   10 pounds
C.   13 pounds
D.   26 pounds

KEY (CORRECT ANSWERS)

1. A
2. D
3. D
4. D

TEST 2

DIRECTIONS: Questions 1 to 6 test knowledge of tools and how to use them. For each question, decide which one of the four things shown in the boxes labeled A, B, C, or D normally is used with or goes best with the thing in the picture on the left. Then *PRINT THE LETTER OF THE CORRECT ANSWER IN THE SPACE AT THE RIGHT.*

NOTE: All tools are NOT drawn to the same scale.

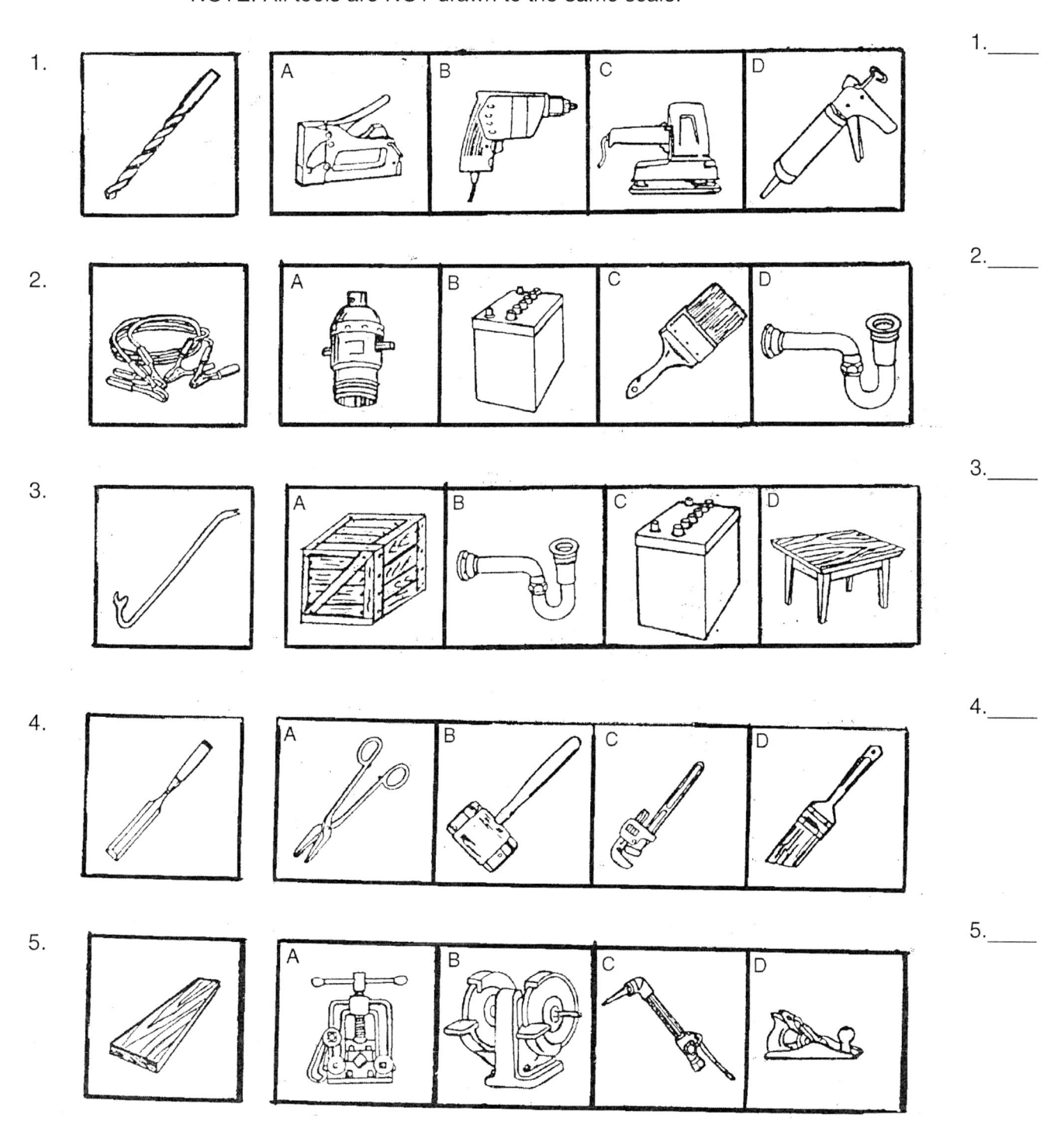

1. ____

2. ____

3. ____

4. ____

5. ____

6.

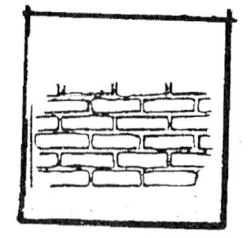

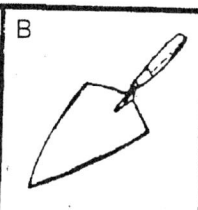

A	B	C	D
file	trowel	hammer	awl

(brick wall shown on left)

KEY (CORRECT ANSWERS)

1. B   4. B
2. B   5. D
3. A   6. B

MECHANICAL APTITUDE

EXAMINATION SECTION
TEST 1

QUESTIONS 1-6.

Questions 1 through 6 are questions designed to test your ability to distinguish identical forms from unlike forms.

In each question, there are five drawings, lettered A, B, C, D, and E. Four of the drawings are alike. You are to find the one drawing that is different from the other four in the question. Then, on the Answer Sheet, blacken the space lettered the same as the figure that you have selected.

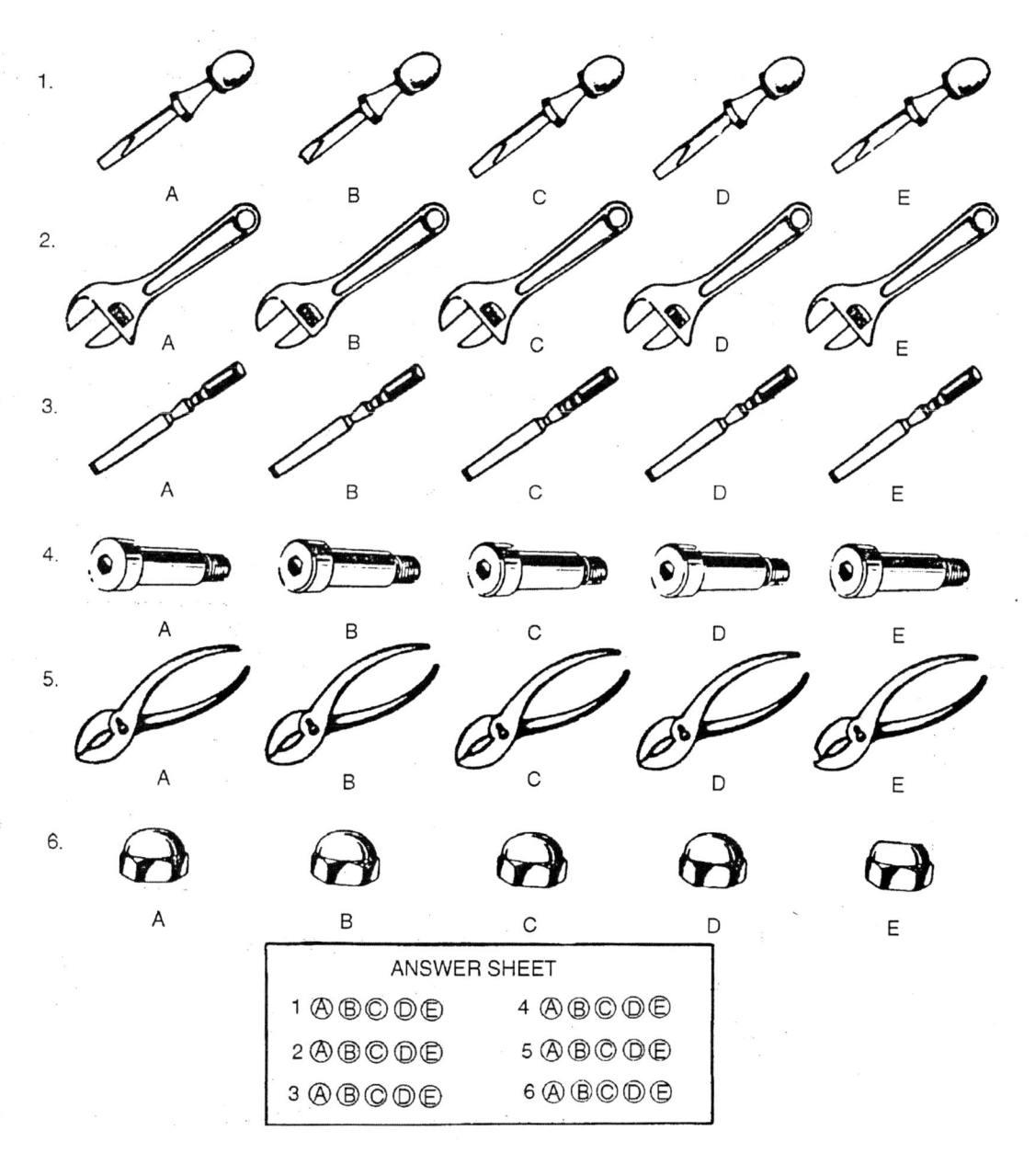

ANSWER SHEET

1 Ⓐ Ⓑ Ⓒ Ⓓ Ⓔ   4 Ⓐ Ⓑ Ⓒ Ⓓ Ⓔ
2 Ⓐ Ⓑ Ⓒ Ⓓ Ⓔ   5 Ⓐ Ⓑ Ⓒ Ⓓ Ⓔ
3 Ⓐ Ⓑ Ⓒ Ⓓ Ⓔ   6 Ⓐ Ⓑ Ⓒ Ⓓ Ⓔ

QUESTIONS 7-8.

Questions 7 and 8 are questions designed to test your knowledge of pattern matching.

Questions 7 and 8 present problems found in making patterns. Each shows, at the left side, two or more separate flat pieces. In each question, select the arrangement lettered A, B, C, or D that shows how these pieces at the left can be fitted together without gaps or overlapping. The pieces may be turned around or turned over in any way to make them fit together.

On the Answer Sheet blacken the space lettered the same as the figure that you have selected.

Now, look at the questions below.

7. From these pieces, which one of these arrangements can you make?

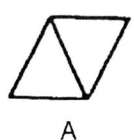

In question 7, only the arrangement D can be made from the pieces shown at the left, so space D is marked for Question 7 on the answer sheet below. (Note that it is necessary to turn the pieces around so that the short sides are at the bottom in the arrangement lettered D. None of the other arrangements show pieces of the given size and shape.)

8. From these pieces, which one of these arrangements can you make?

ANSWER SHEET

7 Ⓐ Ⓑ Ⓒ Ⓓ

8 Ⓐ Ⓑ Ⓒ Ⓓ

QUESTIONS 9-10.

Questions 9 and 10. are questions designed to test your ability to identify forms of *LIKE* and *UNLIKE* proportions.
In each of the questions, select from the drawings of objects labeled A, B, C, and D, the one that would have the Top, Front, and Right views shown in the drawing at the left. Then on your Answer Sheet blacken the space that has the same letter as your answer.

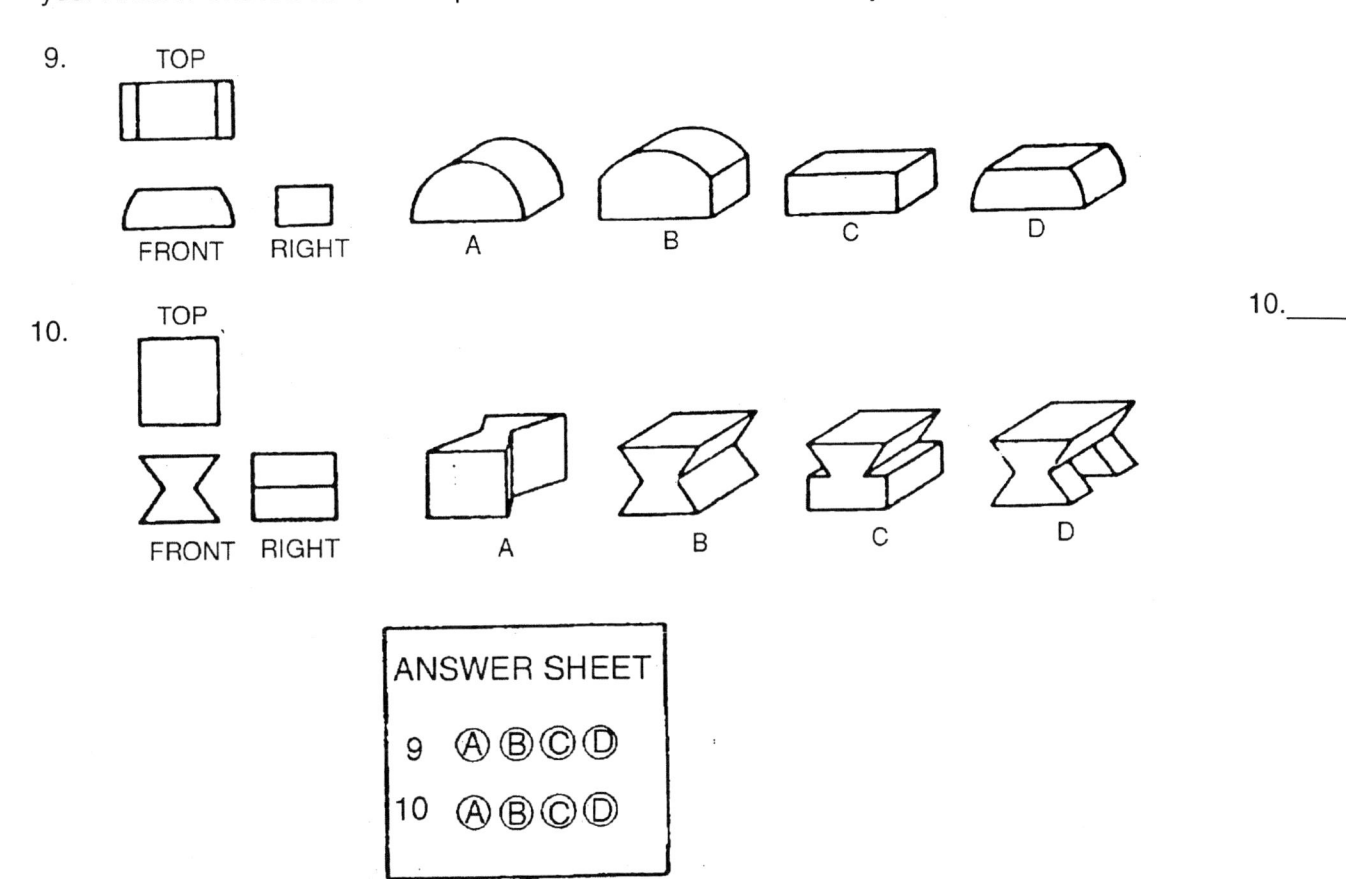

9. TOP / FRONT / RIGHT

10. TOP / FRONT / RIGHT

10.____

ANSWER SHEET

9 Ⓐ Ⓑ Ⓒ Ⓓ

10 Ⓐ Ⓑ Ⓒ Ⓓ

QUESTIONS 11-14.

Explanation and Commentary:
In each question, ONE rectangle is clearly WRONG. For each question, use the measuirng gage to check each of the rectangles and to find the WRONG one. Do this by putting the measuring gage rectangle on the question rectangle with the same letter so that the rectangles slightly overlap and the thin lines are parallel, like the one at the right. In this case, the height of the question rectangle exactly matches the height of the measuring gage rectangle, so the question rectangle is the right height. In this case, you do NOT mark your answer sheet.

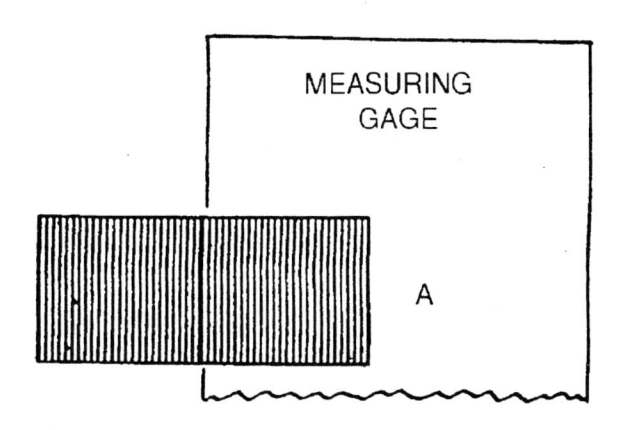

MEASURING GAGE

A

Once in every question, when you put a measuring gage rectangle on a question rectangle, you will find that the heights do NOT match and that the question rectangle is clearly wrong, like the one at the right. In this case, you mark on the answer sheet the space with the same letter as the wrong rectangle. REMEMBER TO LINE UP THE MEASURING RECTANGLE WITH EACH QUESTION RECTANGLE SO THAT THE THIN LINES ARE EXACTLY PARALLEL.

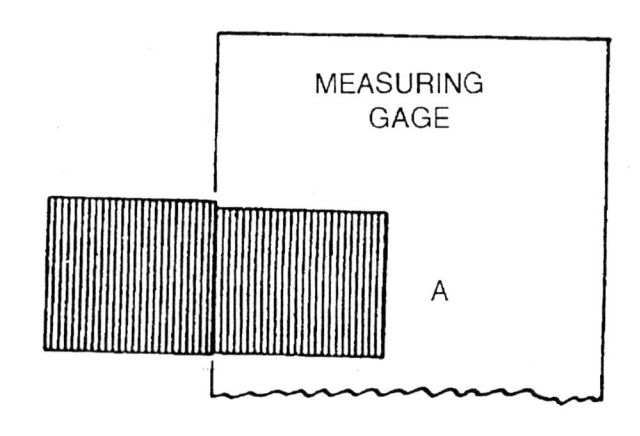

Now, cut out the measuring gage on the last page and practice on the questions. The test will be timed, so practice doing them rapidly and accurately.

Questions 11 through 14 test how quickly and accurately you can check the heights of rectangles with a measuring gage. Each question has five rectangles of different heights. The height is the dimension that runs the same way as the thin lines.

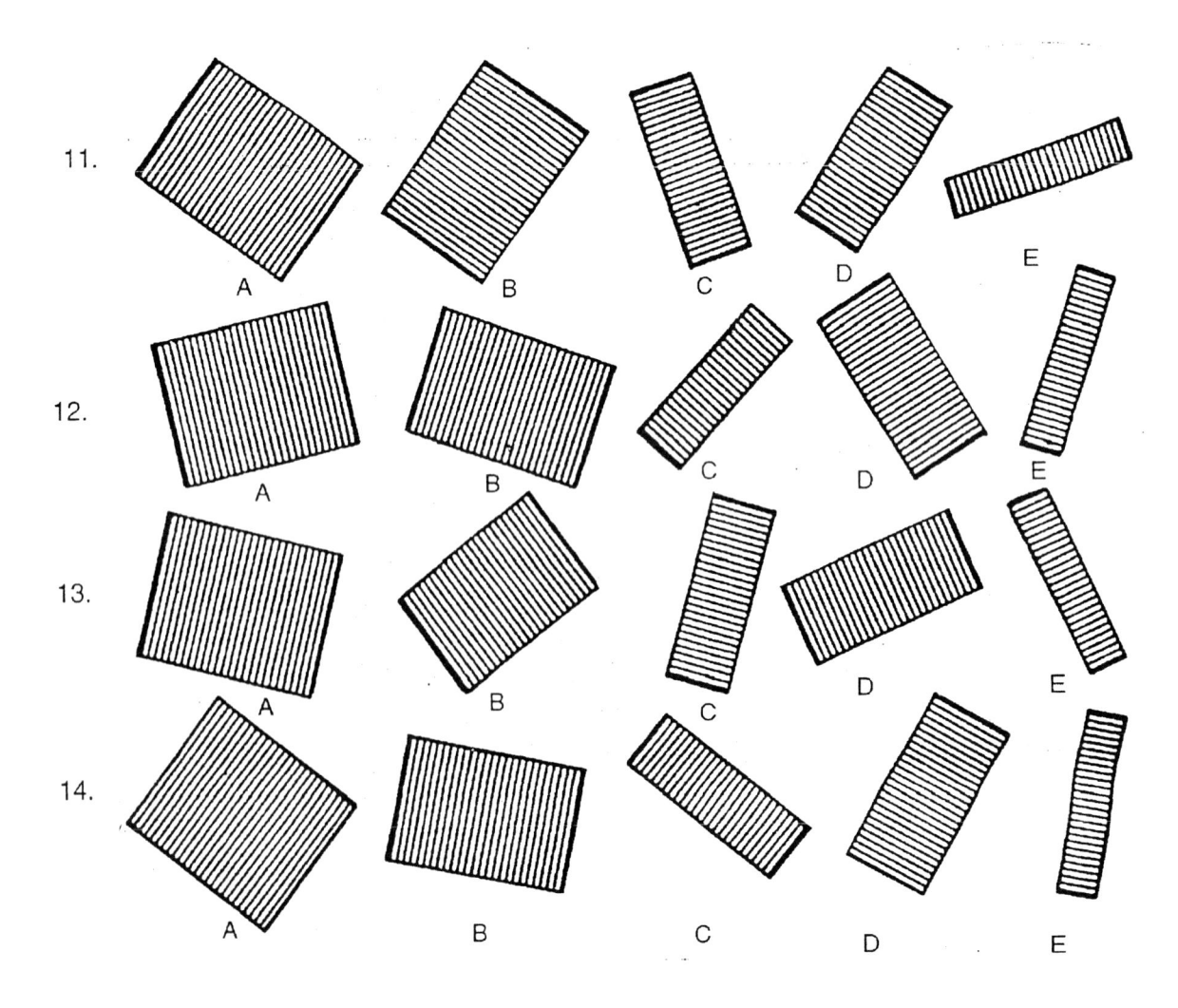

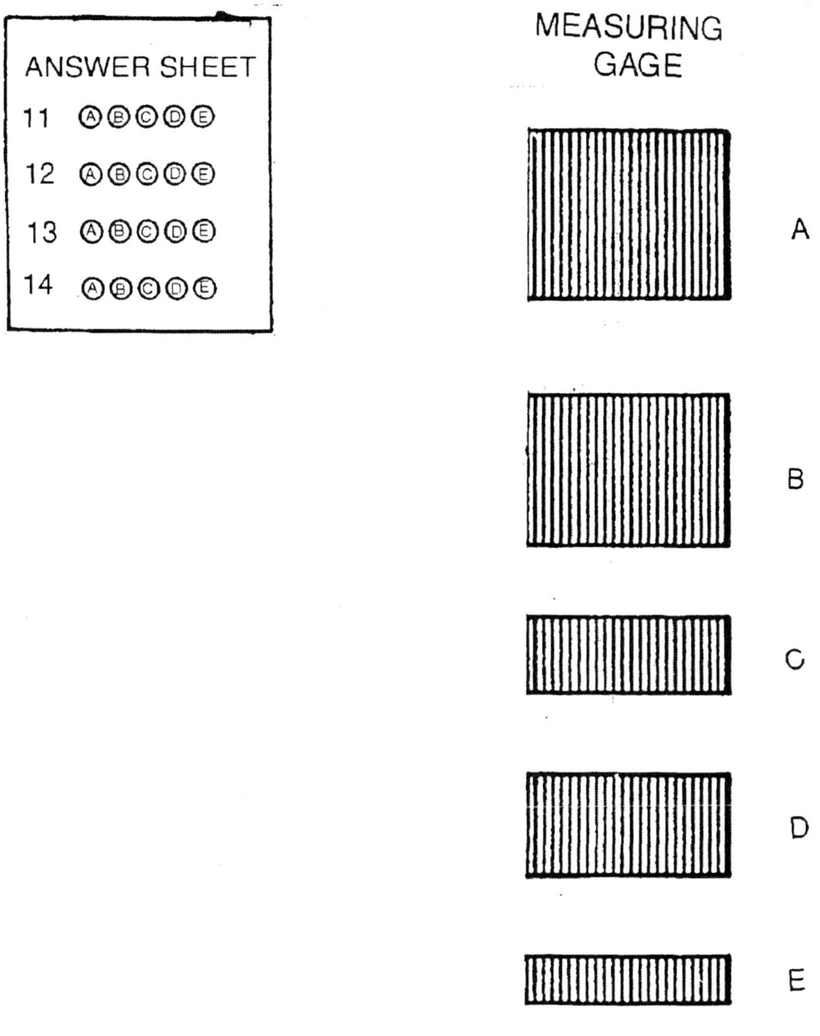

ANSWER SHEET

11 Ⓐ Ⓑ Ⓒ Ⓓ Ⓔ
12 Ⓐ Ⓑ Ⓒ Ⓓ Ⓔ
13 Ⓐ Ⓑ Ⓒ Ⓓ Ⓔ
14 Ⓐ Ⓑ Ⓒ Ⓓ Ⓔ

MEASURING GAGE

A

B

C

D

E

KEY (CORRECT ANSWERS)

1. B
2. B
3. C
4. A
5. E
6. E
7. D
8. B
9. D
10. B
11. D
12. C
13. B
14. A

MECHANICAL APTITUDE
TOOLS AND THEIR USE

EXAMINATION SECTION
TEST 1

Questions 1-16.

DIRECTIONS: Questions 1 through 16 refer to the tools shown below. The numbers in the answers refer to the numbers beneath the tools.
NOTE: These tools are NOT shown to scale

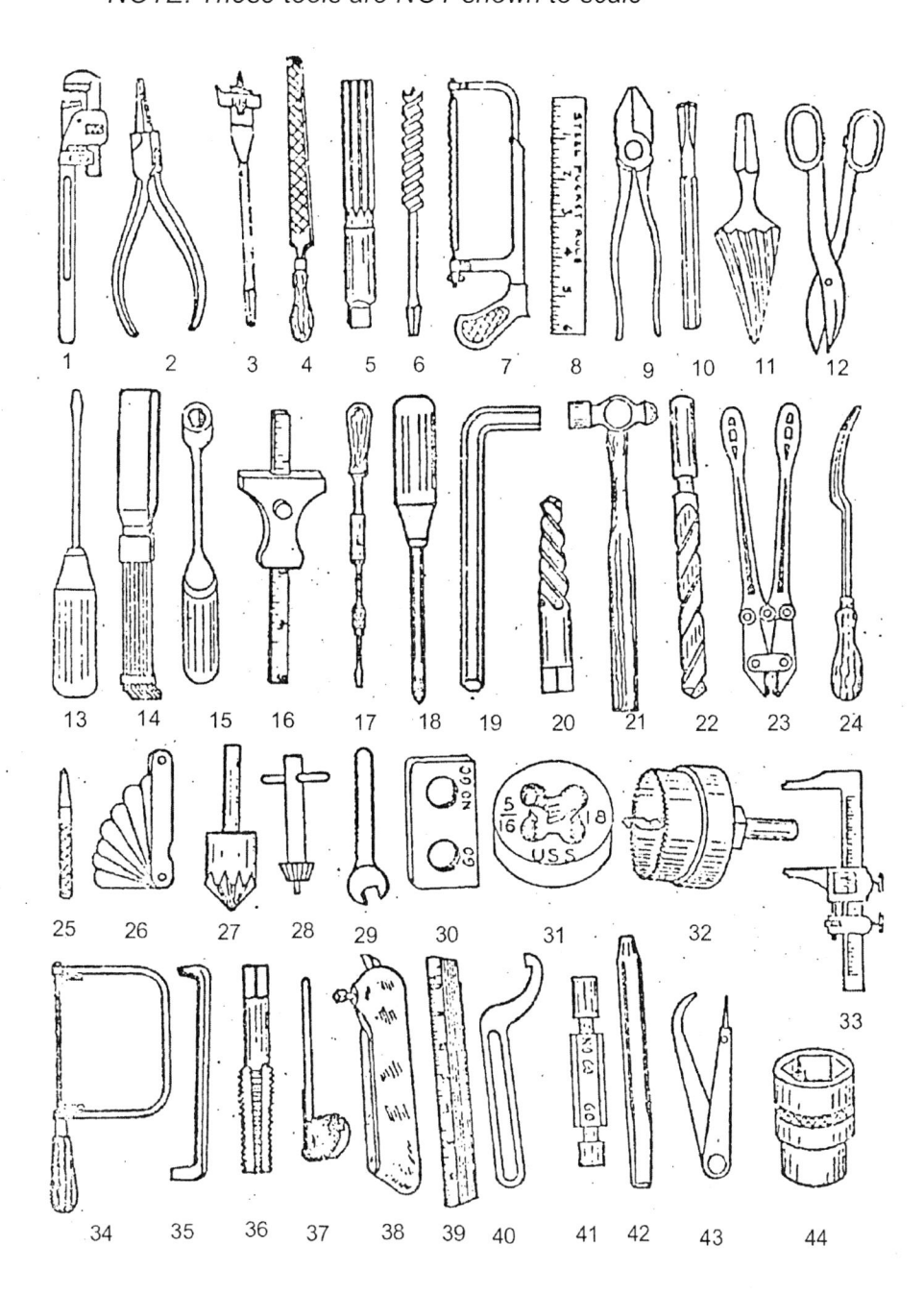

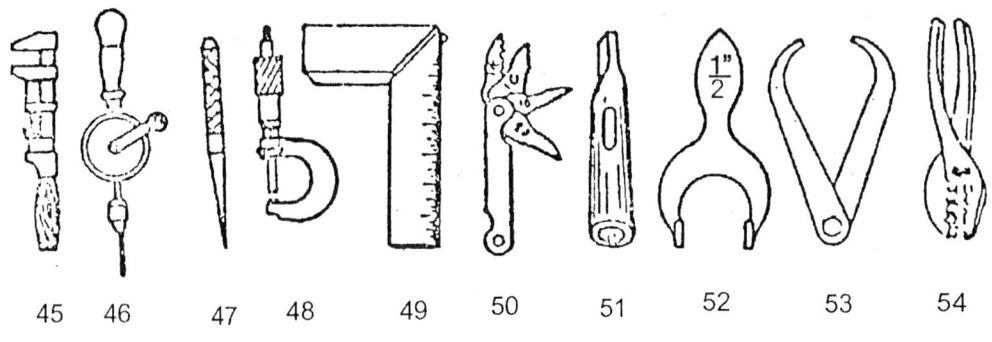

45 46 47 48 49 50 51 52 53 54

1. A 1" x 1" x 1/8" angle iron should be cut by using tool number
   A. 7   B. 12   C. 23   D. 42

2. To peen an iron rivet, you should use tool number
   A. 4   B. 7   C. 21   D. 43

3. The star "drill" is tool number
   A. 5   B. 10   C. 20   D. 22

4. To make holes in sheet metal for sheet metal screws, you should use tool number.
   A. 6   B. 10   C. 36   D. 46

5. To cut through a 3/8" diameter wire rope, you should use tool number
   A. 12   B. 23   C. 42   D. 54

6. To remove cutting burrs from the inside of a steel pipe, you should use tool number
   A. 5   B. 11   C. 14   D. 20

7. The depth of a bored hole may be measured MOST accurately with tool number
   A. 8   B. 16   C. 26   D. 41

8. If the marking on the blade of tool number 7 reads:12"-32", the 32 refers to the
   A. length   B. thickness   C. weight
   D. number of teeth per inch

9. If tool number 6 bears the mark "5", it should be used to drill holes having a diameter of
   A. 5/32"   B. 5/16"   C. 5/8"   D. 5"

10. To determine MOST quickly the number of threads per inch on a bolt, you should use tool number
    A. 8   B. 16   C. 26   D. 50

11. Wood screws, located in positions where the headroom does not permit the use of an ordinary screwdriver, may be removed by using tool number
    A. 17   B. 28   C. 35   D. 46

12. To remove a broken-off piece of 1/2" diameter pipe from a fitting, you should use tool number   12.____
    A. 5   B. 11   C. 20   D. 36

13. The outside diameter of a bushing may be measured MOST accurately with tool number   13.____
    A. 8   B. 26   C. 33   D. 43

14. To re-thread a stud hole in the casting of an elevator motor, you should use tool number   14.____
    A. 5   B. 20   C. 22   D. 36

15. To enlarge slightly a bored hole in a steel plate, you should use tool number   15.____
    A. 5   B. 11   C. 20   D. 36

16. The term "16 oz." should be applied to tool number   16.____
    A. 1   B. 12   C. 21   D. 42

KEYS (CORRECT ANSWERS)

1.	A	9.	B
2.	C	10.	D
3.	B	11.	C
4.	D	12.	C
5.	B	13.	C
6.	B	14.	D
7.	B	15.	A
8.	D	16.	C

TEST 2

Questions 1-11.

DIRECTIONS: Questions 1 through 11 refer to the instruments listed below. Each instrument is listed with an identifying number in front of it.

1 - Hygrometer	6 - Oscilloscope	11 - 6-foot folding rule
2 - Ammeter	7 - Frequency meter	12 - Architect's scale
3 - Voltmeter	8 - Micrometer	13 - Planimeter
4 - Wattmeter	9 - Vernier calliper	14 - Engineer's scale
5 - Megger	10 - Wire gage	15 - Ohmmeter

1. The instrument that should be used to *accurately* measure the resistance of a 4,700-ohm resistor is number

    A. 3   B. 4   C. 7   D. 15

2. To measure the current in an electrical circuit, the instrument that should be used is number

    A. 2   B. 7   C. 8   D. 15

3. To measure the insulation resistance of a rubber-covered electrical cable, the instrument that should be used is number

    A. 4   B. 5   C. 8   D. 15

4. An AC motor is hooked up to a power distribution box. In order to check the voltage at the motor terminals, the instrument that should be used is number

    A. 2   B. 3   C. 4   D. 7

5. To measure the shaft diameter of a motor *accurately* to one-thousandth of an inch, the instrument that should be used is number

    A. 8   B. 10   C. 11   D. 14

6. The instrument that should be used to determine whether 25 Hz. or 60 Hz. is present in an electrical circuit is number

    A. 4   B. 5   C. 7   D. 8

7. Of the following, the *proper* instrument to use to determine the diameter of the conductor of a piece of electrical hookup wire is number

    A. 10   B. 11   C. 12   D. 14

8. The amount of electrical power being used in a balanced three-phase circuit should be measured with number

    A. 2   B. 3   C. 4   D. 5

9. The electrical wave form at a given point in an electronic circuit can be observed with number

    A. 2   B. 3   C. 6   D. 7

10. The *proper* instrument to use for measuring the width of a door is number

    A. 11   B. 12   C. 13   D. 14

11. A one-inch hole with a tolerance of plus or minus three-thousandths is reamed in a steel block. The *proper* instrument to accurately check the diameter of the hole is number

    A. 8   B. 9   C. 11   D. 14

12. An oilstone is LEAST likely to be used correctly to sharpen a

    A. scraper   B. chisel   C. knife   D. saw

13. To cut the ends of a number of lengths of wood at an angle of 45 degrees, it would be BEST to use a

    A. mitre-box   B. protractor   C. triangle   D. wooden rule

14. A gouge is a tool used for

    A. planing wood smooth
    B. grinding metal
    C. drilling steel
    D. chiseling wood

15. Holes are usually countersunk when installing

    A. carriage bolts
    B. lag screws
    C. flat-head screws
    D. square nuts

16. A tool that is *generally* used to slightly elongate a round hole in scrap-iron is a

    A. rat-tail file   B. reamer   C. drill   D. rasp

17. When the term "10-24" is used to specify a machine screw, the number 24 refers to the

    A. number of screws per pound
    B. diameter of the screw
    C. length of the screw
    D. number of threads per inch

18. If you were unable to tighten a nut by means of a ratchet wrench because, although the nut turned on with the forward movement of the wrench, it turned off with the backward movement, you should

    A. make the nut hand-tight before using the wrench
    B. reverse the ratchet action
    C. put a few drops of oil on the wrench
    D. use a different socket in the handle

19. If you were installing a long wood screw and found you were unable to drive this screw more than three-quarters of its length by the use of a properly-fitting straight-handled screwdriver, the *proper* SUBSEQUENT action would be for you to

    A. take out the screw and put soap on it
    B. change to the use of a screwdriver-bit and brace
    C. take out the screw and drill a shorter hole before redriving
    D. use a pair of pliers on the blade of the screwdriver

20. Good practice requres that the end of a pipe to be installed in a plumbing system be reamed to remove the inside burr after it has been cut to length. The *purpose* of this reaming is to

    A. restore the original inside diameter of the pipe at the end
    B. remove loose rust
    C. make the threading of the pipe easier
    D. finish the pipe accurately to length

20.____

KEYS (CORRECT ANSWERS)

1.	D	11.	B
2.	A	12.	D
3.	B	13.	A
4.	B	14.	D
5.	A	15.	C
6.	C	16.	A
7.	A	17.	D
8.	C	18.	A
9.	C	19.	A
10.	A	20.	A

ARITHMETIC
EXAMINATION SECTION
TEST 1

DIRECTIONS: Each question or incomplete statement is followed by several suggested answers or completions. Select the one that BEST answers the question or completes the statement. *PRINT THE LETTER OF THE CORRECT ANSWER IN THE SPACE AT THE RIGHT.*

1. $34\overline{)17136}$

    A. 54   B. 503 24/34   C. 504   D. 505 4/34   E. NG

    1._____

2. 141606
   -94679

    A. 46,837   B. 46,927   C. 46,937   D. 47,027   E. NG

    2._____

3. $86\overline{)8342}$

    A. 96   B. 96 76/86   C. 97 6/86   D. 97 16/86   E. NG

    3._____

4. $1\frac{2}{3}$
   $+1\frac{5}{6}$

    A. 2 1/6   B. 2 1/2   C. 3 1/2   D. 3 1/3   E. NG

    4._____

5. $3\overline{)128.94}$

    A. 42.98   B. 4.298   C. 429.8   D. 4298   E. NG

    5._____

6. 709
   x864

    A. 612,576   B. 602,576   C. 611,576   D. 612,566   E. NG

    6._____

7. 138057
   -54368

    A. 83,679   B. 83,689   C. 83,789   D. 84,689   E. NG

    7._____

8. $3\frac{3}{5} \div \frac{9}{10} =$

    A. 1/4   B. 2 1/2   C. 2 3/5   D. 3 3/5   E. NG

    8._____

9. $7\overline{)21.441}$

    A. 3.063   B. 3.63   C. .363   D. 3063   E. NG

    9._____

10. $\dfrac{9}{10} - \dfrac{1}{2} =$

    A. 3/5   B. 2/5   C. 1/2   D. 1 2/5   E. NG

10.___

11. $\dfrac{2}{3} \times 2\dfrac{1}{4} =$

    A. 1   B. 2 1/2   C. 2   D. 1 1/2   E. NG

11.___

12.
```
  7646
  6799
  3389
 +6597
```

    A. 23,431   B. 24,331   C. 24,431   D. 24,421   E. NG

12.___

13. $\dfrac{5}{6} + 1\dfrac{3}{4}$

    A. 2 7/12   B. 1 4/5   C. 1 1/12   D. 2 1/2   E. NG

13.___

14. Round to tenths: 22.3 - 1.21 =

    A. 21.0   B. 21.5   C. 21.8   D. 21.9   E. NG

14.___

15. Round to 2 digits:

```
  9.05
 x 5.9
```

    A. 53   B. 5.4   C. 5.3   D. 54   E. NG

15.___

16.
```
   608
  x970
```

    A. 58,776   B. 58,876   C. 588,760   D. 589,760   E. NG

16.___

17.
```
  6567
  8999
  6877
 +8789
```

    A. 30,232   B. 31,132   C. 31,222   D. 31,232   E. NG

17.___

18.
```
  4987
  x 96
```

    A. 468,752   B. 477,752   C. 478,742   D. 478,752   E. NG

18.___

19. $3\frac{1}{3} - 1\frac{3}{4}$

    A. 1 5/12   B. 1 7/12   C. 2 1/2   D. 2 7/12| E. NG

20. What is 4% of $500?

    A. $20.00   B. $1.25   C. $2.00   D. $80.00   E. NG

21. $16 \times 10\frac{3}{4}$

    A. 160   B. 160 3/4   C. 167 1/2   D. 172   E. NG

22. If $\frac{16}{K} = 8$, then K =

    A. 1/2   B. 8   C. 128   D. 2   E. NG

23. Round to tenths:

    4.35 × 0.32

    A. 1.3   B. 13.9   C. 1.4   D. 14.0   E. NG

24. What is $2\frac{1}{2}$% of $50?

    A. $12.50   B. $1.25   C. $25.00   D. $125.00   E. NG

25. 89)6267.38

    A. 7.42   B. 74.2   C. 7042   D. 70.42   E. NG

26. $10 is what percent of $400?

    A. 4   B. 25   C. 2 1/2   D. 40   E. NG

27. .68)31.96

    A. 0.47   B. 47   C. 4.7   D. 470   E. NG

28. $\frac{4}{6} = \frac{N}{24}$

    A. 6   B. 18   C. 16   D. 36   E. NG

29. 6÷10=

    A. 2/3   B. 3/5   C. 1 2/3   D. 6   E. NG

30. $\dfrac{3}{10} = \dfrac{15}{N}$

    A. 5   B. 40   C. 45   D. 150   E. NG

30.____

31. $\dfrac{3a}{4} = 6$

    a =

    A. 2   B. 24   C. 8   D. 72   E. NG

31.____

32. $40 is what percent of $1600?

    A. 20   B. 6.40   C. 2 1/2   D. 40   E. NG

32.____

33. $25 is 5% of what amount?

    A. $1.25   B. $125.00   C. $5000.00   D. $500.00   E. NG

33.____

34. (-3)
    x 6
    ―――

    A. 9   B. 15   C. 18   D. -18   E. NG

34.____

35. $160 is 4% of what amount?

    A. $4000.00   B. $64.00   C. $400.00   D. $6.40   E. NG

35.____

36. $\dfrac{N}{12} = \dfrac{13}{39}$

    N =

    A. 4   B. 3   C. 13   D. 36   E. NG

36.____

37. - 4 + 2 =

    A. -6   B. -2   C. 2   D. 8   E. NG

37.____

38. 5N = 8N - 12
    N =

    A. 5/8   B. 4   C. 3   D. 13   E. NG

38.____

39. $\dfrac{16}{-8} =$

    A. 2   B. 8   C. 12   D. -2   E. NG

39.____

40. 2a - 4 = 14 - a
    a =

    A. 6   B. 3 1/3   C. 5   D. 10   E. NG

40.____

KEY (CORRECT ANSWERS)

1.	C	11.	D	21.	D	31.	C
2.	B	12.	C	22.	D	32.	C
3.	E	13.	A	23.	C	33.	D
4.	C	14.	E	24.	B	34.	D
5.	A	15.	A	25.	D	35.	A
6.	A	16.	D	26.	C	36.	A
7.	B	17.	D	27.	B	37.	B
8.	E	18.	D	28.	C	38.	B
9.	A	19.	B	29.	B	39.	D
10.	B	20.	A	30.	E	40.	A

SOLUTIONS TO PROBLEMS

1. $17{,}136 \div 34 = 504$

2. $141{,}606 - 94{,}679 = 46{,}927$

3. $8342 \div 86 = 97$

4. $1\frac{2}{3} + 1\frac{5}{6} = 1\frac{4}{6} + 1\frac{5}{6} = 2\frac{9}{6} = 3\frac{1}{2}$

5. $128.94 \div 3 = 42.98$

6. $709 \times 864 = 612{,}576$

7. $138{,}057 - 54{,}368 = 83{,}689$

8. $3\frac{3}{5} \div \frac{9}{10} = \frac{18}{5} \times \frac{10}{9} = \frac{180}{45} = 4$

9. $21.441 \div 7 = 3.063$

10. $\frac{9}{10} - \frac{1}{2} = \frac{9}{10} - \frac{5}{10} = \frac{4}{10} = \frac{2}{5}$

11. $\frac{2}{3} \times 2\frac{1}{4} = \frac{2}{3} \times \frac{9}{4} = \frac{18}{12} = 1\frac{1}{2}$

12. $7646 + 6799 + 3389 + 6597 = 24{,}431$

13. $\frac{5}{6} + 1\frac{3}{4} = \frac{10}{12} + 1\frac{9}{12} = 1\frac{19}{12} = 2\frac{7}{12}$

14. $22.3 - 1.21 = 21.09 = 21.1$ rounded to nearest tenth

15. $9.05 \times 5.9 = 53.395 = 53$ rounded to two digits

16. $608 \times 970 = 589{,}760$

17. $6567 + 8999 + 6877 + 8789 = 31{,}232$

18. $4987 \times 96 = 478{,}752$

19. $3\frac{1}{3} - 1\frac{3}{4} = 3\frac{4}{12} - 1\frac{9}{12} = 2\frac{16}{12} - 1\frac{9}{12} = 1\frac{7}{12}$

20. 4% of $500 = (.04)($500) = $20

21. $16 \times 10\frac{3}{4} = \frac{16}{1} \times \frac{43}{4} = \frac{688}{4} = 172$

22. $\frac{16}{K} = 8,\ 16 = 8K,\ K = 2$

23. $4.35 \times .32 = 1.3920 = 1.4$ rounded to nearest tenth

24. $2\frac{1}{2}\%$ of $\$50 = (.025)(\$50) = \$1.25$

25. $6267.38 \div 89 = 70.42$

26. $\frac{\$10}{\$400} = \frac{1}{40} = 2\frac{1}{2}\%$

27. $31.96 \div .68 = 47$

28. $\frac{4}{6} = \frac{N}{24},\ 6N = 96,\ N = 16$

29. $6 \div 10 = \frac{6}{10} = \frac{3}{5}$

30. $\frac{3}{10} = \frac{15}{N},\ 3N = 150,\ N = 50$

31. $\frac{3a}{4} = 6,\ 3a = 24,\ a = 8$

32. $\frac{\$40}{\$1600} = \frac{1}{40} = 2\frac{1}{2}\%$

33. $\$25 = 5\%$ of x, $\$25 = .05x$, $x = \frac{\$25}{.05} = \$500$

34. $(-3) \times (6) = -18$

35. $\$160 = 4\%$ of x, $\$160 = .04x$, $x = \frac{\$160}{.04} = \$4000$

36. $\frac{N}{12} = \frac{13}{39} = \frac{1}{3},\ 3N = 12,\ N = 4$

37. $-4 + 2 = -2$

38.   5N = 8N - 12, -3N = -12, N = 4

39. $\dfrac{16}{-8} = -2$

40.   2a - 4 = 14 - a, 3a - 4 = 14, 3a = 18, a = 6

TEST 2

DIRECTIONS: Each question or incomplete statement is followed by several suggested answers or completions. Select the one that BEST answers the question or completes the statement. *PRINT THE LETTER OF THE CORRECT ANSWER IN THE SPACE AT THE RIGHT.*

1. 6 is what part of 9? 1.____
   A. 1/6 B. 1/3 C. 2/3 D. 1 1/2

2. What is 1.48 rounded to tenths? 2.____
   A. 1.4 B. 1.5 C. 1.40 D. 1.50

3. If N times 6 is less than 63, then N may be 3.____
   A. 378 B. 69 C. 9 D. 12

4. What is the smallest common denominator for 1/5, 1/2, and 1/3? 4.____
   A. 2 B. 3 C. 30 D. 10

5. What does CXC mean? 5.____
   A. 210 B. 190 C. 200 D. 201

6. ☐ x 3 = 18. 6.____
   Which numbers, if put into the box, would make the sentence TRUE?
   A. 3 x 3 B. 4 + 5 C. 9 - 2 D. 12 + 2

7. Two-thirds of what number is 8? 7.____
   A. 12 B. 2 2/3 C. 16 D. 24

8. What is 2.0094 rounded to the nearest hundredth? 8.____
   A. 2.009 B. 2.01 C. 2.10 D. 2.010

9. Here are decimal fractions written in four bases. 9.____
   Which would be the LARGEST part of the same pie?
   A. 0.3_{four} B. 0.3_{five} C. 0.3_{six} D. 0.3_{eight}

10. Ten thousand is how many hundreds? 10.____
    A. 1 B. 10 C. 1000 D. 100

11. Interest is found by using the formula 11.____
    A. lwh B. prh C. prt D. hrw

12. What number is 200% of 25? 12.____
    A. 4 B. 40
    C. No such number D. 50

13. What is the value of N in $\frac{25}{75} = \frac{N}{24}$?

    A. 3   B. 49   C. 12   D. 8

14. What is the product of 3 x (-4)?

    A. +12   B. 1/12
    C. -12   D. Can't be multiplied

15. What is the square of (4+2)?

    A. 36   B. 16   C. 8   D. 6

16. 0.26 x 558 is approximately

    A. 140   B. 2300   C. 1400   D. 230

17. $\sqrt{1600}$ is equal to

    A. 4   B. 40   C. 400   D. 4000

18. How many hours pass from 9:45 A.M. to 1:30 P.M.?

    A. $8\frac{1}{4}$ B. $4\frac{1}{4}$ C. $4\frac{3}{4}$ D. $3\frac{3}{4}$

19. Without multiplying, find the difference between 29 x 347 and 28 x 347.

    A. 1   B. 347   C. 29   D. 28

20. What is the dividend if the quotient is 8 and the divisor is 2?

    A. 2   B. 4   C. 16   D. 6

21. 5^3 equals

    A. 15   B. 25   C. 625   D. 125

22. Which fraction is expressed in lowest terms?

    A. $\frac{49}{280}$ B. $\frac{99}{301}$ C. $\frac{475}{1320}$ D. $\frac{998}{1106}$

23. 4 x 253 equals

    A. (4x3) + (4x5) + (4x2)   B. (4x200) + (4x5) + (4x3)
    C. (4x20) + (4x50) + (4x3)   D. (4x250) + (4x3)

24. Which number comes next in this set: 1248?

    A. 16   B. 12   C. 14   D. 10

25. Which of these is the BEST estimate of $0.80 \div 0.04$?

    A. 0.02   B. 0.20   C. 2.0   D. 20

26. By the distributive property of numbers, we know that 246 x z equals   26.____

   A. 2Z + 4Z + 6Z   B. 200Z x 40Z x 6Z
   C. 200Z + 40Z + 6Z   D. 6Z + 4Z + ZZ

27. If (N+4) times 3 is more than 24, you can be sure that N is   27.____

   A. more than 8   B. less than 3
   C. less than 8   D. more than 4

28. There are 2 black balls and 3 white balls in a hat. What are the chances that the first one drawn out will be white?   28.____

   A. 1 in 2   B. 3 in 5   C. 2 in 3   D. 1 in 3

29. If N stands for the same number in each of the following, which will be the smallest?   29.____

   A. $N+\frac{1}{2}$ B. $N+\frac{1}{3}$ C. $N+\frac{2}{3}$ D. $N+\frac{1}{4}$

30. By the commutative property of numbers, we know that   30.____

   A. □ + △ = △ + □   B. □ × △ = △ ÷ □
   C. □ × △ = △ + □   D. □ − △ = △ − □

31. By estimation, choose the example which will have the largest quotient.   31.____

   A. $23\overline{)401}$ B. $46\overline{)800}$ C. $23\overline{)400}$ D. $46\overline{)801}$

32. $16\frac{2}{3}$% of $25 is nearest   32.____

   A. 25¢   B. $4.00   C. $2.50   D. 40¢

33. The volume of a right rectangular prism is found by using the formula   33.____

   A. lw   B. hr^2 C. s^2h D. lwh

34. Which of these is a prime number?   34.____

   A. 109   B. 378   C. 126   D. 417

35. If you know that R + S is less than N, then you know that   35.____

   A. R + 1/2 is greater than N
   B. R + S is greater than 1/2N
   C. 1/2R + 1/2S is less than 1/2N
   D. (1/2R) + S is less than 1/2N

36. Which would tell you that a number is evenly divisible by 9?   36.____

   A. The last two digits.   B. The last three digits
   C. The sum of the digits   D. The number is odd

Questions 37-38.

DIRECTIONS: Questions 37 and 38 are to be answered on the basis of the following sets.

　　Set K: Los Angeles, Yosemite, Mr. Whitney
　　Set L: Chicago, Denver, Los Angeles, Pittsburgh
　　Set M: Mt. McKinley, Pikes Peak, Denver

37. How many elements (different places) are in the union of the three sets, K, L, and M?　　37._____

　　A.　3　　　　B.　8　　　　C.　4　　　　D.　11

38. Which two sets, if any, are disjoint, that is, have no common members?　　38._____

　　A.　M and L　　　　　　　　B.　M and K
　　C.　L and K　　　　　　　　D.　No two sets

39. How many x's are there if counted in a base of eight instead of a base of ten?　　39._____
　　X X X X X X X X X X X X X X X X X X X X X

　　A.　25_{eight}　　B.　21_{eight}　　C.　26_{eight}　　D.　168_{eight}

40. The sum of the digits of a five-place numeral is 24.　　40._____
　　You know the number is evenly divisible (no remainder) by

　　A.　4　　　　B.　3　　　　C.　6　　　　D.　8

KEY (CORRECT ANSWERS)

1.	C	11.	C	21.	D	31.	A
2.	B	12.	D	22.	B	32.	B
3.	C	13.	D	23.	D	33.	D
4.	C	14.	C	24.	A	34.	A
5.	B	15.	A	25.	D	35.	C
6.	D	16.	A	26.	C	36.	C
7.	A	17.	B	27.	D	37.	B
8.	B	18.	D	28.	B	38.	B
9.	A	19.	B	29.	C	39.	A
10.	D	20.	C	30.	A	40.	B

SOLUTIONS TO PROBLEMS

1. $\dfrac{6}{9} = \dfrac{2}{3}$

2. 1.48 = 1.5 rounded to nearest tenth

3. 6N < 63, so N < 10.5; so N may be 9

4. The smallest common denominator for 5, 2, and 3 is 30.

5. CXC = 190

6. $12 \div 2 \times 3 = 18$

7. $\dfrac{2}{3}N = 8,\ N = \dfrac{8}{1} \times \dfrac{3}{2} = 12$

8. 2.0094 = 2.01 rounded to nearest hundredth

9. $.3_{four} = 3 \times 4^{-1} = .75_{ten}$; $.3_{five} = 3 \times 5^{-1} = .6_{ten}$;
   $.3_{six} = 3 \times 6^{-1} = .5_{ten}$; $.3_{eight} = 3 \times 8^{-1} = .375_{ten}$
   Thus, $.3_{four}$ is largest.

10. $10{,}000 \div 100 = 100$

11. I = prt

12. 200% of 25 = (2)(25) = 50

13. $\dfrac{25}{75} = \dfrac{1}{3} = \dfrac{N}{24}$, 3N = 24, N = 8

14. $3 \times (-4) = -12$

15. $(4+2)^2 = 6^2 = 36$

16. $.26 \times 558 = 145.08 \approx 140$

17. $\sqrt{1600} = 40$

18. 9:45 A.M. to 1:30 P.M. = $3\dfrac{3}{4}$ hours

19. $29 \times 347 - 28 \times 347 = 1 \times 347 = 347$

20. $N \div 2 = 8$, so N = 16

21. $5^3 = 5 \times 5 \times 5 = 125$

22. $\dfrac{99}{301}$ is expressed in lowest terms

23. 4 x 253 = (4x250) + (4x3)

24. 1, 2, 4, 8,.... Each number is double its predecessor. Thus, the fifth number = 16

25. $.80 \div .04 = 20$

26. 246 x Z = 200Z + 40Z + 6Z, using the distributive property.

27. (N+4) x 3 > 24, N + 4 > 8, N > 4

28. Probability of drawing a white ball = $\dfrac{3}{2+3}$ = 3 in 5

29. $N \div \dfrac{2}{3}$ is smallest, provided N > 0

30. □ + △ = △ + □ , by the commutative property

31. $401 \div 23$ is the largest of the given selections.

32. $16\dfrac{2}{3}\%$ of $25 = $\dfrac{1}{6}$ x $25 ≈ $4

33. Volume = lwh

34. 109 is a prime number, since its only divisors are 1 and 109

35. If R + S < N, then 1/2 R + 1/2 S < 1/2 N

36. A number is divisible by 9 if the sum of its digits is divisible by 9.

37. The union of sets K, L, M = {Los Angeles, Yosemite, Mt. Whitney, Chicago, Denver, Pittsburgh, Mt. McKinley, Pikes Peak}, which is 8 elements.

38. Sets M and K are disjoint, that is, they have no common elements.

39. $21_{ten} = 25_{eight}$

40. If the sum of the digits is 24, the number must be divisible by 3, since 24 is divisible by 3.

TEST 3

DIRECTIONS: Each question or incomplete statement is followed by several suggested answers or completions. Select the one that BEST answers the question or completes the statement. *PRINT THE LETTER OF THE CORRECT ANSWER IN THE SPACE AT THE RIGHT.*

1. What is the volume in cubic inches of the item shown at the right?
   A. 24
   B. 26
   C. 48
   D. 64
   E. NG

   1.____

2. How much cheaper are a dozen pencils at 49¢ a dozen than a dozen sold at 2 for 9¢?

   A. $4\frac{1}{2}$ ¢   B. 5¢   C. 54¢   D. 58¢   E. NG

   2.____

Questions 3-5.

DIRECTIONS: Questions 3 through 5 are to be answered on the basis of the following chart.

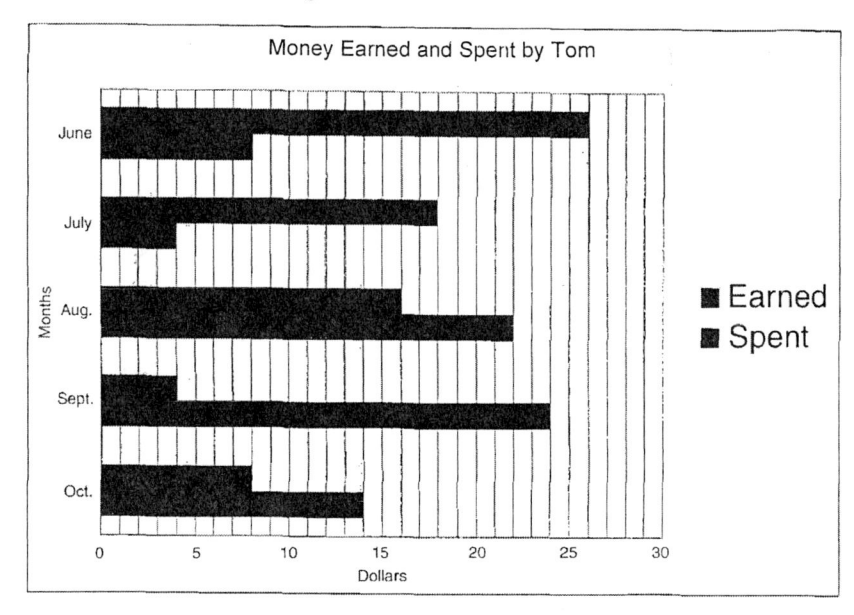

Money Earned and Spent by Tom

3. In which month(s) did Tom spend over twice as much as he earned?

   A. June and July   B. August   C. September
   D. October   E. None

   3.____

4. How did Tom's earnings compare with what he spent during the 5 months shown?

   A. $1 more   B. He broke even
   C. $2 less   D. $3 more
   E. NG

   4.____

5. In which month did Tom save the MOST money? 5.____

   A. June B. July C. August
   D. September E. October

Questions 6-11.

DIRECTIONS: Several Scouts went by bus to a national park. Questions 6 through 11 are some of their problems.

6. If the bus averages 40 miles per hour for 8 hours, how far will it go in that time? 6.____
   _____ miles.

   A. 5   B. 32   C. 48   D. 320   E. NG

7. At the camp store some candy bars are 3 for 25¢. What would 24 cost at that rate? 7.____

   A. $3.00   B. $4.00   C. $6.00   D. $8.00   E. NG

8. We are scheduled to be home at 6:15 P.M. 8.____
   If the trip home takes 7 1/2 hours, when should we start?
   _____ A.M.

   A. 1:45   B. 8:30   C. 9:45   D. 10:45   E. NG

9. At the park, Bill counted 60 trailers. He estimated that this was 1/3 of the total. 9.____
   If so, what was the TOTAL number of trailers?

   A. 180   B. 30   C. 60   D. 20   E. NG

10. Jerry is drawing a map of the park to send home. A 6-inch line will equal 40 miles of the park. 10.____
    His scale will be

    A. 1 in. = 10 mi.   B. $1\frac{1}{2}$ in = $6\frac{2}{3}$ mi.

    C. $1\frac{1}{2}$ in = 10 mi.   D. 2 in. = 15 mi.

    E. NG

11. How will the Scouts determine equal shares of the cost? 11.____

    A. Total cost x number of people
    B. Total cost + the average
    C. Number of people x average
    D. Total cost + number of shares

Questions 12-13.

DIRECTIONS: Questions 12 and 13 are to be answered on the basis of the following graph.

DAVID'S DAY (TOTAL 24 HOURS)

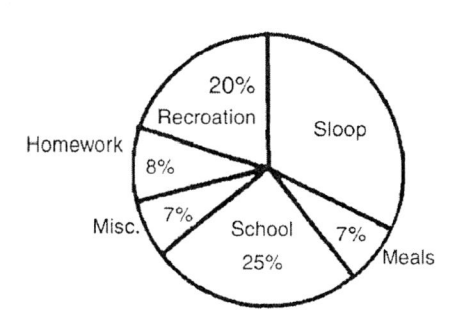

12. What percent of David's day is spent in sleep? 12.____
    A. 33   B. 23   C. 8   D. 37   E. NG

13. How many hours does David spend a day in school? 13.____
    A. 6   B. 7   C. 8   D. 25   E. NG

Questions 14-16.

DIRECTIONS: Questions 14 through 16 are to be answered on the basis of the following chart.

BOXES OF COOKIES SOLD

BOXES OF COOKIES SOLD

Ruth	🍪 🍪 🍪 🍪
Betty	🍪 🍪
Nancy	🍪 🍪 🍪 🍪 🍪 🍪
Sue	🍪 🍪 🍪 🍪 🍪
Mary	🍪 🍪 🍪

Each 🍪 equals 5 boxes

14. Who sold 3 times as many boxes as Betty sold? 14.____
    A. Nancy   B. Ruth   C. Mary   D. Sue   E. No one

15. Sue sold how many more boxes than Ruth sold? 15.____
    A. 1   B. 2   C. 6   D. 15   E. NG

16. How many boxes did Betty sell? 16.____
    A. 2   B. 20   C. 11   D. 10   E. NG

Questions 17-19.

DIRECTIONS: Marvin's mother and father both work downtown. Questions 17 through 19 are some of their problems.

17. Marvin's mother and father have one car but are considering buying another for $2,000. Father figures that it will cost $50.00 a month to run each car.
How much will it cost to buy the second car and to use it for a year?

    A. $2050   B. $2600   C. $2500   D. $3200   E. NG

17.____

18. The total cost for a babysitter is $7.00 a day for a 5-day week. Mother's take-home pay is $3740 for 48 weeks' work.
How much is left of her yearly pay after she pays the babysitter for 48 weeks?

    A. $1480   B. $1680   C. $2060   D. $2140   E. NG

18.____

19. Father and Mother together earn $12,000 a year. To find how much Father earns a month, you would

    A. divide sum of both salaries by 2; then divide by 12
    B. subtract Mother's salary from sum of both salaries; multiply by 12
    C. divide 12 by sum of both salaries; then subtract Mother's salary
    D. subtract Mother's salary from sum of both; then divide by 12
    E. do none of the above

19.____

20. What is the circumference of the circle shown in the figure at the right?

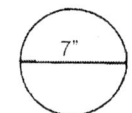

Use $\pi = 3\frac{1}{7}$

    A. 11 in.
    B. 21 in.
    C. 22 in.
    D. 154 in.
    E. NG

20.____

Questions 21-23.

DIRECTIONS: Questions 21 through 23 are to be answered on the basis of the following chart.

Number of Problems Worked and Time Spent

Pupil	Time	Problems
Larry	1'15"	25
Meg	45"	15
Joe	40"	10
Sue	1'30"	30
Bill	50"	25

21. What was the average number of problems worked?   21.____

    A. 15   B. 21   C. 19   D. 25   E. NG

22. What was the median length of time spent?   22.____

    A. 40"   B. 50"   C. 60"   D. 15"   E. NG

23. Who is the fastest worker per problem?   23.____

    A. Meg   B. Sue   C. Joe   D. Bill   E. NG

Questions 24-26.

DIRECTIONS: Jack is planting a hedge 30 feet long. Questions 24 through 26 are some of his problems.

24. He can put 30 small plants, costing 15¢ each, 12 inches apart. Or, he can put large plants, costing 40¢ each, 18 inches apart.   24.____
How much more will it cost to buy the large plants?

    A. No more   B. $3.50   C. $4.50   D. $8.00   E. NG

25. Hedge clippers cost $30.00. They can be rented for $1.50 a day. Jack would need them for 4 days each year.   25.____
How many years will it take for the rent to equal the cost?

    A. 4 1/2   B. 5   C. 6   D. 7 1/2   E. NG

26. Jack waters the hedge every day for 15 days, every other day for the next 30 years, and twice a week for the following 16 weeks. Each watering costs about 5¢.   26.____
How much does it cost to water it during this time?

    A. $3.10   B. $3.05   C. $1.90   D. $4.50   E. NG

27. How long is the diagonal line shown in the figure at the right?   27.____
    A. 8 1/2'
    B. 14'
    C. 15'
    D. 17'
    E. NG

28. How tall is a flagpole that makes a shadow of 20 feet when a yardstick makes a shadow of 1 foot 6 inches?   28.____

    A. 20 ft.   B. 40 ft.   C. 21 ft. 6 in.
    D. 60 ft.   E. NG

29. The figure shown at the right was once a regular prism, but some of the blocks have been taken away. How many are left?
    A. 23
    B. 24
    C. 32
    D. 36
    E. NG

30. A mixture formula reads, *Use 1/2 oz. per pint of water.*
    A pound will make how many gallons?
    A. 1   B. 2   C. 4   D. 8   E. NG

31. If all of x is part of y, and part of y is all of z, you know that
    A. all of x is z
    B. y is all of x and all of z
    C. some of x is z
    D. none of z is part of x
    E. x must equal 2 of y

32. How many different triangles are there in the figure shown at the right? Some of them overlap.
    A. 4
    B. 5
    C. 6
    D. 7
    E. NG

33. The amount of $1.00 at 4% interest compounded annually for 5 years is $1.2167. What would be the amount for $50.00 at 4% for 5 years?
    A. $52.00   B. $60.00   C. $60.20   D. $60.84   E. $68.35

34. A house that cost $20,000 is rented for $150 a month. Taxes, depreciation, and other costs amount to $600 for a year.
    What percent does the investment net for the year?
    A. 6   B. 4 1/2   C. 5   D. 4   E. NG

35. Jim tossed a coin 7 times. It came up heads twice.
    What are the chances that the next toss will be heads?
    A. 1 in 2   B. 5 in 8   C. 3 in 7   D. 1 in 8   E. NG

KEY (CORRECT ANSWERS)

1. C	11. D	21. B	31. B
2. B	12. A	22. B	32. D
3. C	13. A	23. D	33. D
4. B	14. A	24. B	34. E
5. A	15. E	25. B	35. A
6. D	16. D	26. A	
7. E	17. B	27. E	
8. D	18. C	28. B	
9. A	19. D	29. D	
10. C	20. C	30. C	

SOLUTIONS TO PROBLEMS

1. Volume = (2")(3")(8") = 48 cu.in.

2. Difference in price = (.09)(12/2) -.49 = .05

3. In September, he spent $24 but only earned $4.

4. Total earnings = $26 + $18 + $16 + $4 + $8 = $72, whereas total spending = $8 + $4 + $22 + $24 + $14 = $72. He broke even.

5. In June, Tom saved $26 - $8 = $18, which was highest.

6. (40)(8) = 320 miles

7. (.25)(24/3) = $2.00

8. 6:15 P.M. - 7 1/2 hrs. = 10:45 A.M.

9. $60 \div \frac{1}{3}$ = 180 trailers

10. $\frac{40}{6} = 1$ in for $6\frac{2}{3}$ mi. $= 1\frac{1}{2}$ in. for 10 mi.

11. Total cost ÷ number of shares = cost per share

12. Sleep = 100% - 20% - 8% - 7% - 25% - 7% = 33%

13. Hours in school = (.25)(24) = 6

14. Nancy sold 30 boxes, which is 3 times as many as Betty sold.

15. Sue sold 25 boxes, which is 5 more than Ruth sold.

16. Betty sold 10 boxes.

17. $2000 + (12)($50) = $2600

18. $3740 - ($35)(48) = $2060

19. To find Father's monthly earnings, subtract Mother's salary from the sum of both, then divide by 12.

20. Circumference = $(\pi)(7") \approx (3\frac{1}{7})(7") = 22$ in

21. (25+15+10+30+25)/5 = 105÷5 = 21

22. Median = 3rd value from lowest to highest = 50 sec.
    (Times are 40", 45", 50", 1'15", 1'30")

23. Rates per problem are as follows:
    Larry: 75 sec/25 = 3 sec; Meg: 45 sec/15 = 3 sec.
    Joe: 40 sec/10 = 4 sec; Sue: 90 sec/30 = 3 sec.
    Bill: 50 sec/25 = 2 sec; so, Bill is fastest.

24. $30 \div 1.5 = 20$ Then, $(20)(.40) - (30)(.15) = \$3.50$

25. $(\$1.50)(4) = \$6.00$ rental cost per year. Then $\$30 \div \$6 = 5$ years.

26. Total cost = $(.05)(15) + (.05)(15) + (.05)(32) = \$3.10$

27. Diagonal = $\sqrt{5^2 + 12^2} = \sqrt{169} = 13$ ft.

28. Let x = height of flagpole. $\dfrac{3}{1\frac{1}{2}} = \dfrac{x}{20}$, $1\frac{1}{2}x = 60$, x = 40 ft.

29. 1st layer: 15 blocks; 2nd layer: 10 blocks; 3rd layer: 8 blocks; 4th layer: 3 blocks. Total = 36 blocks.

30. 1 lb. $\div \dfrac{1}{2}$ oz = 32. Then, 32 pints = $\dfrac{32}{8} = 4$ gallons.

31. There are 3 possible diagrams:

32. 1 large triangle, 4 separate smaller triangles, 2 "half" triangles. Total of 7 triangles. There are ACE, BCD, ABD, ADF, FDE, ACD, ADE.

33. $(50)(\$1.2167) = \$60.835 \approx 60.84$

34. $(\$150)(12) = \$1800$. Then, $\dfrac{\$1800}{\$20,600} \approx 8.7\%$

35. Regardless of the results of previous tosses, the probability that the next toss is heads = 1/2 = 1 in 2.

NUMBER SERIES

DIRECTIONS: The numbers in each series below proceed according to some rule. For each series you are to find the *next number*. *PRINT THE LETTER OF THE CORRECT ANSWER IN THE SPACE AT THE RIGHT.*

PRACTICE PROBLEMS

In the first series below, each number is 2 larger than the preceding number. The *next number* in the series would be 14. Of the five answers below, answer E, therefore, is correct.

1. 2 4 6 8 10 12
    A. 1   B. 11   C. 12   D. 13   E. 14   1.____

2. 20 19 18 17 16 15
    A. 10   B. 12   C. 14   D. 15   E. 16   2.____

3. 10 8 1 9 12 10
    A. 9   B. 10   C. 11   D. 12   E. 13   3.____

4. 8 11 14 17 20 23
    A. 10   B. 13   C. 23   D. 25   E. 26   4.____

5. 27 27 23 23 19 19
    A. 15   B. 16   C. 17   D. 18   E. 19   5.____

6. 16 17 19 20 22 23
    A. 18   B. 20   C. 22   D. 24   E. 25   6.____

KEY (CORRECT ANSWERS)

1. E
2. C
3. E
4. E
5. A
6. E

EXAMINATION SECTION
TEST 1

DIRECTIONS: The numbers in each series below proceed according to some rule. For each series you are to find the *next number*. PRINT THE LETTER OF THE CORRECT ANSWER IN THE SPACE AT THE RIGHT.

1. 3 5 7 9 11 13 15
   A. 11   B. 13   C. 15   D. 17   E. 19   1.____

2. 17 20 23 26 29 32 35
   A. 37   B. 38   C. 39   D. 40   E. 41   2.____

3. 2 4 8 16 32 64 128
   A. 129   B. 160   C. 192   D. 256   E. 512   3.____

4. 8 11 9 12 10 13 11
   A. 7   B. 9   C. 12   D. 14   E. 15   4.____

5. 2 2 3 3 5 5 8
   A. 5   B. 8   C. 9   D. 10   E. 11   5.____

6. 10 11 10 9 10 11 10
   A. 8   B. 9   C. 10   D. 12   E. 13   6.____

7. 17 19 16 18 15 17 14
   A. 11   B. 12   C. 13   D. 15   E. 16   7.____

8. 22 20 23 21 24 22 25
   A. 21   B. 23   C. 25   D. 27   E. 28   8.____

9. 5 9 10 14 15 19 20
   A. 21   B. 24   C. 25   D. 26   E. 30   9.____

10. 3 6 8 16 18 36 38
    A. 40   B. 48   C. 68   D. 76   E. 80   10.____

11. 3 2 4 3 6 5 10
    A. 4   B. 9   C. 10   D. 12   E. 20   11.____

12. 8 24 12 36 18 54 27
    A. 3   B. 9   C. 12   D. 54   E. 81   12.____

13. 8 9 12 13 16 17 20
    A. 19   B. 20   C. 21   D. 22   E. 23   13.____

14. 70 68 34 32 16 14 7
    A. 0   B. 1   C. 3   D. 4   E. 5   14.____

2 (#1)

15. 0 1 3 6 10 15 21
    A. 23   B. 25   C. 28   D. 29   E. 30   15.____

16. 14 15 13 16 12 17 11
    A. 5   B. 13   C. 18   D. 22   E. 23   16.____

17. 18 20 17 21 16 22 15
    A. 8   B. 17   C. 21   D. 23   E. 30   17.____

18. 4 7 6 6 9 8 8
    A. 5   B. 7   C. 8   D. 10   E. 11   18.____

19. 0 1 10 2 20 3 30
    A. 1   B. 2   C. 3   D. 4   E. 40   19.____

20. 14 16 19 13 15 18 12
    A. 6   B. 10   C. 14   D. 15   E. 18   20.____

21. 20 25 30 36 42 49 56
    A. 59   B. 60   C. 62   D. 63   E. 64   21.____

22. 50 43 37 31 26 21 17
    A. 12   B. 13   C. 14   D. 15   E. 16   22.____

23. 20 16 8 24 20 10 30
    A. 15   B. 23   C. 26   D. 28   E. 90   23.____

24. 0 1 3 4 5 7 8
    A. 6   B. 7   C. 8   D. 9   E. 10   24.____

25. 4 6 3 7 9 6 10
    A. 5   B. 7   C. 12   D. 14   E. 15   25.____

26. 54 45 37 30 24 19 15
    A. 12   B. 13   C. 14   D. 16   E. 17   26.____

27. 32 16 19 20 10 13 14
    A. 7   B. 14   C. 15   D. 17   E. 28   27.____

28. 45 54 18 27 9 18 6
    A. 2   B. 8   C. 9   D. 12   E. 15   28.____

29. 11 14 18 22 27 32 38
    A. 40   B. 43   C. 44   D. 45   E. 46   29.____

30. 89 78 87 76 67 56 65
    A. 45   B. 54   C. 56   D. 74   E. 76   30.____

KEY (CORRECT ANSWERS)

1.	D	11.	B	21.	E
2.	B	12.	E	22.	B
3.	D	13.	C	23.	C
4.	D	14.	E	24.	D
5.	B	15.	C	25.	C
6.	B	16.	C	26.	A
7.	E	17.	D	27.	A
8.	B	18.	E	28.	E
9.	B	19.	D	29.	C
10.	D	20.	C	30.	B

TEST 2

DIRECTIONS: The numbers in each series below proceed according to some rule. For each series you are to find the *next number*. PRINT THE LETTER OF THE CORRECT ANSWER IN THE SPACE AT THE RIGHT.

1. 14 18 22 26 30 34 38
   A. 39   B. 40   C. 41   D. 42   E. 43   1._____

2. 8 8 8 7 7 7 6
   A. 5   B. 6   C. 7   D. 8   E. 9   2._____

3. 1 2 3 4 1 2 3
   A. 0   B. 2   C. 3   D. 4   E. 5   3._____

4. 6 9 7 10 8 11 9
   A. 7   B. 10   C. 12   D. 13   E. 14   4._____

5. 21 20 22 20 23 20 24
   A. 16   B. 20   C. 24   D. 28   E. 29   5._____

6. 10 12 16 18 22 24 28
   A. 30   B. 32   C. 34   D. 36   E. 38   6._____

7. 8 6 4 12 10 8 16
   A. 6   B. 10   C. 12   D. 14   E. 16   7._____

8. 90 82 74 66 58 50 42
   A. 32   B. 34   C. 36   D. 38   E. 40   8._____

9. 15 15 13 10 10 8 5
   A. 2   B. 3   C. 4   D. 5   E. 6   9._____

10. 6 7 5 8 9 7 10
    A. 8   B. 9   C. 10   D. 11   E. 13   10._____

11. 5 7 14 16 32 34 68
    A. 70   B. 72   C. 74   D. 76   E. 78   11._____

12. 72 36 40 20 24 12 16
    A. 4   B. 8   C. 12   D. 16   E. 20   12._____

13. 3 4 6 9 13 18 24
    A. 29   B. 30   C. 31   D. 32   E. 33   13._____

14. 5 10 7 14 11 22 19
    A. 16   B. 20   C. 24   D. 32   E. 38   14._____

15. 76 38 36 18 16 8 6
    A. 1   B. 2   C. 3   D. 4   E. 5

16. 9 10 8 24 6 7 5
    A. 3   B. 6   C. 15   D. 16   E. 20

17. 17 14 7 21 18 9 27
    A. 15   B. 21   C. 24   D. 45   E. 81

18. 14 16 13 17 12 18 11
    A. 15   B. 16   C. 17   D. 18   E. 19

19. 1 2 5 11 12 15 21
    A. 22   B. 24   C. 25   D. 27   E. 30

20. 3 6 5 5 8 7 7
    A. 6   B. 7   C. 10   D. 13   E. 14

21. 8 10 12 10 12 14 12
    A. 10   B. 12   C. 14   D. 16   E. 18

22. 2 3 5 5 10 11 13
    A. 13   B. 15   C. 16   D. 26   E. 28

23. 44 40 42 14 10 12 4
    A. 0   B. 2   C. 6   D. 7   E. 10

24. 24 27 9 18 21 7 14
    A. 11   B. 17   C. 22   D. 28   E. 33

25. 81 27 54 18 36 12 24
    A. 4   B. 8   C. 21   D. 24   E. 48

26. 7 9 12 8 3 9 16
    A. 8   B. 9   C. 19   D. 23   E. 24

27. 22 16 11 7 4 2 1
    A. 1   B. 2   C. 4   D. 7   E. 11

28. 6 42 7 12 48 16 18
    A. 6   B. 18   C. 20   D. 23   E. 24

29. 95 92 46 42 21 16 8
    A. 2   B. 4   C. 6   D. 8   E. 10

30. 8 6 12 14 7 5 10
    A. 5   B. 6   C. 12   D. 15   E. 20

15.____
16.____
17.____
18.____
19.____
20.____
21.____
22.____
23.____
24.____
25.____
26.____
27.____
28.____
29.____
30.____

KEY (CORRECT ANSWERS)

1.	D	11.	A	21.	C
2.	B	12.	B	22.	A
3.	D	13.	C	23.	A
4.	C	14.	E	24.	B
5.	B	15.	C	25.	B
6.	A	16.	C	26.	A
7.	D	17.	C	27.	A
8.	B	18.	E	28.	B
9.	D	19.	A	29.	A
10.	D	20.	C	30.	C

TEST 3

DIRECTIONS: The numbers in each series below proceed according to some rule. For each series you are to find the *next number*. PRINT THE LETTER OF THE CORRECT ANSWER IN THE SPACE AT THE RIGHT.

1. 9 12 15 18 21 24 27
   A. 30   B. 31   C. 32   D. 33   E. 36   1.____

2. 2 3 9 10 30 31 93
   A. 89   B. 91   C. 92   D. 93   E. 94   2.____

3. 82 73 64 55 46 37 28
   A. 14   B. 18   C. 19   D. 20   E. 27   3.____

4. 18 21 17 20 16 19 15
   A. 11   B. 13   C. 16   D. 18   E. 19   4.____

5. 20 18 21 17 22 16 23
   A. 9   B. 12   C. 15   D. 21   E. 24   5.____

6. 24 48 12 24 6 12 3
   A. 6   B. 12   C. 18   D. 24   E. 48   6.____

7. 16 18 21 14 16 19 12
   A. 5   B. 8   C. 9   D. 13   E. 14   7.____

8. 4 4 0 5 5 1 6
   A. 2   B. 4   C. 6   D. 8   E. 11   8.____

9. 3 8 5 10 7 12 9
   A. 6   B. 12   C. 14   D. 17   E. 18   9.____

10. 4 5 6 7 5 6 7
    A. 3   B. 6   C. 7   D. 8   E. 9   10.____

11. 60 64 32 36 18 22 11
    A. 0   B. 5   C. 7   D. 10   E. 15   11.____

12. 2 6 3 9 6 18 15
    A. 12   B. 20   C. 30   D. 45   E. 50   12.____

13. 8 9 12 13 15 16 19
    A. 17   B. 20   C. 21   D. 23   E. 24   13.____

14. 1 2 4 7 11 16 22
    A. 24   B. 25   C. 26   D. 27   E. 29   14.____

15. 2 5 6 5 8 9 8
    A. 4   B. 7   C. 9   D. 11   E. 12

16. 28 27 25 22 18 13 7
    A. 0   B. 5   C. 7   D. 8   E. 9

17. 5 3 4 6 4 5 7
    A. 4   B. 5   C. 6   D. 8   E. 9

18. 1 2 4 8 10 20 22
    A. 24   B. 40   C. 44   D. 46   E. 48

19. 4 8 9 18 22 23 46
    A. 48   B. 50   C. 69   D. 70   E. 90

20. 12 15 19 23 28 33 39
    A. 41   B. 43   C. 44   D. 45   E. 46

21. 88 90 45 48 16 20 5
    A. 1   B. 8   C. 9   D. 10   E. 25

22. 10 14 16 19 23 25 28
    A. 30   B. 31   C. 32   D. 33   E. 34

23. 16 61 15 51 14 41 13
    A. 12   B. 13   C. 14   D. 21   E. 31

24. 22 15 21 16 20 17 19
    A. 13   B. 13   C. 16   D. 18   E. 21

25. 22 20 10 12 6 4 2
    A. 2   B. 4   C. 6   D. 8   E. 10

26. 45 36 28 21 15 10 6
    A. 2   B. 3   C. 4   D. 12   E. 16

27. 41 37 38 19 15 16 8
    A. 1   B. 2   C. 3   D. 4   E. 5

28. 21 18 9 27 24 12 36
    A. 12   B. 18   C. 33   D. 42   E. 72

29. 84 21 63 65 64 16 48
    A. 13   B. 16   C. 24   D. 47   E. 50

30. 5 10 13 9 18 21 17
    A. 13   B. 20   C. 27   D. 30   E. 34

15.____
16.____
17.____
18.____
19.____
20.____
21.____
22.____
23.____
24.____
25.____
26.____
27.____
28.____
29.____
30.____

KEY (CORRECT ANSWERS)

1.	A	11.	E	21.	D
2.	E	12.	D	22.	C
3.	C	13.	B	23.	E
4.	D	14.	E	24.	D
5.	C	15.	D	25.	B
6.	A	16.	A	26.	B
7.	E	17.	B	27.	D
8.	C	18.	C	28.	C
9.	C	19.	B	29.	E
10.	D	20.	D	30.	E

TEST 4

DIRECTIONS: The numbers in each series below proceed according to some rule. For each series you are to find the *next number*. PRINT THE LETTER OF THE CORRECT ANSWER IN THE SPACE AT THE RIGHT.

1. 9 13 17 21 25 29 33
   A. 34   B. 35   C. 37   D. 40   E. 41   1.____

2. 7 8 7 6 7 8 7
   A. 5   B. 6   C. 7   D. 9   E. 10   2.____

3. 19 22 18 21 17 20 16
   A. 12   B. 17   C. 19   D. 20   E. 21   3.____

4. 4 4 5 5 7 7 10
   A. 10   B. 11   C. 12   D. 13   E. 14   4.____

5. 18 20 23 16 18 21 14
   A. 6   B. 7   C. 13   D. 16   E. 19   5.____

6. 1 2 4 8 16 32 64
   A. 63   B. 66   C. 68   D. 106   E. 128   6.____

7. 56 28 32 16 20 10 14
   A. 2   B. 7   C. 10   D. 16   E. 18   7.____

8. 21 19 22 18 23 17 24
   A. 14   B. 16   C. 17   D. 31   E. 32   8.____

9. 17 17 15 12 12 10 7
   A. 7   B. 8   C. 9   D. 10   E. 11   9.____

10. 4 3 6 5 10 9 18
   A. 8   B. 9   C. 17   D. 19   E. 36   10.____

11. 78 76 38 36 18 16 8
   A. 3   B. 4   C. 5   D. 6   E. 7   11.____

12. 4 8 6 12 10 20 18
   A. 16   B. 34   C. 36   D. 68   E. 72   12.____

13. 11 2 12 3 13 4 14
   A. 4   B. 5   C. 6   D. 15   E. 16   13.____

14. 14 11 15 16 13 17 18
   A. 15   B. 19   C. 22   D. 23   E. 36   14.____

2 (#4)

15. 5 6 7 8 6 7 8
    A. 4   B. 7   C. 8   D. 9   E. 10

16. 50 42 35 29 24 20 17
    A. 11   B. 12   C. 13   D. 14   E. 15

17. 12 6 8 16 14 7 9
    A. 7   B. 11   C. 12   D. 18   E. 36

18. 3 6 7 6 9 10 9
    A. 5   B. 8   C. 10   D. 12   E. 13

19. 9 10 13 14 16 17 20
    A. 21   B. 22   C. 24   D. 25   E. 26

20. 98 87 76 65 54 43 32
    A. 21   B. 23   C. 31   D. 32   E. 34

21. 6 8 10 8 10 12 10
    A. 8   B. 10   C. 12   D. 14   E. 16

22. 1 5 11 19 29 41 55
    A. 58   B. 63   C. 67   D. 39   E. 71

23. 0 1 2 3 6 7 14
    A. 7   B. 12   C. 14   D. 15   E. 28

24. 37 31 26 21 17 13 10
    A. 5   B. 6   C. 7   D. 8   E. 9

25. 20 2 12 60 6 16 80
    A. 2   B. 4   C. 6   D. 8   E. 100

26. 1 7 10 40 8 14 17
    A. 12   B. 16   C. 20   D. 68   E. 71

27. 25 27 30 15 5 7 10
    A. 5   B. 11   C. 13   D. 20   E. 30

28. 9 5 10 13 9 18 21
    A. 17   B. 24   C. 42   D. 45   E. 63

29. 6 12 24 16 32 64 56
    A. 28   B. 48   C. 56   D. 64   E. 112

30. 4 3 6 3 12 7 42
    A. 21   B. 35   C. 36   D. 40   E. 84

15.____
16.____
17.____
18.____
19.____
20.____
21.____
22.____
23.____
24.____
25.____
26.____
27.____
28.____
29.____
30.____

KEY (CORRECT ANSWERS)

1.	C	11.	D	21.	C
2.	B	12.	C	22.	E
3.	C	13.	B	23.	D
4.	A	14.	A	24.	C
5.	D	15.	D	25.	D
6.	E	16.	E	26.	D
7.	B	17.	D	27.	A
8.	B	18.	D	28.	A
9.	A	19.	A	29.	E
10.	C	20.	A	30.	B

TEST 5

DIRECTIONS: The numbers in each series below proceed according to some rule. For each series you are to find the *next number*. PRINT THE LETTER OF THE CORRECT ANSWER IN THE SPACE AT THE RIGHT.

1. 13 17 21 25 29 33 37
    A. 38   B. 39   C. 41   D. 44   E. 45   1._____

2. 8 12 11 15 14 18 17
    A. 16   B. 18   C. 20   D. 21.   E. 24   2._____

3. 6 7 6 5 6 7 6
    A. 5   B. 6   C. 7   D. 8   E. 9   3._____

4. 13 14 16 19 23 28 34
    A. 36   B. 38   C. 40   D. 41   E. 42   4._____

5. 18 9 10 5 6 3 4
    A. 1   B. 2   C. 3   D. 4   E. 5   5._____

6. 19 21 18 22 17 23 16
    A. 12   B. 24   C. 26   D. 28   E. 30   6._____

7. 56 28 32 16 20 10 14
    A. 7   B. 14   C. 15   D. 17   E. 18   7._____

8. 10 6 24 28 7 3 12
    A. 3   B. 6   C. 16   D. 24   E. 48   8._____

9. 9 12 8 10 13 9 11
    A. 10   B. 11   C. 14   D. 16   E. 17   9._____

10. 4 7 6 6 9 8 8
    A. 5   B. 7   C. 8   D. 10   E. 11   10._____

11. 31 24 18 13 9 6 4
    A. 0   B. 1   C. 2   D. 3   E. 4   11._____

12. 82 73 64 55 46 37 28
    A. 14   B. 18   C. 19   D. 20   E. 27   12._____

13. 6 4 8 5 15 11 44
    A. 39   B. 40   C. 41   D. 49   E. 55   13._____

14. 12 3 13 4 14 5 15
    A. 5   B. 6   C. 7   D. 16   E. 17   14._____

2 (#5)

15. 20 25 30 36 42 49 56
    A. 59   B. 60   C. 62   D. 63   E. 64   15.____

16. 32 8 16 4 8 2 4
    A. 0   B. 1   C. 2   D. 6   E. 8   16.____

17. 16 16 8 24 6 30 5
    A. 30   B. 34   C. 35   D. 36   E. 40   17.____

18. 2 5 10 17 26 37 50
    A. 59   B. 61   C. 63   D. 64   E. 65   18.____

19. 24 26 13 16 8 12 6
    A. 3   B. 5   C. 10   D. 11   E. 12   19.____

20. 97 98 49 52 13 18 3
    A. 0   B. 1   C. 6   D. 7   E. 10   20.____

21. 5 3 9 7 21 19 57
    A. 55   B. 59   C. 63   D. 114   E. 171   21.____

22. 25 36 49 64 81 100 121
    A. 132   B. 144   C. 156   D. 169   E. 256   22.____

23. 52 40 30 22 16 12 10
    A. 4   B. 6   C. 8   D. 9   E. 10   23.____

24. 1 6 30 120 360 720 720
    A. 0   B. 120   C. 360   D. 720   E. 1440   24.____

25. 15 22 11 18 9 16 8
    A. 1   B. 4   C. 8   D. 15   E. 16   25.____

26. 24 27 9 18 21 7 14
    A. 11   B. 17   C. 22   D. 28   E. 33   26.____

27. 4 5 7 7 14 15 17
    A. 17   B. 18   C. 19   D. 24   E. 34   27.____

28. 65 60 30 26 13 10 5
    A. 0   B. 1   C. 2   D. 3   E. 4   28.____

29. 3 6 12 6 12 24 18
    A. 12   B. 18   C. 24   D. 30   E. 36   29.____

30. 9 3 6 18 15 5 8
    A. 5   B. 11   C. 24   D. 32   E. 40   30.____

KEY (CORRECT ANSWERS)

1.	C	11.	D	21.	A
2.	D	12.	C	22.	B
3.	A	13.	A	23.	E
4.	D	14.	B	24.	A
5.	B	15.	E	25.	D
6.	B	16.	B	26.	B
7.	A	17.	C	27.	A
8.	C	18.	E	28.	D
9.	C	19.	D	29.	E
10.	E	20.	E	30.	C

ABSTRACT REASONING
EXAMINATION SECTION
COMMENTARY

Since intelligence exists in many forms or phases and the theory of differential aptitudes is now firmly established in testing, other manifestations and measurements of intelligence than verbal or purely arithmetical must be identified and measured.

Classification inventory, or figure classification, involves the aptitude of form perception, i.e., the ability to perceive pertinent detail in objects or in pictorial or graphic material. It involves making visual comparisons and discriminations and discerning slight differences in shapes and shading figures and widths and lengths of lines.

Leading examples of presentation are the figure analogy and the figure classification. The Section that follows presents progressive and varied samplings of this type of question.

SAMPLE QUESTIONS

DIRECTIONS: In each of these sample questions, look at the symbols in the first two boxes. Something about the three symbols in the first box makes them alike; something about the two symbols in the other box with the question mark makes them alike. Look for some characteristic that is common to all symbols in the same box, yet makes them different from the symbols in the other box. Among the five answer choices, find the symbol that can BEST be substituted for the question mark, because it is *like* the symbols in the second box, and, *for the same reason*, different from those in the first box.

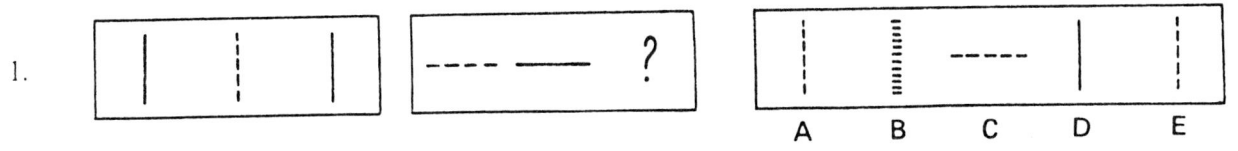

1.

In sample question 1, all the symbols in the first box are vertical lines. The second box has two lines, one broken and one solid. Their *likeness* to each other consists in their being horizontal; and their being horizontal makes them *different* from the vertical lines in the other box. The answer must be the only one of the five lettered choices that is a horizontal line, either broken or solid. Therefore, the CORRECT answer is C.

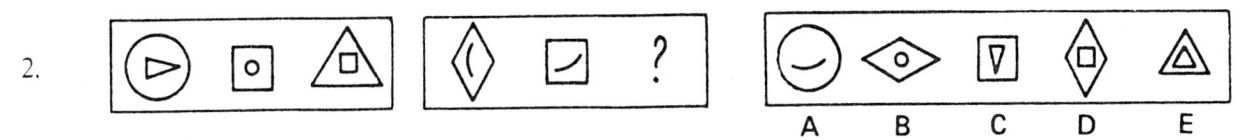

2.

The CORRECT answer is A.

EXAMINATION SECTION

DIRECTIONS FOR THIS SECTION: In each of these questions, look at the symbols in the first two boxes. Something about the three symbols in the first box makes them alike; something about the two symbols in the other box with the question mark makes them alike. Look for some characteristic that is common to all symbols in the same box, yet makes them different from the symbols in the other box. Among the five answer choices, find the symbol that can BEST be substituted for the question mark, because it is *like* the symbols in the second box, and, *for the same reason*, different from those in the first box.

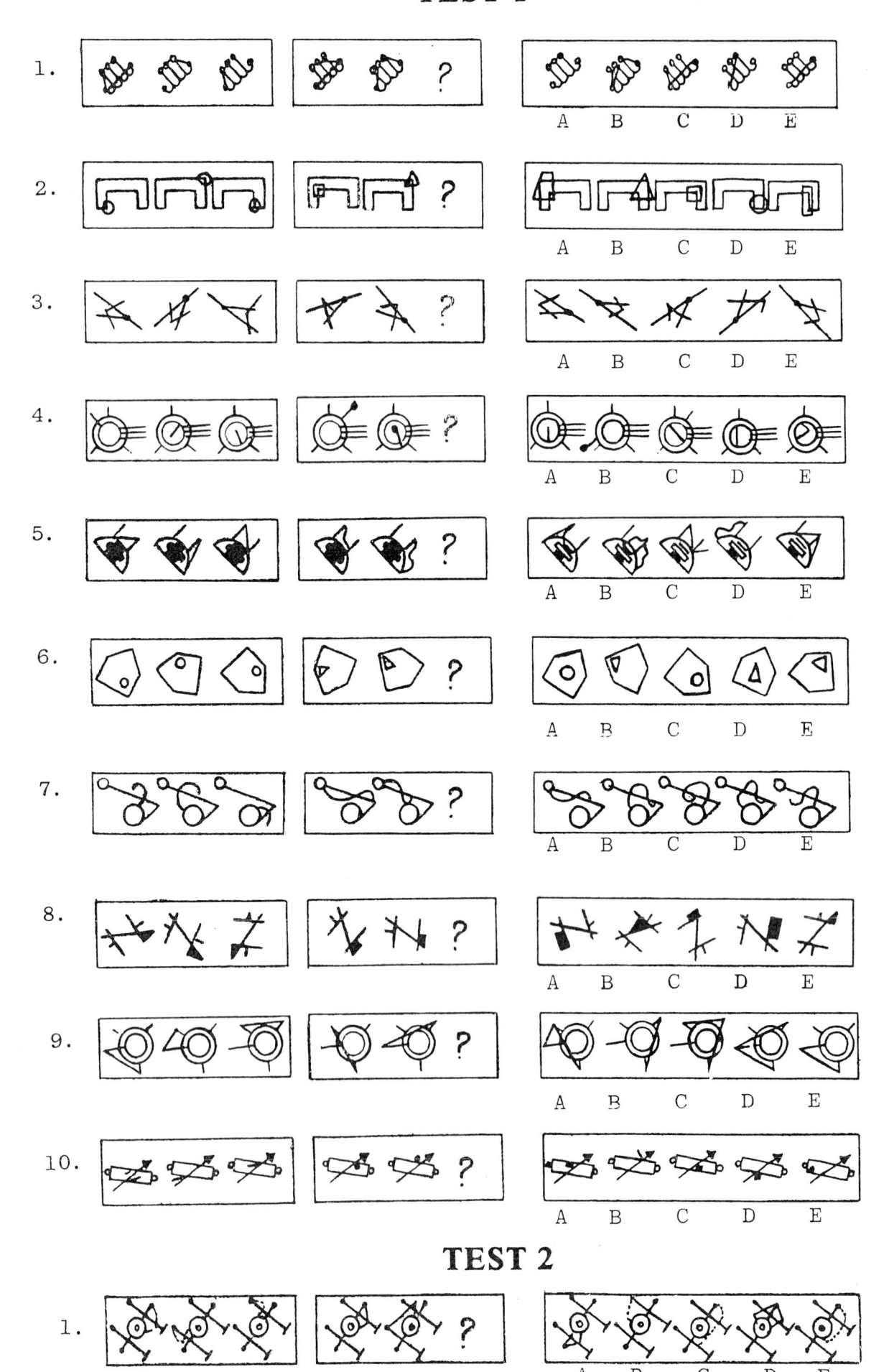

TEST 1

1.
2.
3.
4.
5.
6.
7.
8.
9.
10.

TEST 2

1.

TEST 2/3

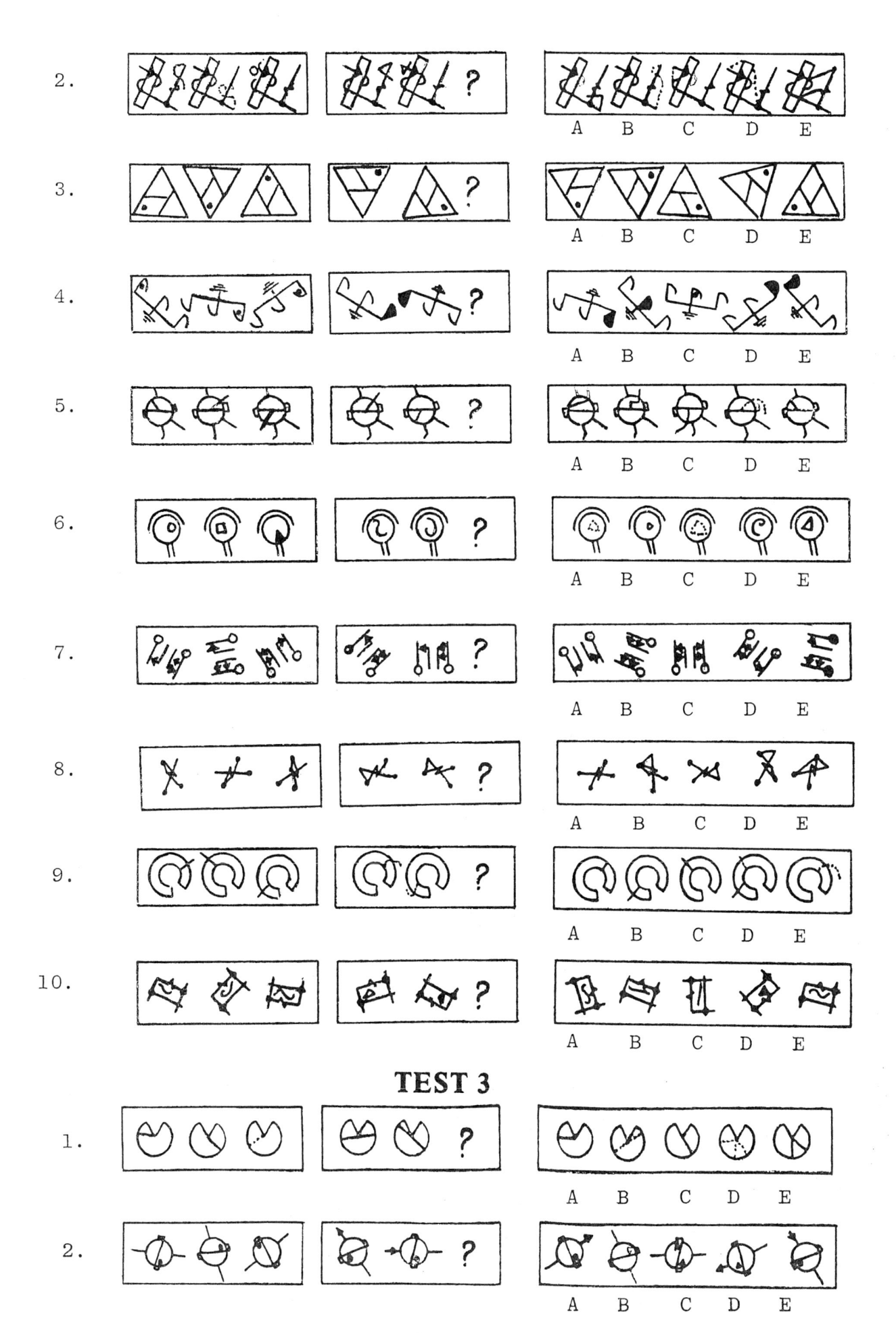

TEST 3

TEST 3/KEYS

3.
4.
5.
6.
7.
8.
9.
10.

KEY (CORRECT ANSWERS)

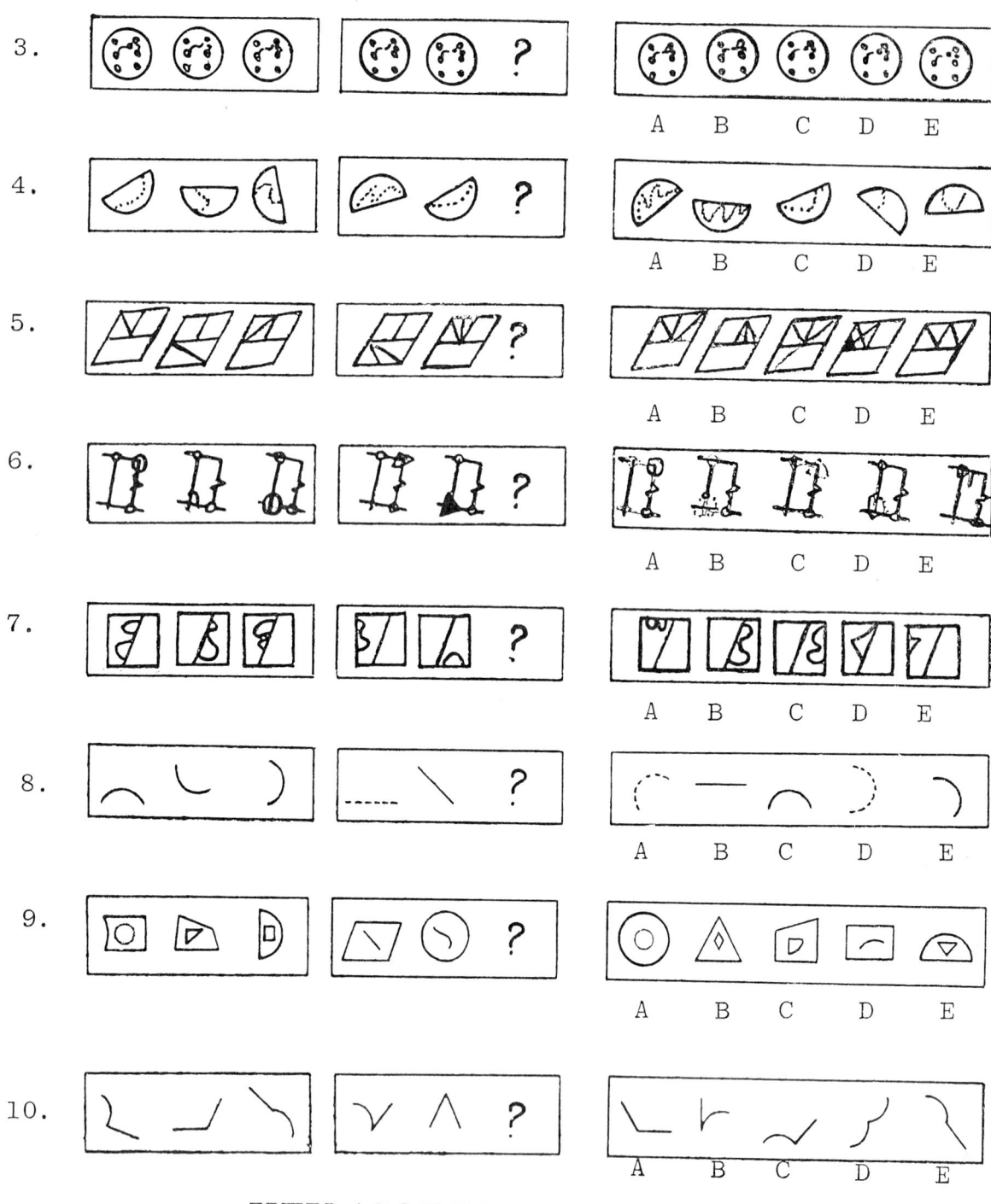

TEST 1	TEST 2	TEST 3
1. B	1. A	1. B
2. C	2. A	2. E
3. C	3. A	3. C
4. B	4. D	4. A
5. D	5. E	5. B
6. B	6. D	6. C
7. A	7. D	7. C
8. C	8. C	8. B
9. B	9. E	9. D
10. D	10. D	10. B

GLOSSARY OF ELECTRONIC TERMS

TABLE OF CONTENTS

Page

Acorn Tube ... Bias	1
Biasing Resistor ... Coefficient of Coupling (K)	2
Condenser ... Dielectric	3
Dielectric Constant ... Electrostatic Field	4
Equivalent Circuit ... Henry (h)	5
Helmholts Coil ... Klystron	6
Lag ... Neutralisation	7
Node ... Plate Resistance (r_p)	8
Positive Feedback ... Relaxation Oscillator	9
Reluctance ... Solenoid	10
Space Charge ... Unbalanced Line	11
Unidirectional ... Z	12

ELECTRONICS SYMBOLS	
Amplifier ... Cell, Photosensitive	13
Circuit Breaker ... Discontinuity	14
Electron Tube ... Inductor	15
Key, Telegraph ... Meter, Instrument	16
Mode Transducer ... Semiconductor Device	17
Squib ... Transformer	18
Vibrator, Interrupter ... Visual Signaling Device	19
TRANSISTOR SYMBOLS	19
TUBE SYMBOLS	20

GLOSSARY OF ELECTRONIC TERMS

Acorn tube. An acorn-shaped vacuum tube designed for ultra-high-frequency circuits. The tube has short electron transit time and low inter-electrode capacitance because of close spacing and small size electrodes.

Align. To adjust the tuned circuits of a receiver or transmitter for maximum signal response.

Alternation. One-half of a complete cycle.

Ammeter. An instrument for measuring the electron flow in amperes.

Ampere (amp). The basic unit of current or electron flow.

Amplification (A). The process of increasing the strength of a signal.

Amplification factor (ft). The ratio of a small change in plate voltage to a small change in grid voltage, with all other electrode voltages constant, required to produce the same small change in plate current.

Amplifier. A device used to increase the signal voltage, current, or power, generally composed of a vacuum tube and associated circuit called a stage. It may contain several stages in order to obtain a desired gain.

Amplitude. The maximum instantaneous value of an alternating voltage or current, measured in either the positive or negative direction.

Amplitude distortion. The changing of a waveshape so that it is no longer proportional to its original form. Also known as harmonic distortion.

Anode. A positive electrode; the plate of a vacuum tube.

Antenna. A device used to radiate or absorb r-f energy.

Aquadag. A graphite coating on the inside of certain cathode-ray tubes for collecting secondary electrons emitted by the screen.

Array (antenna). An arrangement of antenna elements, usually di-poles, which results in desirable directional characteristics.

Attenuation. The reduction in the strength of a signal.

Audio frequency (a-f). A frequency which can be detected as a sound by the human ear. The range of audio frequencies extends approximately from 20 to 20,000 cycles per second.

Autodyne circuit. A circuit in which the same elements and vacuum tube are used as an oscillator and as a detector. The output has a frequency equal to the difference between the frequencies of the received signal and the oscillator signal.

Automatic gain control (age) A method of automatically regulating the gain of a receiver so that the output tends to remain constant though the incoming signal may vary in strength.

Automatic volume control (avc). See Automatic gain control.

Autotransformer. A transformer in which part of the primary winding is used as a secondary winding, or vice versa.

Azimuth. The angular measurement in a horizontal plane and in a clockwise direction, beginning at a point oriented to north.

Ballast resistance. A self-regulating resistance, usually connected in the primary circuit of a power transformer to compensate for variations in the line voltage.

Ballast tube. A tube which contains a ballast resistance.

Band of frequencies. The frequencies existing between two definite limits.

Band-pass filter. A circuit designed to pass with nearly equal response all currents having frequencies within a definite band, and to reduce substantially the amplitudes of currents of all frequencies outside that band.

Bazooka. See Line-balance converter.

Beam-power tube. A high vacuum tube in which the electron stream is directed in concentrated beams from the cathode to the plate. Variously termed beam-power tetrode and beam-power pentode.

Beat frequency. A frequency resulting from the combination of two different frequencies. It is numerically equal to the difference between or the sum of these two frequencies.

Beat note. See Beat frequency.

Bias. The average d-c voltage maintained between the cathode and control grid of a vacuum tube.

Biasing resistor. A resistor used to provide the voltage drop for a required bias.

Blanking. See Gating.

Bleeder. A resistance connected in parallel with a power-supply output to protect equipment from excessive voltages if the load is removed or substantially reduced; to improve the voltage regulation, and to drain the charge remaining in the filter capacitors when the unit is turned off.

Blocking capacitor. A capacitor used to block the flow of direct current while permitting the flow of alternating current.

Break-down voltage. The voltage at which an insulator or dielectric ruptures, or at which ionization and conduction take place in a gas or vapor.

Brilliance modulation. See Intensity modulation.

Buffer amplifier. An amplifier used to isolate the output of an oscillator from the effects produced by changes in voltage or loading in following circuits.

Buncher. The electrode of a velocity-modulated tube which alters the velocity of electrons in the constant current beam causing the electrons to become bunched in a drift space beyond the buncher electrode.

Bypass capacitor. A capacitor used to provide an alternating current path of comparatively low impedance around a circuit element.

Capacitance. The property of two or more bodies which enables them to store electrical energy in an electrostatic field between the bodies.

Capacitive coupling. A method of transferring energy from one circuit to another by means of a capacitor that is common to both circuits.

Capacitive reactance (X_c). The opposition offered to the flow of an alternating current by capacitance, expressed in ohms.

Capacitor. Two electrodes or sets of electrodes in the form of plates, separated from each other by an insulating material called the dielectric.

Carrier. The r-f component of a transmitted wave upon which an audio signal or other form of intelligence can be impressed.

Catcher. The electrode of a velocity-modulated tube which receives energy from the bunched electrons.

Cathode (K). The electrode in a vacuum tube which is the source of electron emission. Also a negative electrode.

Cathode bias. The method of biasing a tube by placing the biasing resistor in the common cathode return circuit, making the cathode more positive, rather than the grid more negative, with respect to ground.

Cathode follower. A vacuum-tube circuit in which the input signal is applied between the control grid and ground, and the output is taken from the cathode and ground. A cathode follower has a high input impedance and a low output impedance.

Characteristic impedance (Z_0). The ratio of the voltage to the current at every point along a transmission line on which there are no standing waves.

Choke. A coil which impedes the flow of alternating current of a specified frequency range because of its high inductive reactance at that range.

Chopping. See Limiting.

Clamping circuit. A circuit which maintains either amplitude extreme of a waveform at a certain level of potential.

Class A operation. Operation of a vacuum tube so that plate current flows throughout the entire operating cycle and distortion is kept to a minimum.

Class AB operation. Operation of a vacuum tube with grid bias so that the operating point is approximately halfway between Class A and Class B.

Class B operation. Operation of a vacuum tube with bias at or near cut-off so that plate current flows during approximately one-half cycle.

Class C operation. Operation of a vacuum tube with bias considerably beyond cut-off so that plate current flows for less than one-half cycle.

Clipping. See Limiting.

Coaxial cable. A transmission line consisting of two conductors concentric with and insulated from each other.

Coefficient of coupling (K). A numerical indication of the degree of coupling existing between two circuits, expressed in terms of either a decimal or a percentage.

Condenser. See Capacitor.

Conductance (G). The ability of a material to conduct or carry an electric current. It is the reciprocal of the resistance of the material, and is expressed in *ohms*.

Continuous waves. Radio waves which maintain a constant amplitude and a constant frequency.

Control grid (G). The electrode of a vacuum tube other than a diode upon which the signal voltage is impressed in order to control the plate current.

Control-grid-plate transconductance. See Transconductance.

Conversion transconductance (gc). A characteristic associated with the mixer function of vacuum tubes, and used in the same manner as transconductance is used. It is the ratio of the i-f current in the primary of the first i-f transformer to the r-f signal voltage producing it.

Converter. See Mixer.

Converter tube. A multielement vacuum tube used both as a mixer and as an oscillator in a superheterodyne receiver. It creates a local frequency and combines it with an incoming signal to produce an intermediate frequency.

Counting circuit. A circuit which receives uniform pulses representing units to be counted and produces a voltage in proportion to their frequency.

Coupled impedance. The effect produced in the primary winding of a transformer by the influence of the current flowing in the secondary winding.

Coupling. The association of two circuits in such a way that energy may be transferred from one to the other.

Coupling element. The means by which energy is transferred from one circuit to another; the common impedance necessary for coupling.

Critical coupling. The degree of coupling which provides the maximum transfer of energy between two resonant circuits at the resonant frequency.

Crystal (Xtal). (1) A natural substance, such as quartz or tourmaline, which is capable of producing a voltage stress when under pressure, or producing pressure when under an applied voltage. Under stress it has the property of responding only to a given frequency when cut to a given thickness.

(2) A nonlinear element such as gelena or silicon, in which case the piezo-electric characteristic is not exhibited.

Crystal mixer. A device which employs the nonlinear characteristic of a crystal (nonpiezo-electric type) and a point contact to mix two frequencies.

Crystal oscillator. An oscillator circuit in which a piezoelectric crystal is used to control the frequency and to reduce frequency instability to a minimum.

Current (J). Flow of electrons; measured in amperes.

Cut-off (c.o.). The minimum value of negative grid bias which prevents the flow of plate current in a vacuum tube.

Cut-off limiting. Limiting the maximum output voltage of a vacuum-tube circuit by driving the grid beyond cut-off.

Cycle. One complete positive and one complete negative alternation of a current or voltage.

Damped waves. Waves which decrease exponentially in amplitude.

Decoupling network. A network of capacitors and chokes, or resistors, placed in leads which are common to two or more circuits to prevent unwanted interstage coupling.

Deflection sensitivity (CRT). The quotient of the displacement of the electron beam at the place of impact by the change in the deflecting field. It is usually expressed in millimeters per volt applied between the deflection electrodes, or in millimeters per gauss of the deflecting magnetic field.

Degeneration. The process whereby a part of the output signal of an amplifying device is returned to its input circuit in such a manner that it tends to cancel the input.

De-ionization potential. The potential at which ionization of the gas within a gas-filled tube ceases and conduction stops.

Demodulation. See Detection.

Detection. The process of separating the modulation component from the received signal.

Dielectric. An insulator; a term applied to the

insulating material between the plates of a capacitor.

Dielectric constant. The ratio of the capacitance of a capacitor with a dielectric between the electrodes to the capacitance with air between the electrodes.

Differentiating circuit. A circuit which produces an output voltage substantially in proportion to the rate of change of the input voltage.

Diode. A two-electrode vacuum tube containing a cathode and a plate.

Diode detector. A detector circuit employing a diode tube.

Dipole antenna. Two metallic elements, each approximately one quarter wavelength long, which radiate r-f energy fed to them by the transmission line.

Directly heated cathode. A filament cathode which carries its own heating current for electron emission, as distinguished from an indirectly heated cathode.

Director (antenna). A parasitic antenna placed in front of a radiating element so that r-f radiation is aided in the forward direction.

Distortion. The production of an output waveform which is not a true reproduction of the input waveform. Distortion may consist of irregularities in amplitude, frequency, or phase.

Distributed capacitance. The capacitance that exists between the turns in a coil or choke, or between adjacent conductors or circuits, as dis- tinguished from the capacitance which is concentrated in a capacitor.

Distributed inductance. The inductance that exists along the entire length of a conductor, as distinguished from the self-inductance which is concentrated in a coil.

Doorknob tube. A doorknob-shaped vacuum tube designed for ultra-high-frequency circuits. This tube has short electron transit time and low interelectrode capacitance, because of the close spacing and small size of electrodes.

Dropping resistor. A resistor used to decrease a given voltage to a lower value.

Dry electrolytic capacitor. An electrolytic capacitor using a paste instead of a liquid electrolyte. *See* Electrolytic capacitor.

Dynamic characteristics. The relation between the instantaneous plate voltage and plate current of a vacuum tube as the voltage applied to the grid is moved; thus, the characteristics of a vacuum tube during operation.

Dynatron. A negative resistance device; particularly, a tetrode operating on that portion of its i_p vs. e_p characteristic where secondary emission exists to such an extent that an increase in plate voltage actually causes a decrease in plate current, and, therefore, makes the circuit behave like a negative resistance.

Eccles-Jordan circuit (trigger circuit). A direct coupled multivibrator circuit possessing two conditions of stable equilibrium. Also known as a flip-flop circuit.

Effective value. The equivalent heating value of an alternating current or voltage, as compared to a direct current or voltage. It is 0.707 times the peak value of a sine wave. It is also called the rms value.

Efficiency. The ratio of output to input power, generally expressed as a percentage.

Electric field. A space in which an electric charge will experience a force exerted upon it.

Electrode. A terminal at which electricity passes from one medium into another.

Electrolyte. A water solution of a substance which is capable of conducting electricity. An electrolyte may be in the form of either a liquid or a paste.

Electrolytic capacitor. A capacitor employing a metallic plate and an electrolyte as the second plate separated by a dielectric which is produced by electrochemical action.

Electromagnetic field. A space field in which electric and magnetic vectors at right angles to each other travel in a direction at right angles to both.

Electron. The negatively charged particles of matter. The smallest particle of matter.

Electron emission. The liberation of electrons from a bo]difference.

Electronic switch. A circuit which causes a start-and-stop action or a switching action by electronic means.

Electronic voltmeter. *See* Vacuum tube voltmeter.

Electrostatic field. The field of influence

between two charged bodies.

Equivalent circuit. A diagrammatic arrangement of coils, resistors, and capacitors, representing the effects of a more complicated circuit in order to permit easier analysis.

Farad (f). The unit of capacitance.

Feedback. A transfer of energy from the output circuit of a device back to its input.

Field. The space containing electric or magnetic lines of force.

Field intensity. Electrical strength of a field.

Filament. See Directly heated cathode.

Filter. A combination of circuit elements designed to pass a definite range of frequencies, attenuating all others.

Firing potential. The controlled potential at which conduction through a gas-filled tube begins.

First detector. See Mixer.

Fixed bias. A bias voltage of constant value, such as one obtained from a battery, power supply, or generator.

Fixed capacitor. A capacitor which has no provision for varying its capacitance.

Fixed resistor. A resistor which has no provision for varying its resistance.

Fluorescence. The property of emitting light as the immediate result of electronic bombardment.

Fly-back. The portion of the time base during which the spot is returning to the starting point. This is usually not seen on the screen of the cathode-ray tube, because of gating action or the rapidity with which it occurs.

Free electrons. Electrons which are loosely held and consequently tend to move at random among the atoms of the material.

Free oscillations. Oscillatory currents which continue to flow in a tuned circuit after the impressed voltage has been removed. Their frequency is the resonant frequency of the tuned circuit.

Frequency (f). The number of complete cycles per second existing in any form of wave motion; such as the number of cycles per second of an alternating current.

Frequency distortion. Distortion which occurs as a result of failure to amplify or attenuate equally all frequencies present in a complex wave.

Frequency modulation. See Modulation.

Frequency stability. The ability of an oscillator to maintain its operation at a constant frequency.

Full-wave rectifier circuit. A circuit which utilizes both the positive and the negative alternations of an alternating current to produce a direct current.

Gain (A). The ratio of the output power, voltage, or current to the input power, voltage, or current, respectively.

Gas tube. A tube filled with gas at low pressure in order to obtain certain desirable characteristics.

Gating (cathode-ray tube). Applying a rectangular voltage to the grid or cathode of a cathode-ray tube to sensitize it during the sweep time only.

Grid current. Current which flows between the cathode and the grid whenever the grid becomes positive with respect to the cathode.

Grid detection. Detection by rectification in the grid circuit of a detector.

Grid leak. A high resistance connected across the grid capacitor or between the grid and the cathode to provide a d-c path from grid to cathode and to limit the accumulation of charge on the grid.

Grid limiting. Limiting the positive grid voltage (minimum output voltage) of vacuum-tube circuit by means of a large series grid resistor.

Ground. A metallic connection with the earth to establish ground potential. Also, a common return to a point of zero r-f potential, such as the chassis of a receiver or a transmitter.

Half-wave rectification. The process of rectifying an alternating current wherein only one-half of the input cycle is passed and the other half is blocked by the action of the rectifier, thus producing pulsating direct current.

Hard tube. A high vacuum electronic tube.

Harmonic. An integral multiple of a fundamental frequency. (The second harmonic is twice the frequency of the fundamental or first harmonic.)

Harmonic distortion. Amplitude distortion.

Heater. The tube element used to indirectly heat a cathode.

Henry (h). The basic unit of inductance.

Helmholts coil. A variometer having horizontal and vertical balanced coil windings, used to vary the angle of phase difference between any two similar waveforms of the same frequency.

Heterodyne. To beat or mix two signals of different frequencies.

High-frequency resistance. The resistance presented to the flow of high-frequency current. *See* Skin effect.

Horn radiator. Any open-ended metallic device for concentrating energy from a waveguide and directing this energy into space.

Hysteresis. A lagging of the magnetic flux in a magnetic material behind the magnetizing force which is producing it.

Image frequency. An undesired signal capable of beating with the local oscillator signal of a superheterodyne receiver which produces a difference frequency within the bandwidth of the i-f channel.

Impedance (Z). The total opposition offered to the flow of an alternating current. It may consist of any combination of resistance, inductive reactance, and capacitive reactance.

Impedance coil. *See* Choke.

Impedance coupling. The use of a tuned circuit or an impedance coil as the common coupling element between two circuits.

Impulse. Any force acting over a comparatively short period of time, such as a momentary rise in voltage.

Indirectly heated cathode. A cathode which is brought to the temperature necessary for electron emission by a separate heater element. Compare *Directly heated cathode.*

Inductance (L). The property of a circuit which tends to oppose a change in the existing current.

Induction. The act or process of producing voltage by the relative motion of a magnetic field across a conductor.

Inductive reactance (X_1). The opposition to the flow of alternating or pulsating current caused by the inductance of a circuit. It is measured in ohms.

Inductor. A circuit element designed so that its inductance is its most important electrical property; a coil.

Infinite. Extending indefinitely; having innumerable parts, capable of endless division within itself.

In phase. Applied to the condition that exists when two waves of the same frequency pass through their maximum and minimum values of like polarity at the same instant.

Instantaneous value. The magnitude at any particular instant when a value is continually varying with respect to time.

Integrating circuit. A circuit which produces an output voltage substantially in proportion to the frequency and amplitude of the input voltage.

Intensify. To increase the brilliance of an image on the screen of a cathode-ray tube.

Intensity modulation. The control of the brilliance of the trace on the screen of a cathode-ray tube in conformity with the signal.

Interelectrode capacitance. The capacitance existing between the electrodes in a vacuum tube.

Intermediate frequency (i-f). The fixed frequency to which r-f carrier waves are converted in a superheterodyne receiver.

Inverse peak voltage. The highest instantaneous negative potential which the plate can acquire with respect to the cathode without danger of injuring the tube.

Ion. An elementary particle of matter or a small group of such particles having a net positive or negative charge.

Ionization. Process by which ions are produced in solids, liquids, or gases.

Ionization potential. The lowest potential at which ionization takes place within a gas-filled tube.

Ionosphere. A region composed of highly ionized layers of atmosphere from 70 to 250 miles above the surface of the earth.

Kilo (k). A prefix meaning 1,000.

Kilocycle (kc). One thousand cycles; conversationally used to indicate 1,000 cycles per second.

Klystron. A tube in which oscillations are generated by the bunching of electrons (that is, velocity modulation). This tube utilizes the transit time between two given electrodes to deliver pulsating energy to a cavity resonator in order to sustain oscillations within the cavity.

Lag. The amount one wave is behind another in time; expressed in electrical degrees.

Lead The opposite of *lag.* Also, a wire or connection.

Leakage. The electrical loss due to poor insulation.

Lecher line. A section of open-wire transmission line used for measurements of standing waves.

Limiting. Removal by electronic means of one or both extremities of a waveform at a predetermined level.

Linear. Having an output which varies in direct proportion to the input.

Line-balance converter. A device used at the end of a coaxial line to isolate the outer conductor from ground.

Load. The impedance to which energy is being supplied.

Local oscillator. The oscillator used in a superheterodyne receiver the output of which is mixed with the desired r-f carrier to form the intermediate frequency.

Loose coupling. Less than critical coupling; coupling providing little transfer of energy.

Magnetic circuit. The complete path of magnetic lines of force.

Magnetic field (H). The space in which a magnetic force exists.

Magnetron. A vacuum-tube oscillator containing two electrodes, in which the flow of electrons from cathode to anode is controlled by an externally applied magnetic field.

Matched impedance. The condition which exists when two coupled circuits are so adjusted that their impedances are equal.

Meg (mega) (m). A prefix meaning one million.

Megacycle (M_c). One million cycles. Used conversationally to mean 1,000,000 cycles per second.

Metallic insulator. A shorted quarter-wave section of a transmission line which acts as an electrical insulator at a frequency corresponding to its quarter-wave length.

Mho. The unit of conductance.

Micro (μ). A prefix meaning one-millionth.

Microsecond (μs). One-millionth of a second.

Milli (m). A prefix meaning one-thousandth.

Milliampera (ma). One-thousandth of an ampere.

Mixer. A vacuum tube or crystal and suitable circuit used to combine the incoming and local-oscillator frequencies to produce an intermediate frequency. *See* Beat frequency.

Modulation. The process of varying the amplitude (amplitude modulation), the frequency (frequency modulation), or the phase (phase modulation) of a carrier wave in accordance with other signals in order to convey intelligence. The modulating signal may be an audiofrequency signal, video signal (as in television), or electrical pulses or tones to operate relays, etc.

Modulator. The circuit which provides the signal that varies the ampli- tude, frequency, or phase of the oscillations generated in the transmitter tube.

Multielectrode tube. A vacuum tube containing more than three electrodes associated with a single electron stream.

Multiunit tube. A vacuum tube containing within one envelope two or more groups of electrodes, each associated with separate electron streams.

Multivibrator. A type of relaxation oscillator for the generation of nonsinusoidal waves in which the output of each of its two tubes is coupled to the input of the other to sustain oscillations.

Mutual conductance (g_m). *See* Transconductance.

Mutual inductance. A circuit property existing when the relative position of two inductors causes the magnetic lines of force from one to link with the turns of the other.

Negative feedback. *See* Degeneration.

Neon bulb. A glass bulb containing two electrodes in neon gas at low pressure.

Network. Any electrical circuit containing two or more interconnected elements.

Neutralisation. The process of nullifying the voltage fed back through the interelectrode capacitance of an amplifier tube, by providing an equal voltage of opposite phase; generally necessary only with triode tubes.

Node. A zero point; specifically, a current node is a point of zero current and a voltage node is a point of zero voltage.

Noninductive capacitor. A capacitor in which the inductive effects at high frequencies are reduced to the minimum.

Noninductive circuit. A circuit in which inductance is reduced to a minimum or negligible value.

Nonlinear. Having an output which does not vary in direct proportion to the input.

Ohm (ω). The unit of electrical resistance.

Open circuit. A circuit which does not provide a complete path for the flow of current.

Optimum coupling. See Critical coupling.

Oscillator. A circuit capable of converting direct current into alternating current of a frequency determined by the constants of the circuit. It generally uses a vacuum tube.

Oscillatory circuit. A circuit in which oscillations can be generated or sustained.

Oscillograph. See Oscilloscope.

Oscilloscope. An instrument for showing, visually, graphical representations of the waveforms encountered in electrical circuits.

Overdriven amplifier. An amplifier designed to distort the input signal waveform by a combination of cut-off limiting and saturation limiting.

Overload. A load greater than the rated load of an electrical device.

Parallel feed. Application of a d-c voltage to the plate or grid of a tube in parallel with an a-c circuit so that the d-c and a-c components flow in separate paths. Also called shunt feed.

Parallel-resonant circuit. A resonant circuit in which the applied voltage is connected across a parallel circuit formed by a capacitor and an inductor.

Paraphase amplifier. An amplifier which converts a single input into a push-pull output.

Parasitic suppressor. A resistor in a vacuum-tube circuit to prevent un-wanted oscillations.

Peaking circuit. A type of circuit which converts an input to a peaked output waveform.

Peak plate current. The maximum instantaneous plate current passing through a tube.

Peak value. The maximum instantaneous value of a varying current, voltage, or power. It is equal to 1.414 times the effective value of a sine wave.

Pentode. A five-electrode vacuum tube containing a cathode, control, grid, screen grid, suppressor grid, and plate.

Phase difference. The time in electrical degrees by which one wave leads or lags another.

Phase inversion. A phase difference of 180 between two similar waveshapes of the same frequency.

Phase-splitting circuit. A circuit which produces from the same input waveform two output waveforms which differ in phase from each other.

Phosphorescence. The property of emitting light for some time after excitation by electronic bombardment.

Piezoelectric effect. The effect of producing a voltage by placing a stress, either by compression, by expansion, or by twisting, on a crystal, and, conversely, the effect of producing a stress in a crystal by applying a voltage to it.

Plate (P). The principal electrode in a tube to which the electron stream is attracted. See Anode.

Plate circuit. The complete electrical circuit connecting the cathode and plate of a vacuum tube.

Plate current (i_p). The current flowing in the plate circuit of a vacuum tube.

Plate detection. The operation of a vacuum-tube detector at or near cutoff so that the input signal is rectified in the plate circuit.

Plate dissipation. The power in watts consumed at the plate in the form of heat.

Plate efficiency. The ratio of the a-c power output from a tube to the average d-c power supplied to the plate circuit.

Plate impedance. See Plate resistance.

Plate-load impedance (R_L or Z_L). The impedance in the plate circuit across which the output signal voltage is developed by the alternating component of the plate current.

Plate modulation. Amplitude modulation of a class-C r-f amplifier by varying the plate voltage in accordance with the signal.

Plate resistance (r_p). The internal resistance to

the flow of alternating current between the cathode and plate of tube. It is equal to a small change in plate voltage divided by the corresponding change in plate current, and is expressed in ohms. It is also called a-c resistance, internal impedance, plate impedance, and dynamic plate impedance. The static plate resistance, or resistance to the flow of *direct current* is a different value. It is denoted by R_p.

Positive feedback. See Regeneration.

Potentiometer. A variable voltage divider; a resistor which has a variable contact arm so that any portion of the potential applied between its ends may be selected.

Power. The rate of doing work or the rate of expending energy. The unit of electrical power is the watt.

Power amplification. The process of amlifying a signal to produce a gain in power, as distinguished from voltage amplification. The gain in the ratio of the alternating power output to the alternating power input of an amplifier.

Power factor. The ratio of the actual power of an alternating or pulsating current, as measured by a wattmeter, to the apparent power, as indicated by ammeter and voltmeter readings. The power factor if an inductor, capacitor, or insulator is an expression of the losses.

Power tube. A vacuum tube designed to handle a greater amount of power than the ordinary voltage-amplifying tube.

Primary circuit. The first, in electrical order, of two or more coupled circuits, in which a change in current induces a voltage in the other or secondary circuits; such as the primary winding of a transformer.

Propagation. See Wave propagation.

Pulsating current. A unidirectional current which increases and decreases in magnitude.

Push-pull circuit. A push-pull circuit usually refers to an amplifier circuit using two vacuum tubes in such a fashion that when one vacuum tube is operating on a positive alternation, the other vacuum tube operates on a negative alternation.

Q. The figure of merit of efficiency of a circuit or coil. Numerically it is equal to the inductive reactance divided by the resistance of the circuit or coil.

Radiate. To send out energy, such as r-f waves, into space.

Radiation resistance. A fictitious resistance which may be considered to dissipate the energy radiated from the antenna.

Radio frequency (r-f). Any frequency of electrical energy capable of propagation into space. Radio frequencies normally are much higher than sound-wave frequencies.

Radio-frequency amplification. The amplification of a radio wave by a receiver before detection, or by a transmitter before radiation.

Radio-frequency choke (RFC). An air-core or powdered iron core coil used to impede the flow of r-f currents.

Radio-frequency component. See Carrier.

Ratio. The value obtained by dividing one number by another, indicating their relative proportions.

Reactance (X). The opposition offered to the flow of an alternating current by the inductance, capacitance, or both, in any circuit.

Reciprocal. The value obtained by dividing the number 1 by any quantity.

Rectifier. A device used to change alternating current to unidirectional current.

Reflected impedance. See Coupled impedance.

Reflection. The turning back of a radio wave caused by reradiation from any conducting surface which is large in comparison to the wavelength of the radio wave.

Reflector. A metallic object placed behind a radiating antenna to prevent r-f radiation in an undesired direction and to reinforce radiation in a desired direction.

Regeneration. The process of returning a part of the output signal of an amplifier to its input circuit in such a manner that it reinforces the grid excitation and thereby increases the total amplification.

Regulation (voltage). The ratio of the change in voltage due to a load to the open-circuit voltage, expressed in per cent.

Relaxation oscillator. A circuit for the generation of nonsinusoidal waves by gradually storing and quickly releasing energy either in the electric field of a capacitor or in the magnetic field of an inductor.

Reluctance. The opposition to magnetic flux.

Resistance (R). The opposition to the flow of current caused by the nature and physical dimensions of a conductor.

Resistor. A circuit element whose chief characteristic is resistance; used to oppose the flow of current.

Resonance. The condition existing in a circuit in which the inductive and capacitive reactances cancel.

Resonance curve. A graphical representation of the manner in which a resonant circuit responds to various frequencies at and near the resonant frequency.

Rheostat. A variable resistor.

Ripple voltage. The fluctuations in the output voltage of a rectifier, filter, or generator.

rms. Abbreviation of root mean square. *See* Effective value.

Saturation. The condition existing in any circuit when an increase in the driving signal produces no further change in the resultant effect.

Saturation limiting. Limiting the minimum output voltage of a vacuum-tube circuit by operating the tube in the region of plate-current saturation (not to be confused with emission saturation).

Saturation point. The point beyond which an increase in either grid voltage, plate voltage, or both produces no increase in the existing plate current.

Screen dissipation. The power dissipated in the form of heat on the screen grid as the result of bombardment by the electron stream.

Screen grid (S_c). An electrode placed between the control grid and the plate of a vacuum tube to reduce interelectrode capacitance.

Secondary. The output coil of a transformer. *See* Primary circuit.

Secondary emission. The emission of electrons knocked loose from the plate, grid, or fluorescent screen of a vacuum tube by the impact or bombardment of electrons arriving from the cathode.

Selectivity. The degree to which a receiver is capable of discriminating between signals of different carrier frequencies.

Self-bias. The bias of a tube created by the voltage drop developed across a resistor through which either its cathode current or its grid current flows.

Self-excited oscillator. An oscillator depending on its resonant circuits for frequency determination. *See* Crystal oscillator.

Self-induction. The production of a counter-electromotive force in a conductor when its own magnetic field collapses or expands with a change in current in the conductor.

Sensitivity. The degree of response of a circuit to signals of the frequency to which it is tuned.

Series feed. Application of the d-c voltage to the plate or grid of a tube through the same impedance in which the alternating current flows. Compare *Parallel feed.*

Series resonance. The condition existing in a circuit when the source of voltage is in series with an inductor and capacitor whose reactances cancel each other at the applied frequency and thus reduce the impedance to a minimum.

Series-resonant circuit. A resonant circuit in which the capacitor and the inductor are in series with the applied voltage.

Shielding. A metallic covering used to prevent magnetic or electrostatic coupling between adjacent circuits.

Short-circuit. A low-impedance or zero-impedance path between two points.

Shunt. Parallel. A parallel resistor placed in an ammeter to increase its range.

Shunt feed. *See* Parallel feed. *Sine wave.* The curve traced by the projection on a uniform time scale of the end of a rotating arm, or vector. Also known as a sinusoidal wave.

Skin effect. The tendency of alternating currents to flow near the surface of a conductor, thus being restricted to a small part of the total cross-sectional area. This effect increases the resistance and becomes more marked as the frequency rises.

Soft tube. A vacuum tube the characteristics of which are adversely affected by the presence of gas in the tube; not to be confused with tubes designed to operate with gas inside them.

Solenoid. A multiturn coil of wire wound in a

uniform layer or layerson a hollow cylindrical form.

Space charge. The cloud of electrons existing in the space between the cathode and plate in a vacuum tube, formed by the electrons emitted from the cathode in excess of those immediately attracted to the plate.

Space current. The total current flowing between the cathode and all the other electrodes in a tube. This includes the plate current, grid current, screen-grid current, and any other electrode current which may be present.

Stability. Freedom from undesired variation.

Standing wave. A distribution of current and voltage on a transmission line formed by two sets of waves traveling in opposite directions, and characterized by the presence of a number of points of successive maxima and minima in the distribution curves.

Static. A fixed nonvarying condition; without motion.

Static characteristics. The characteristics of a tube with no output load and with d-c potentials applied to the grid and plate.

Superheterodyne. A receiver in which the incoming signal is mixed with a locally generated signal to produce a predetermined intermediate frequency.

Suppressor grid (Su). An electrode used in a vacuum tube to minimize the harmful effects of secondary emission from the plate.

Surge. Sudden changes of current or voltage in a circuit.

Surge impedance (Co). See Characteristic impedance.

Sweep circuit. The part of a cathode-ray oscilloscope which provides a time-reference base.

Swing. The variation in frequency or amplitude of an electrical quantity.

Swinging choke. A choke with an effective inductance which varies with the amount of current passing through it. It is used in some power-supply filter circuits.

Synchronous. Happening at the same time; having the same period and phase.

Tank circuit. See Parallel-resonant circuit.

Tetrode. A four-electrode vacuum tube containing a cathode, control grid, screen grid, and plate.

Thermionic emission. Electron emission caused by heating an emitter.

Thermocouple ammeter. An ammeter which operates by means of a voltage produced by the heating effect of a current passed through the junction of two dissimilar metals. It is used for r-f measurements.

Thyratron. A hot-cathode, gas-discharge tube in which one or more electrodes are used to control electrostatically the starting of an unidirectional flow of current.

Tight coupling. Degree of coupling in which practically all of the magnetic lines of force produced by one coil link a second coil.

Trace. A visible line or lines appearing on the screen of a cathode-ray tube in operation.

Transconductance (G_m). The ratio of the change in plate current to the change in grid voltage producing this change in plate current, while all other electrode voltages remain constant.

Transformer. A device composed of two or more coils, linked by magnetic lines of force, used to transfer energy from one circuit to another.

Transient. The voltage or current which exists as the result of a change from one steady-state condition to another.

Transit time. The time which electrons take to travel between the cathode and the plate of a vacuum tube.

Transmission lines. Any conductor or system of conductors used to carry electrical energy from its source to a load.

Triggering. Starting an action in another circuit, which then functions for a time under its own control.

Triode. A three-electrode vacuum tube, containing a cathode, control grid, and plate.

Tuned circuit. A resonant circuit.

Tuning. The process of adjusting a radio circuit so that it resonates at the desired frequency.

Unbalanced line. A transmission line in which the voltages on the two conductors are not equal with respect to ground; for example, a coaxial line.

Unidirectional. In one direction only.

Vacuum-tube voltmeter (VTVM). A device which uses either the amplifier characteristic or the rectifier characteristic of a vacuum tube or both to measure either d-c or a-c voltages. Its input impedance is very high, and the current used to actuate the meter movement is not taken from the circuit being measured. It can be used to obtain accurate measurements in sensitive circuits.

Variable-u tube. A vacuum tube in which the control grid is irregularly spaced, so that the grid exercises a different amount of control on the electron stream at different points within its operating range.

Variocoupler. Two independent inductors, so arranged mechanically that their mutual inductance (coupling) can be varied.

Variometer. A variocoupler having its two coils connected in series, and so mounted that the movable coil may be rotated within the fixed coil, thus changing the total inductance of the unit.

Vector. A line used to represent both direction and magnitude.

Velocity modulation. A method of modulation in which the input signal voltage is used to change the velocity of electrons in a constant-current electron beam so that the electrons are grouped into bunches.

Video amplifier. A circuit capable of amplifying a very wide range of frequencies, including and exceeding the audio band of frequencies.

Volt (V). The unit of electrical potential.

Voltage amplification. The process of amplifying a signal to produce a gain in voltage. The voltage gain of an amplifier is the ratio of its alternating-voltage output to its alternating-voltage input.

Voltage divider. An impedance connected across a voltage source. The load is connected across a fraction of this impedance so that the load voltage is substantially in proportion to this fraction.

Voltage doubler. A method of increasing the voltage by rectifying both halves of a cycle and causing the outputs of both halves to be additive.

Voltage regulation. A measure of the degree to which a power source maintains its output-voltage stability under varying load conditions.

Watt (w). The unit of electrical power.

Wave. Loosely, an electromagnetic impulse, periodically changing in intensity and traveling through space. More specifically, the graphical representation of the intensity of that impulse over a oeriod of time.

Waveform. The shape of the wave obtained when instantaneous values of an a-c quantity are plotted againsi: time in rectangular coordinates.

Wavelength (A). The distance, usually expressed in meters, traveled by a wave during the time interval of one complete cycle. It is equal to the velocity divided by the frequency.

Wave propagation. The transmission of r-f energy through space.

Wien-bridge circuit. A circuit in which the various values of capacitance and resistance are made to balance with each other at a certain frequency.

X. The symbol for reactance.

Z. The symbol for impedance.

ELECTRONICS SYMBOLS

AMPLIFIER (2)

general

with two inputs

with two outputs

with adjustable gain

with associated power supply

with associated attenuator

with external feedback path

Amplifier Letter Combinations (amplifier-use identification in symbol if required)

BDG	Bridging
BST	Booster
CMP	Compression
DC	Direct Current
EXP	Expansion
LIM	Limiting
MON	Monitoring
PGM	Program
PRE	Preliminary
PWR	Power
TRQ	Torque

ANTENNA (3)

general

dipole

loop

counterpoise

ARRESTER, LIGHTNING (4)

general

carbon block

electrolytic or aluminum cell

horn gap

protective gap

sphere gap

valve or film element

multigap

ATTENUATOR, FIXED
(see PAD) (57)
(same symbol as variable attenuator, without variability)

ATTENUATOR, VARIABLE (5)

balanced

unbalanced

AUDIBLE SIGNALING DEVICE (6)

bell, electrical; ringer, telephone

buzzer

horn, electrical; loud-speaker; siren; under-water sound hydrophone, projector or transducer

Horn, Letter Combinations (if required)

*HN	Horn, electrical	
*HW	Howler	
*LS	Loudspeaker	
*SN	Siren	
‡EM	Electromagnetic with moving coil	
‡EMN	Electromagnetic with moving coil and neutralizing winding	
‡MG	Magnetic armature	
‡PM	Permanent magnet with moving coil	

identification replaces (*) asterisk and (‡) dagger)

sounder, telegraph

BATTERY (7)

generalized direct current source; one cell

multicell

CAPACITOR (8)

general

polarized

adjustable or variable

continuously adjustable or variable differential

phase-shifter

split-stator

feed-through

CELL, PHOTOSENSITIVE
(Semiconductor) (9)

asymmetrical photoconductive transducer

symmetrical photoconductive transducer

ELECTRONICS SYMBOLS

photovoltaic transducer; solar cell

CIRCUIT BREAKER (11)

general

with magnetic overload

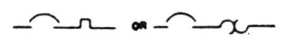

drawout type

CIRCUIT ELEMENT (12)

general

Circuit Element Letter Combinations (replaces (*) asterisk)

EG	Equalizer
FAX	Facsimile set
FL	Filter
FL-BE	Filter, band elimination
FL-BP	Filter, band pass
FL-HP	Filter, high pass
FL-LP	Filter, low pass
PS	Power supply
RG	Recording unit
RU	Reproducing unit
DIAL	Telephone dial
TEL	Telephone station
TPR	Teleprinter
TTY	Teletypewriter

Additional Letter Combinations (symbols preferred)

AR	Amplifier
AT	Attenuator
C	Capacitor
CB	Circuit breaker
HS	Handset
I	Indicating or switchboard lamp
L	Inductor
J	Jack
LS	Loudspeaker
MIC	Microphone
OSC	Oscillator
PAD	Pad
P	Plug
HT	Receiver, headset
K	Relay
R	Resistor
S	Switch or key switch
T	Transformer
WR	Wall receptacle

CLUTCH; BRAKE (14)

disengaged when operating means is de-energized

engaged when operating means is de-energized

COIL, RELAY and OPERATING (16)

semicircular dot indicates inner end of wiring

CONNECTOR (18)

assembly, movable or stationary portion; jack, plug, or receptacle

jack or receptacle

plug

separable connectors

two-conductor switchboard jack

two-conductor switchboard plug

jacks normalled through one way

jacks normalled through both ways

2-conductor nonpolarized, female contacts

2-conductor polarized, male contacts

waveguide flange

plain, rectangular

choke, rectangular

engaged 4-conductor; the plug has 1 male and 3 female contacts, individual contact designations shown

coaxial, outside conductor shown carried through

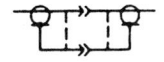

coaxial, center conductor shown carried through; outside conductor not carried through

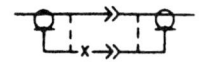

mated choke flanges in rectangular waveguide

COUNTER, ELECTROMAGNETIC; MESSAGE REGISTER (26)

general

with a make contact

COUPLER, DIRECTIONAL (27)
(common coaxial/waveguide usage)

(common coaxial/waveguide usage)

E-plane aperture-coupling, 30-decibel transmission loss

COUPLING (28)

by loop from coaxial to circular waveguide, direct-current grounds connected

CRYSTAL, PIEZO-ELECTRIC (62)

DELAY LINE (31)

general

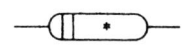

tapped delay

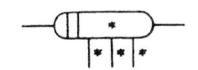

bifilar slow-wave structure (commonly used in traveling-wave tubes)

(length of delay indication replaces (*) asterisk)

DETECTOR, PRIMARY; MEASURING TRANSDUCER (30)
(see HALL GENERATOR and THERMAL CONVERTER)

DISCONTINUITY (33)
(common coaxial/waveguide usage)

equivalent series element, general

capacitive reactance

inductive reactance

inductance-capacitance circuit, infinite reactance at resonance

ELECTRONICS SYMBOLS

inductance-capacitance circuit, zero reactance at resonance

resistance

equivalent shunt element, general

capacitive susceptance

conductance

inductive susceptance

inductance-capacitance circuit, infinite susceptance at resonance

inductance-capacitance circuit, zero susceptance at resonance

ELECTRON TUBE (34)

triode

pentode, envelope connected to base terminal

twin triode, equipotential cathode

typical wiring figure to show tube symbols placed in any convenient position

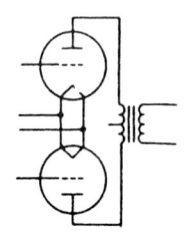

rectifier; voltage regulator (see LAMP, GLOW)

phototube, single and multiplier

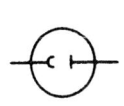

cathode-ray tube, electrostatic and magnetic deflection

mercury-pool tube, ignitor and control grid (see RECTIFIER)

resonant magnetron, coaxial output and permanent magnet

reflex klystron, integral cavity, aperture coupled

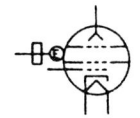

transmit-receive (TR) tube gas filled, tunable integral cavity, aperture coupled, with starter

traveling-wave tube (typical)

forward-wave traveling-wave-tube amplifier shown with four grids, having slow-wave structure with attenuation, magnetic focusing by external permanent magnet, rf input and rf output coupling each E-plane aperture to external rectangular waveguide

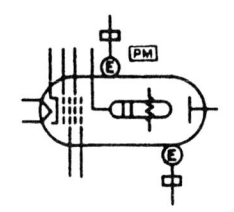

FERRITE DEVICES (100)

field polarization rotator

field polarization amplitude modulator

FUSE (36)

high-voltage primary cutout, dry

high-voltage primary cutout, oil

GOVERNOR (Contact-making) (37)

contacts shown here as closed

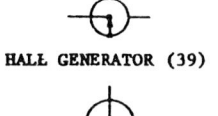

HALL GENERATOR (39)

HANDSET (40)

general

operator's set with push-to talk switch

HYBRID (41)

general

junction (common coaxial/waveguide usage)

circular

(E, H or HE transverse field indicators replace (*) asterisk)

rectangular waveguide and coaxial coupling

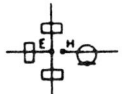

INDUCTOR (42)

general

ELECTRONICS SYMBOLS

magnetic core

tapped

adjustable, continuously adjustable

KEY, TELEGRAPH (43)

LAMP (44)

ballast lamp; ballast tube

lamp, fluorescent, 2 and 4 terminal

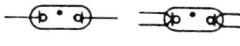

lamp, glow; neon lamp
 a-c

 d-c

lamp, incandescent

indicating lamp; switchboard lamp
(see VISUAL SIGNALING DEVICE)

LOGIC (see 806B and Y32-14) (including some duplicate symbols; left and right-hand symbols are not mixed)

AND function

OR function

EXCLUSIVE-OR function

((*) input side of logic symbols in general)

condition indicators

 state (logic negation)

 a Logic Negation output becomes 1-state if and only if the input is not 1-state

 an AND func. where output is low if and only if all inputs are high

electric inverter

(elec. invtr. output becomes 1-state if and only if the input is 1-state)
(elec. invtr. output is more pos. if and only if input is less pos.)

level (relative)

 1-state is   1-state is
 less +   more +

(symbol is a rt. triangle pointing in direction of flow)

an AND func. with input 1-states at more pos. level and output 1-state at less pos. level

single shot (one output)

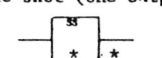

(waveform data replaces inside/outside (*))

schmitt trigger, waveform and two outputs

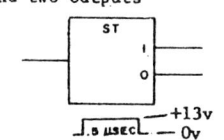

flip-flop, complementary

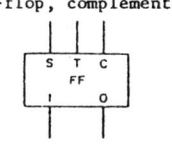

flip-flop, latch

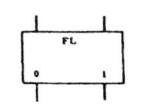

register

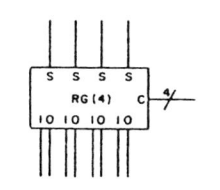

(binary register denoting four flip-flops and bits)

amplifier (see AMPLIFIER)

channel path(s) (see PATH, TRANSMISSION)

magnetic heads (see PICK-UP HEAD)

oscillator (see OSCILLATOR)

relay, contacts (see CONTACT, ELECTRICAL)
relay, electromagnetic (see RELAY COIL RECOGNITION)

signal flow (see DIRECTION OF FLOW)

time delay (see DELAY LINE)

time delay with typical delay taps:
 1.5 MS
 5 MS
 3 MS

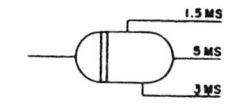

functions not otherwise symbolized

(identification replaces (*))

Logic Letter Combinations

S	set
C	clear (reset)
T	toggle (trigger)
(N)	number of bits
BO	blocking oscillator
CF	cathode follower
EF	emitter follower
FF	flip-flop
SS	single shot
ST	schmitt trigger
RG(N)	register (N stages)
SR	shift register

MACHINE, ROTATING (46)

generator

motor

METER, INSTRUMENT (48)

identification replaces (*) asterisk)

Meter Letter Combinations

A	Ammeter
AH	Ampere-hour
CMA	Contact-making (or breaking) ammeter
CMC	Contact-making (or breaking) clock
CMV	Contact-making (or breaking) voltmeter
CRO	Oscilloscope or cathode-ray oscillograph
DB	DB (decibel) meter
DBM	DBM (decibels referred to 1 milliwatt) meter
DM	Demand meter
DTR	Demand-totalizing relay
F	Frequency meter
G	Galvanometer
GD	Ground detector
I	Indicating
INT	Integrating
μA or UA	Microammeter
MA	Milliammeter
NM	Noise meter
OHM	Ohmmeter
OP	Oil pressure

ELECTRONICS SYMBOLS

MODE TRANSDUCER (53)

(common coaxial/waveguide usage)

transducer from rectangular waveguide to coaxial with mode suppression, direct-current grounds connected

MOTION, MECHANICAL (54)

rotation applied to a resistor

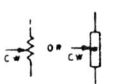

(identification replaces (*) asterisk)

**NUCLEAR-RADIATION DETECTOR, gas filled;
IONIZATION CHAMBER;
PROPORTIONAL COUNTER TUBE;
GEIGER-MULLER COUNTER TUBE (50)**
(see RADIATION-SENSITIVITY INDICATOR)

PATH, TRANSMISSION (58)

cable; 2-conductor, shield grounded and 5-conductor shielded

PICKUP HEAD (61)

general

writing; recording

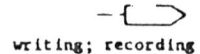

reading; playback

erasing

writing, reading, and erasing

stereo

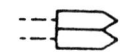

RECTIFIER (65)

semiconductor diode;
metallic rectifier;
electrolytic rectifier;
asymmetrical varistor

mercury-pool tube power rectifier

fullwave bridge-type

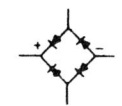

RESISTOR (68)

general

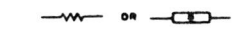

tapped

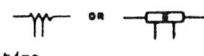

heating

symmetrical varistor resistor, voltage sensitive (silicon carbide, etc.)

(identification marks replace (*) asterisk)

with adjustable contact

adjustable or continuously adjustable (variable)

(identification replaces (*) asterisk)

RESONATOR, TUNED CAVITY (71)

(common coaxial/waveguide usage)

resonator with mode suppression coupled by an E-plane aperture to a guided transmission path and by a loop to a coaxial path

tunable resonator with direct-current ground connected to an electron device and adjustably coupled by an E-plane aperture to a rectangular waveguide

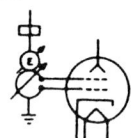

ROTARY JOINT, RF (COUPLER) (72)

general; with rectangular waveguide

(transmission path recognition symbol replaces (*) asterisk)

coaxial type in rectangular waveguide

circular waveguide type in rectangular waveguide

SEMICONDUCTOR DEVICE (73)
(Two Terminal, diode)

semiconductor diode; rectifier

capacitive diode (also Varicap, Varactor, reactance diode, parametric diode)

breakdown diode, unidirectional (also backward diode, avalanche diode, voltage regulator diode, Zener diode, voltage reference diode)

breakdown diode, bidirectional and backward diode (also bipolar voltage limiter)

tunnel diode (also Esaki diode)

temperature-dependent diode

photodiode (also solar cell)

semiconductor diode, PNPN switch (also Shockley diode, four-layer diode and SCR).

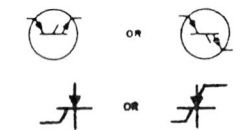

(Multi-Terminal, transistor, etc.)

PNP transistor

NPN transistor

unijunction transistor, N-type base

ELECTRONICS SYMBOLS

unijunction transistor, P-type base

field-effect transistor, N-type base

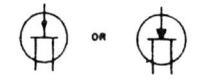

field-effect transistor, P-type base

semiconductor triode, PNPN-type switch

semiconductor triode, NPNP-type switch

NPN transistor, transverse-biased base

PNIP transistor, ohmic connection to the intrinsic region

NPIN transistor, ohmic connection to the intrinsic region

PNIN transistor, ohmic connection to the intrinsic region

NPIP transistor, ohmic connection to the intrinsic region

SQUIB (75)

explosive

igniter

sensing link; fusible link operated

SWITCH (76)

push button, circuit closing (make)

push button, circuit opening (break)

nonlocking; momentary circuit closing (make)

nonlocking; momentary circuit opening (break)

transfer

locking, circuit closing (make)

locking, circuit opening (break)

transfer, 3-position

wafer

(example shown: 3-pole 3-circuit with 2 non-shorting and 1 shorting moving contacts)

safety interlock, circuit opening and closing

2-pole field-discharge knife, with terminals and discharge resistor

(identification replaces (*) asterisk)

SYNCHRO (78)

Synchro Letter Combinations
CDX Control-differential transmitter
CT   Control transformer
CX   Control transmitter
TDR Torque-differential receiver
TDX Torque-differential transmitter
TR   Torque receiver
TX   Torque transmitter
RS   Resolver
B   Outer winding rotatable in bearings

THERMAL ELEMENT (83)

actuating device

thermal cutout; flasher

thermal relay

thermostat (operates on rising temperature), contact)

thermostat, make contact

thermostat, integral heater and transfer contacts

THERMISTOR; THERMAL RESISTOR (84)

with integral heater

THERMOCOUPLE (85)

temperature-measuring

current-measuring, integral heater connected

current-measuring, integral heater insulated

temperature-measuring, semiconductor

current-measuring, semiconductor

TRANSFORMER (86)

general

magnetic-core

one winding with adjustable inductance

separately adjustable inductance

adjustable mutual inductor, constant-current

ELECTRONICS SYMBOLS

autotransformer, 1-phase adjustable

current, with polarity marking

potential, with polarity mark

with direct-current connections and mode suppression between two rectangular waveguides

(common coaxial/waveguide usage)

shielded, with magnetic core

with a shield between windings, connected to the frame

VIBRATOR; INTERRUPTER (87)

typical shunt drive (terminals shown)

typical separate drive (terminals shown)

VISUAL SIGNALING DEVICE (88)

communication switchboard-type lamp

indicating, pilot, signaling, or switchboard light (see LAMP)

(identification replaces (*) asterisk)

indicating light letter combinations

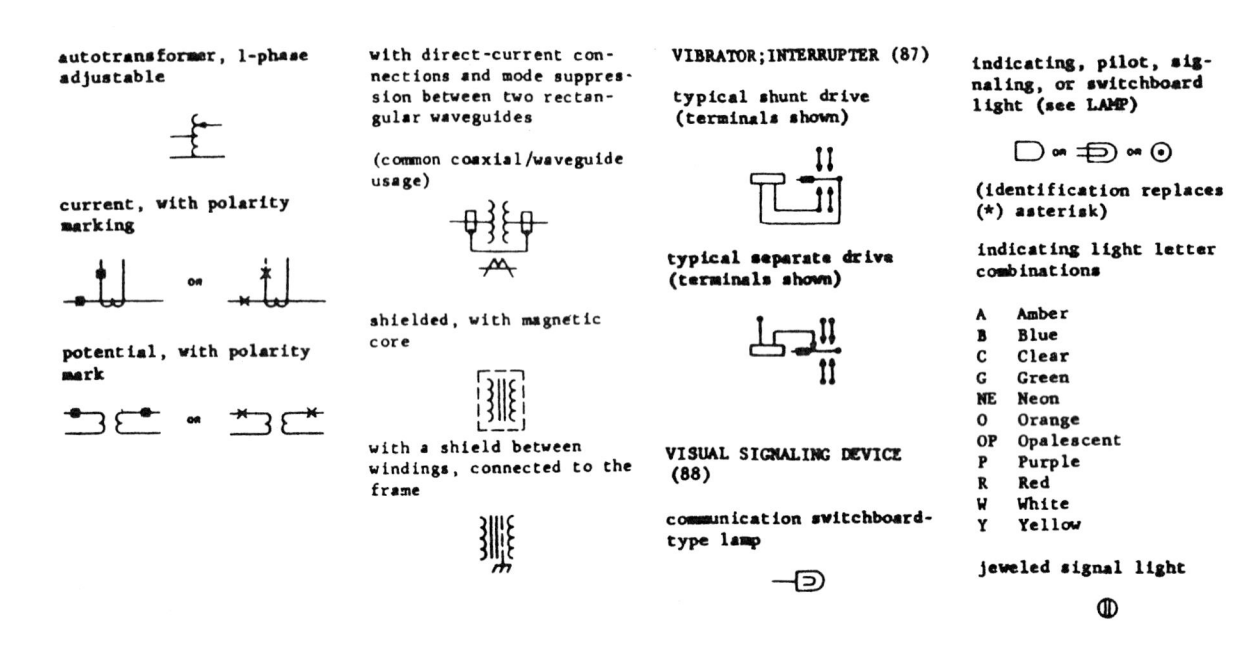

A   Amber
B   Blue
C   Clear
G   Green
NE Neon
O   Orange
OP Opalescent
P   Purple
R   Red
W   White
Y   Yellow

jeweled signal light

TRANSISTOR SYMBOLS

Semiconductor, General
BV .... Breakdown voltage
TA .... Ambient temperature
T_{ep} .... Operating temperature

Transistor
B, b .... Base electrode
C, c .... Collector electrode
C_{ib} .... Input capacitance (common base)
C_{ie} .... Input capacitance (common emitter)
C_{ob} .... Output capacitance (common base)
C_{oe} .... Output capacitance (common emitter)
E, e .... Emitter electrode
I_B .... Base current (dc)
i_b .... Base current (instantaneous)
I_C .... Collector current (dc)
i_c .... Collector current (instantaneous)
I_{CBO} .... Collector cutoff current (dc) emitter open
I_{CEO} .... Collector cutoff current (dc) base open
I_E .... Emitter current
R_B .... External base resistance
$r_{b'}$ .... Base spreading resistance
r_i .... Input junction resistance
V_{BB} .... Base supply voltage
V_C .... Collector voltage (with respect to ground or common point)
V_{BE} .... Base to emitter voltage (dc)
V_{CB} .... Collector to base voltage (dc)
V_{CE} .... Collector to emitter voltage (dc)
V_{ce} .... Collector to emitter voltage (rms)
vce .... Collector to emitter voltage (instantaneous)
$V_{CE\,(sat)}$ ..... Collector to emitter saturation voltage
V_{EBO} .... Emitter to base voltage (static)
V_{CC} .... Collector supply voltage
V_{EE} .... Emitter supply voltage

TUBE SYMBOLS

A_{hf} — High frequency gain
A_{lf} — Low frequency gain
A_v — Voltage gain
C_c — Coupling capacitor
C_d — Distributed capacitance
C_{gk} — Grid-to-cathode capacitance
C_{gp} — Grid-to-plate capacitance
C_i — Input capacitance
C_K — Cathode bypass capacitor
C_O — Output capacitance
C_{pk} — Plate-to-cathode capacitance
C_s — Shunt capacitance ($C_d + C_i + C_o$)
E_b — Plate volts (dc)
E_{bb} — Supply volts (dc)
E_{bo} — Quiescent plate voltage
E_{c1} — Control grid voltage
E_{c2} — Screen grid voltage
E_{cc} — Control grid supply voltage
E_f — Filament terminal voltage
e_b — Instantaneous total plate volts (ac and dc)
e_{c1} — Instantaneous total control grid volts (ac and dc)
e_{c2} — Instantaneous total screen grid volts (ac and dc)
e_{g1} — Instantaneous value of ac control grid volts
e_{g2} — Instantaneous value of ac screen grid volts
e_{po} — Instantaneous value of plate voltage above and below the quiescent value
E_g — RMS value of grid volts
E_p — RMS value of plate volts
gm — Grid-plate transconductance (mutual conductance)

I_b — DC value of plate volts
I_{bo} — Quiescent value of plate current
I_{c1} — DC value of control grid current
I_{C2} — DC value of screen grid current
I_f — Filament or heater current
I_{g1} — RMS value of control grid current
I_{g2} — RMS value of screen grid current
I_{gml} — Crest values of ac current control grid
g_{m2} — Crest values of ac current screen grid
I_p — RMS values of plate current
I_{pm} — Crest value of plate current
I_s — Total electron emission
i_b — Instantaneous total value of plate current
i_{c1} — Instantaneous total value of control grid current
i_{c2} — Instantaneous total value of screen grid current
i_{g1} — Instantaneous ac value of control grid current
i_{g2} — Instantaneous ac value of screen grid current
i_p — Instantaneous ac value of plate current
i_{po} — Instantaneous values of plate current above and below the quiescent value
R_b — DC plate resistance
R_g — DC grid resistance
R_k — DC cathode resistance
R_L — Plate load resistance
r_p — AC plate resistance
μ — Amplification factor

ANSWER SHEET

TEST NO. _____ PART _____ TITLE OF POSITION _____
(AS GIVEN IN EXAMINATION ANNOUNCEMENT - INCLUDE OPTION, IF ANY)

PLACE OF EXAMINATION _____ DATE _____
(CITY OR TOWN)   (STATE)

RATING

USE THE SPECIAL PENCIL. MAKE GLOSSY BLACK MARKS.

#	A B C D E	#	A B C D E	#	A B C D E	#	A B C D E	#	A B C D E
1	:: :: :: :: ::	26	:: :: :: :: ::	51	:: :: :: :: ::	76	:: :: :: :: ::	101	:: :: :: :: ::
2	:: :: :: :: ::	27	:: :: :: :: ::	52	:: :: :: :: ::	77	:: :: :: :: ::	102	:: :: :: :: ::
3	:: :: :: :: ::	28	:: :: :: :: ::	53	:: :: :: :: ::	78	:: :: :: :: ::	103	:: :: :: :: ::
4	:: :: :: :: ::	29	:: :: :: :: ::	54	:: :: :: :: ::	79	:: :: :: :: ::	104	:: :: :: :: ::
5	:: :: :: :: ::	30	:: :: :: :: ::	55	:: :: :: :: ::	80	:: :: :: :: ::	105	:: :: :: :: ::
6	:: :: :: :: ::	31	:: :: :: :: ::	56	:: :: :: :: ::	81	:: :: :: :: ::	106	:: :: :: :: ::
7	:: :: :: :: ::	32	:: :: :: :: ::	57	:: :: :: :: ::	82	:: :: :: :: ::	107	:: :: :: :: ::
8	:: :: :: :: ::	33	:: :: :: :: ::	58	:: :: :: :: ::	83	:: :: :: :: ::	108	:: :: :: :: ::
9	:: :: :: :: ::	34	:: :: :: :: ::	59	:: :: :: :: ::	84	:: :: :: :: ::	109	:: :: :: :: ::
10	:: :: :: :: ::	35	:: :: :: :: ::	60	:: :: :: :: ::	85	:: :: :: :: ::	110	:: :: :: :: ::

Make only ONE mark for each answer. Additional and stray marks may be counted as mistakes. In making corrections, erase errors COMPLETELY.

#	A B C D E	#	A B C D E	#	A B C D E	#	A B C D E	#	A B C D E
11	:: :: :: :: ::	36	:: :: :: :: ::	61	:: :: :: :: ::	86	:: :: :: :: ::	111	:: :: :: :: ::
12	:: :: :: :: ::	37	:: :: :: :: ::	62	:: :: :: :: ::	87	:: :: :: :: ::	112	:: :: :: :: ::
13	:: :: :: :: ::	38	:: :: :: :: ::	63	:: :: :: :: ::	88	:: :: :: :: ::	113	:: :: :: :: ::
14	:: :: :: :: ::	39	:: :: :: :: ::	64	:: :: :: :: ::	89	:: :: :: :: ::	114	:: :: :: :: ::
15	:: :: :: :: ::	40	:: :: :: :: ::	65	:: :: :: :: ::	90	:: :: :: :: ::	115	:: :: :: :: ::
16	:: :: :: :: ::	41	:: :: :: :: ::	66	:: :: :: :: ::	91	:: :: :: :: ::	116	:: :: :: :: ::
17	:: :: :: :: ::	42	:: :: :: :: ::	67	:: :: :: :: ::	92	:: :: :: :: ::	117	:: :: :: :: ::
18	:: :: :: :: ::	43	:: :: :: :: ::	68	:: :: :: :: ::	93	:: :: :: :: ::	118	:: :: :: :: ::
19	:: :: :: :: ::	44	:: :: :: :: ::	69	:: :: :: :: ::	94	:: :: :: :: ::	119	:: :: :: :: ::
20	:: :: :: :: ::	45	:: :: :: :: ::	70	:: :: :: :: ::	95	:: :: :: :: ::	120	:: :: :: :: ::
21	:: :: :: :: ::	46	:: :: :: :: ::	71	:: :: :: :: ::	96	:: :: :: :: ::	121	:: :: :: :: ::
22	:: :: :: :: ::	47	:: :: :: :: ::	72	:: :: :: :: ::	97	:: :: :: :: ::	122	:: :: :: :: ::
23	:: :: :: :: ::	48	:: :: :: :: ::	73	:: :: :: :: ::	98	:: :: :: :: ::	123	:: :: :: :: ::
24	:: :: :: :: ::	49	:: :: :: :: ::	74	:: :: :: :: ::	99	:: :: :: :: ::	124	:: :: :: :: ::
25	:: :: :: :: ::	50	:: :: :: :: ::	75	:: :: :: :: ::	100	:: :: :: :: ::	125	:: :: :: :: ::

ANSWER SHEET

JAN - - 2016

TEST NO. _____ PART _____ TITLE OF POSITION _____
(AS GIVEN IN EXAMINATION ANNOUNCEMENT - INCLUDE OPTION, IF ANY)

PLACE OF EXAMINATION _____ DATE _____
(CITY OR TOWN)   (STATE)

RATING

USE THE SPECIAL PENCIL.   MAKE GLOSSY BLACK MARKS.

Make only ONE mark for each answer. Additional and stray marks may be counted as mistakes. In making corrections, erase errors COMPLETELY.